The Life and Times of General Sir Miles Dempsey

GBE KCB DSO MC

For Nigel

The Life and Times of General Sir Miles Dempsey

GBE KCB DSO MC

Monty's Army Commander

Peter Rostron

Pen & Sword
MILITARY

First published in Great Britain in 2010 by
Pen & Sword Military
An imprint of
Pen & Sword Books Ltd
47 Church Street
Barnsley
South Yorkshire
S70 2AS

ISBN 978 1 84884 252 6

A CIP catalogue record for this book is
available from the British Library

Typeset in 10pt Palatino by Mac Style, Beverley, East Yorkshire
Printed and bound in the UK by MPG Books Group

Pen & Sword Books Ltd incorporates the Imprints of Pen & Sword
Aviation, Pen & Sword Maritime, Pen & Sword Military,
Wharncliffe Local History, Pen & Sword Select, Pen & Sword Military
Classics, Leo Cooper, Remember When, Seaforth Publishing and
Frontline Publishing

For a complete list of Pen & Sword titles please contact
PEN & SWORD BOOKS LIMITED
47 Church Street, Barnsley, South Yorkshire, S70 2AS, England
E-mail: enquiries@pen-and-sword.co.uk
Website: www.pen-and-sword.co.uk

Contents

Preface		vi
Prologue		xi
Chapter 1	'School'	1
Chapter 2	'Execute Orders Received'	6
Chapter 3	'Orderly Room'	15
Chapter 4	'Officers'	25
Chapter 5	'Alarm (for Troops to Turn out under Arms)'	36
Chapter 6	'Retire or Troops About Wheel'	43
Chapter 7	'Draw Swords'	54
Chapter 8	'Head of Column Change Direction Half Right'	69
Chapter 9	'Front'	80
Chapter 10	'Form Line'	95
Chapter 11	'Charge'	112
Chapter 12	'Pursue'	128
Chapter 13	'Halt'	145
Chapter 14	'Stand Fast/Cease Firing'	162
Chapter 15	'Last Post'	173
Chapter 16	'Sunset'	190
Epilogue		202
Notes		203
Select Bibliography		208
Index		210

(Note: chapter headings are named after bugle calls for infantry and mounted infantry).

Preface

When I was first asked to write about Miles Dempsey I knew very little of him. I had studied the Normandy Campaign at Staff College, and walked the course for the D-Day landings and Operation GOODWOOD. I had heard his name and had a hazy idea of his position in the hierarchy. In that respect, I suspect I shared my ignorance with the great majority of the British public.

As I came to know him better, two things became apparent to me – the first, that little had ever been written either by or about him. This was largely due to his reticence, and to old-fashioned notions of loyalty and a dislike of self-aggrandisement. Second, I came to perceive that, in addition to these admirable traits, he possessed in abundance all the military virtues – leadership based on self-confidence, a shrewd tactical brain, calmness in a crisis, total disregard for danger, and a 'big' personality, able to make quick decisions and stick to them. I also realized that he had played an enormously important role in the great events that shaped the world in which we now live. That he had not received his fair share of plaudits was as much due to the desire on the part of others to seek glory as to his own reticence.

No biography had ever been written, largely because of the lack of source material on which to base one. He ordered the majority of his papers to be burned, and produced nothing for the public domain. But, despite this dearth of material, what I did see induced in me huge respect, not least because of the calibre of those who passed favourable judgement on him. These ranged from major figures such as Montgomery, Mountbatten, Leese, Horrocks and de Guingand to Selwyn Lloyd, a wartime soldier who went on to great things in politics, and had no axe to grind on the military front. Not only did they all agree on his unusual ability, they remained loyal for years after all military ties had been severed. It is indeed hard to find anyone with a harsh word to say about him.

I was extremely fortunate to be offered by the Dempsey family a collection of letters, diaries, including trench diaries from the Great War, papers and photographs – the Dempsey Family Collection – which had never been seen before by researchers, and which enabled me to add a human dimension to the otherwise laconic official sources. I owe them, and especially James Dempsey, a great debt of gratitude.

I am also grateful to Dr Peter Caddick-Adams, of the UK Defence Academy, and Dr Stephen Hart of the Royal Military Academy Sandhurst, who gave me much helpful advice. I am grateful to the Liddell Hart Centre for Military Archives of King's College London, for giving me access to their invaluable sources, and to the Imperial War Museum, the Churchill Archives Centre, Churchill College Cambridge, Southampton University Library, the Joint Services Command and Staff College Library, the archives of the Royal Military Academy Sandhurst and the National Archives Kew, for their help.

I have been lucky enough to have received enormous help and encouragement from the successors to Dempsey's old regiment, the Royal Berkshires. After many mutations occasioned by the vagaries of changing defence requirements, their records are now held by the Rifles Wardrobe Museum, Salisbury. Their staff, especially 'Mac' Macintyre and John Peters, led by Lieutenant Colonel Michael Cornwell, have been quite outstanding in their help, and I am most grateful to them, and to Brigadier Patrick Davidson-Houston, Colonel Mike Vernon-Powell and Lieutenant Colonel David Stone, all with strong links to the Berkshires, for their unfailing encouragement. I have been privileged to interview individuals who knew Dempsey, and I am grateful to them for their insights.

I am also grateful to the Royal Irish Fusiliers Museum; the Royal Military Police Museum; Christ Church, Portsdown; Shrewsbury School and in particular the Head of History, Dr O'Morrogh; and all the trustees and copyright holders who have given me permission to quote from works consulted. I have endeavoured to ensure in every case that rights have been respected, and if I have erred in any respect I am ready to make suitable acknowledgement.

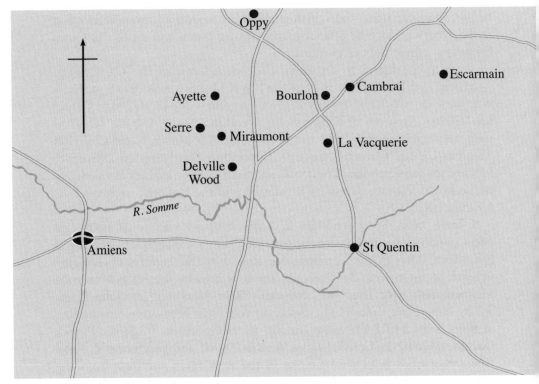

Map 1: Dempsey's Battlefields, 1916–18.

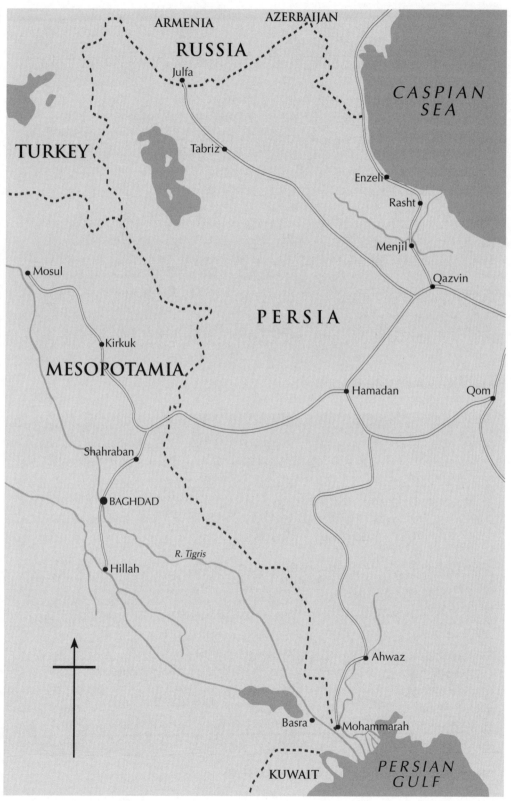

Map 2: Mesopotamia and Northern Persia, 1920–21.

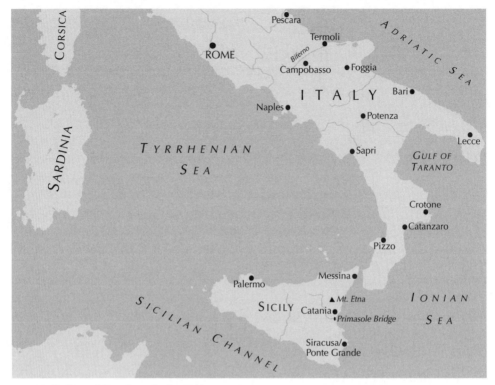

Map 3: Sicily and Southern Italy, 1943.

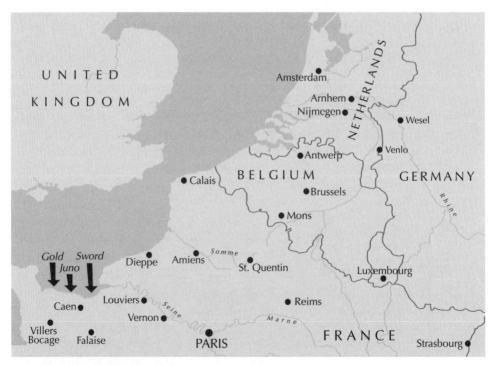

Map 4: Normandy and The Low Countries, 1944–45.

Prologue

On the evening of 4 June 1944, the congregation at Christ Church, Portsdown, was unusually large. Built in 1874, overlooking the English Channel on land donated by the Army, the large, airy church was used by the garrisons of the nearby forts to hold their own services, and to conduct military burials. On this evening there were so many soldiers worshipping that they overflowed into the area outside. The two officiating priests were The Revd R.B.S. Gilman, vicar of Christ Church, and The Revd J.W.J. Steele, Senior Chaplain Second Army. As they entered the church, the congregation stood, led by the tall, imposing figure of their general in the front pew.

Lieutenant General Miles Christopher Dempsey had arranged this service for the officers and men of Headquarters Second Army, on the eve of the planned date for the largest combined military operation the world has ever seen – D-Day, the invasion of Europe. General Sir Bernard Law Montgomery, commanding the British, Canadian and American land forces for the invasion, had already called in a personal message to all those involved, that 'The Lord Mighty in Battle' would go forth with their armies, and that His special providence would aid them in the struggle. Now Dempsey, a devout Christian, called on his men, in the service known as 'The Knight's Vigil', to dedicate to Almighty God the task which lay before them. Accompanied by his Chief of Staff and his Deputy, he led them in that evocative prayer which he had known thirty years before at Shrewsbury;

> Teach us good Lord, to serve Thee as Thou deservest; to give and not to count the cost; to fight and not to heed the wounds; to toil and not to ask for rest; to labour and not to ask for any reward save that of knowing that we do Thy will.

With characteristic modesty, Dempsey asked that someone other than himself should read the lesson. His example during this voluntary act of dedication before the great armada set off expressed many of the fundamentals of his personality: strong religious belief, selfless integrity, professional dedication and extraordinary humility.

Within forty-eight hours thousands of troops under Dempsey's command were fighting in Normandy.

Chapter 1

'School'

The Dempseys originated in Ireland, and Terence O'Dempsey, a senior member of the Gaelic aristocracy, was knighted on the field of battle at Kiltenan in County Limerick by the earl of Essex in 1589. As a result of his faithful service to the Crown, he was later created Viscount Glinmalery and Baron of Philipstown. By 1821, the family had settled in England, and James Dempsey, husband of Ann, was head of Dempsey and Pickard, timber merchants of Liverpool. Of James's six children, Louisa married John Tarr, MP for Liverpool, while Henry and Arthur continued in the timber trade. Arthur, who became a timber broker, moved out to the Cheshire plain, and in 1857 his wife bore a son, Arthur Francis.

Arthur Francis became a marine insurance underwriter's clerk, a profession which enabled him and his wife, Margaret Maud, to buy 7 Sandringham Drive, a comfortable house in the prosperous neighbourhood of New Brighton, Wallasey. Here they lived a typically middle-class life with a housekeeper, a cook and Elizabeth, a nursemaid. Elizabeth looked after the three Dempsey children, all boys, of whom the eldest, James, was born in 1889. Like his brother Patrick who was christened at St Mary's, Wallasey, in October 1893, he had the unusual middle name of De La Fosse, his mother's maiden name. Her father, Major General Henry De La Fosse CB, was one of the few survivors of the Cawnpore massacre in the Indian Mutiny.

In December 1896, a third son, Miles Christopher, was born, but when he was just six years old the family was enveloped in sorrow when their father committed suicide, apparently as a result of financial difficulties. It was an event which Miles would never discuss. Margaret moved to Crawley in Sussex, from where James enrolled at Dartmouth Naval College, and in 1908 Patrick entered Shrewsbury, a well-established public school in Shropshire. A number of Salopians had gained eminence in public life, probably the best known being Darwin, the evolutionist. At the time of Patrick's arrival the school was becoming a little set in its ways, but this changed dramatically with the appointment that year of Cyril Argentine Alington as Headmaster.

Alington, at just thirty-six years of age, was younger than all of the rest of the staff but two. Educated at Marlborough and Trinity, Oxford, he was elected to All Souls in 1896 and ordained in the Church of England in 1901. He came to Shrewsbury from teaching at his old school, where he had already established an impressive reputation. He was blessed with almost every gift to ensure a successful career. Extraordinarily handsome, stimulating, theatrical in voice and manner, endowed with huge charisma and profound oratorical powers, his sermons had a deep and lasting effect on the boys. Nevil Shute, the writer, then Nevil Shute Norway, wrote of 'The restrained, masculine school services in the chapel' which so impressed him, and another described how he had every boy silent, moved and tense on the edge of his pew. Alington was later to become Headmaster of Eton, Chairman of the Headmasters' Conference, and Chaplain to the King from 1921 until 1933.

To Miles, who followed Patrick to Shrewsbury in 1911, probably of equal importance was the Headmaster's sporting prowess. As a young man Alington was a very successful cricketer, fives and rackets player, and both Dempsey boys showed much promise as sportsmen. Patrick, to whom Miles was to remain extremely close throughout his life, was in the school cricket eleven, and by the time his elder brother left, Miles was already establishing a reputation as an outstanding player. He captained the school side for one of their most memorable seasons in 1914, when they lost only one match. The *Salopian* for that year records its hearty congratulations to the Captain, M.C. Dempsey: 'It is always gratifying to those interested in school cricket to see the skipper giving a lead to his crew, and this our skipper has done with rare exceptions at the wicket, where his nerve, pluck and steady patience have been a grand example and encouragement to his followers.'[1]

Describing the 'characters' of the team, the journal notes that Dempsey was a very steady, patient bat, but too fond of driving off his right leg, and diffident of his bowling powers. Among the eleven in this, the last season before the war, were B.H. Ellis, 'a good field and catch', and T. Onslow, 'an improving bowler who could make a run or two'.

Miles had decided early on a military career, possibly influenced by his grandfather and by James, who had run away from Dartmouth at sixteen and joined the French Foreign Legion. He was in the Army Class, on the classical side, when the school broke up for the summer holidays. He attended the OTC tented camp at Rugeley as a sergeant, where with other schools under their own masters as officers, and a small number of regulars, they carried out large-scale manoeuvres based on Boer War tactics. He returned for the Michaelmas term with every intention of completing another year at Shrewsbury, but the events of August 1914 had changed everything for ever, and in October, along with J.P. Moreton and G.F. Maclean, he left for the Royal Military College, Sandhurst; he was aged just seventeen years and nine months. In the course of the next year, every player in the cricket eleven, and all but two of the twenty-one monitors enlisted. By the end of the war, even members of staff were being called up; one of those to go was a brilliant young sixth-form master, Philip Bainbrigge, whose weak build and thick spectacles did not save him from soldiering – and dying – in the ranks.

Dempsey could look back on his time at Shrewsbury with satisfaction. On top of his success on the cricket field, he was a school and house monitor, and played in the second eleven football. As a general rule, a housemaster probably influences a boy's character more than does the headmaster, but Dempsey's housemaster, A.F. Chance, had been in post for thirty years. It is to the effect of the young and enormously energetic Alington's huge persona that the deep religious faith and upright, honourable character, which were to be Dempsey's throughout his life, may largely be attributed. As well as some photographs, Dempsey kept to the end of his life his cricketing records, and a collection of typed handouts on religious themes, such as an analysis of the Bible, from his time at Shrewsbury.

The Royal Military College, to which Dempsey reported, had had to adapt quickly to the demands of war. Although potential gentlemen cadets were still required to pass an entrance exam, and the majority of parents were expected to pay fees (the usual £150 per year in his case), the course had been shortened dramatically so as to produce the maximum number of officers for a rapidly expanding army. Dempsey and Maclean joined the sixty-five cadets of G Company, commanded by Captain Eden, Black Watch, as did Nevil Shute's brother, F.H. Norway. Many of their fellow cadets came from traditional backgrounds, and the fathers of the four next to Dempsey in the College Register were described as 'Lt Colonel', 'Gentleman JP', 'Parliamentary Agent' and 'Gentleman'.

The one-year course at Sandhurst, prior to the outbreak of war, was known for its hard life and strict discipline. Impeccable standards were demanded and the cadets' drill was intended to be the best in the British Army. A famous product of the College wrote: 'One's natural instinct when shooting starts is to lie in a ditch and stay there until it is all over; and it is only through discipline and training that one can make oneself get out and go forward.' The fervour, or lack of it, with which cadets applied themselves to their studies depended in many cases on whether they were desperate to obtain entry to the Indian Army – where an officer could live on his pay – or the British Army, where he probably could not. Cadets had to ride, the cause of heartache to many. The war changed all that.

Eden and the platoon commanders, Captain Robinson, Royal Dublin Fusiliers, and Captain Tonson-Rye, Royal Munster Fusiliers, instructed in organization, minor tactics and the welfare and administration of soldiers.

Colour Sergeant Morris, Coldstream Guards and Sergeant Mulally, Irish Guards, taught drill and musketry.

The course was the second short wartime one, and the civilian clothing on several of the cadets in the photograph of G Company from December 1914 – two months after the course began – points to administrative problems that still needed to be overcome. The course was designed to produce officers in five months, but there was flexibility in the system. Dempsey passed out in February 1915, but others of his intake did not become officers until March, April or even, in the cases of Dashwood of the East Yorks, or Dyer of the Bedfordshire Regiment, until May.

When Dempsey left Sandhurst he was commissioned into the Royal Berkshire Regiment, whose 1st (Regular) Battalion was fighting in France. Before a young officer joined a unit at the front, he had to attend numerous courses, to acquaint him with the mechanics of trench warfare. His first port of call was always to the regiment's depot, where Regimental Headquarters (a purely administrative body) was housed, along with the museum and the Training Company which put new recruits through their induction into the Army. Dempsey reported as a new second lieutenant to Brock Barracks, Reading, home of the Royal Berkshire Regiment, the 49th and 66th Foot. A solid county regiment, the Berkshires had earned honours in every corner of the globe from Brandywine Creek, where they trounced George Washington, to China, and, like every other regiment worth its salt, considered themselves second to none. Dempsey's choice of regiment was a happy one. It was to be his home and inspiration for many years. He was then posted to the 3rd (Special Reserve) Battalion in Dublin to learn his craft.

While Miles was training, James and Patrick enlisted in the 5th (Service) Battalion the Royal Irish Fusiliers, which formed at Dublin. James, who had been bought out of the Foreign Legion, was the first of the family to be commissioned, and was gazetted Second Lieutenant on 19 December 1914, while Miles was still a Gentleman Cadet. Patrick was also commissioned and the brothers were together in the Battalion, part of the 10th (Irish) Division, when it was despatched to the Mediterranean. It was to serve under General Sir Ian Hamilton, whose task was to seize the Dardanelles, and put Turkey out of the war. When the first phase of the campaign had ended in stalemate, Hamilton's operational plan was to make a fresh landing at Suvla Bay, in the hope of gaining surprise and outflanking the Turks. In August, Miles and his mother received grim news of Patrick.

On 6 August 1915, the Fusiliers were still ignorant of the plan when the sound of gunfire and flashes in the night sky had indicated their objective. At 0700 next day, lighters had come alongside and two companies at a time landed on 'C' Beach under fire. At 1100, they were ordered to attack the heights of Lala Baba. The plan was difficult, involving a move in one direction, followed by a change of direction for the final assault. This was difficult enough, but an added problem was that they had to narrow their frontage in order to pass the Salt Lake, where they were under the observed fire of some twenty Turksh guns. As the Fusiliers struggled knee deep through the brackish mud, Patrick was wounded in the stomach. The Battalion suffered heavily in the assault and with great difficulty settled in to hastily dug trenches on Green Hill. The Turks counter-attacked ferociously and on 19 August James was also wounded.

The war had struck home to the Dempsey family. Although both brothers returned to active service, Miles and his mother passed a troubling few weeks. The chances of recovery from wounds were much lower then than today, and the remoteness of the theatre added to their worries. Their concern was only increased when James volunteered for the Royal Flying Corps, in which almost as many pilots were killed in training as in combat. James distinguished himself, winning the Military Cross, and setting a benchmark for Miles.

Meanwhile, B.H. Ellis, the 'good field and catch' of the Shrewsbury 1914 cricket side, was killed by a shell when wounded, serving with the King's Shropshire Light Infantry; 'Fred' Norway of G Company died of wounds in June while serving with the Duke of Cornwall's Light Infantry; and in September, T.S. Woods, Dempsey's fellow monitor, was killed in action with the Royal Field Artillery. With the long shadow of the war beginning to darken everyone's lives, Nevil Shute described the atmosphere at Shrewsbury in these words:

> The list of the school casualties grew every day. Older boys that we knew intimately, one who had perhaps been monitor in one's bedroom, appeared once or twice resplendent in their new uniform, and were dead. We remembered them as we had known them less than a year before, as we knelt praying for their souls in chapel, knowing as we did so that in a year or so the little boys in our own house would be kneeling for us.[2]

Dempsey must have been conscious that he was embarking on a profession that demanded much and gave little. Promoted Lieutenant in August 1915, he attended courses, slowly mastering the role of an infantry officer on active service, and in June 1916 he at last joined the 1st Battalion Royal Berkshires in France. Shortly before Dempsey arrived, another fellow monitor from Shrewsbury, E. Pitcairn Jones, was killed while serving with the Rifle Brigade. The Berkshires were about to take part in the Somme offensive, and Dempsey was about to undergo his baptism of fire.

CHAPTER 2

'Execute Orders Received'

The 1st Battalion, The Royal Berkshire Regiment was at Aldershot when war was declared and reservists soon made up its strength to the wartime establishment of 800. They moved to France, participated in the retreat from Mons and by late September were in trenches at La Metz Farm. Heavily involved from 22 October to 13 November in the First Battle of Ypres, they spent the winter in and out of trenches and were involved in a further three attacks. The summer of 1915 was relatively quiet, but on 5 September the Battalion lost 288 men in one day in the Battle of Loos. At the time Dempsey joined, the Battalion was in billets behind the line, in the Béthune sector of the Somme front. The Battalion was not to move more than 30 miles from here for the remainder of the war. More than half its number had been replaced since 1914, and the total battalion strength was 420. As a result of a comprehensive overhaul and the application of some disciplinary measures, they were still very much a regular battalion, with the standards that that implied. Throughout the war it was the common experience of regular units that, provided a nucleus survived – the Regimental Sergeant Major, the Quartermaster, the Transport Officer, the Orderly Room Sergeant and a few more – a battalion would maintain its ethos.

By the end of June reinforcements had brought the Berkshires' numbers up to twenty-seven officers and 620 other ranks, and they were preparing for the event that is probably more evocative to the British people than any other military action – the Battle of the Somme. The modern view of the First World War, taught in our schools and fostered by much of the media, is of incompetent generals on both sides, unable to understand modern warfare, enormous casualties sustained through stupidity, and the flower of a generation sacrificed for a futile cause. This view does not stand close examination. In contrast to the large, conscript armies of the other major powers, Britain possessed a small, volunteer army, half of which garrisoned the Empire. When required to fight alongside the French, the British contribution, although high in quality, was tiny in comparison to their allies. A massive citizen army had to be mobilized with meagre resources.

Commanders and staffs had to learn how to handle large numbers of barely trained men, while the first line, the regular battalions, then the second line, the Territorials, slowly bled to death. And yet it was the British Army which developed, in the tank, the answer to barbed wire and machine guns; it was the British Army which developed infantry/artillery cooperation to such a fine art that by 1918 it was the most professional in Europe; it was Haig who commanded the final offensive in 1918 that brought the German Army to its knees.

But the narrative of the Somme, and particularly the first day, with its terrible casualty list, is the abiding theme that runs through Britain's popular understanding of the war. The writings of Robert Graves, Siegfried Sassoon, Wilfred Owen and other war poets, and the memoirs of Lloyd George and Winston Churchill, have helped to foster this influence. There are, however, works by others which, while lacking in popular appeal, give a very different view. They are the writings of the small number of regular officers who fought at battalion level throughout the conflict and survived. Three of the most significant are: *The War The Infantry Knew* by Captain J.C. Dunn; *Infantry* by Brigadier General A.W. Pagan; and *The Land Locked Lake* by Lieutenant Colonel A.A. Hanbury-Sparrow.

Dunn was the Regimental Medical Officer of 2nd Battalion Royal Welch Fusiliers, the regular battalion which Graves wrote about in *Goodbye to All That*. Awarded the DSO, MC and bar and mentioned in dispatches, Dunn wrote that he put together the book, which is an amalgam of others' recollections, as a record of a long spell of duty done in the face of difficulty and discouragement.

> What was achieved is made radiant in my memory by the gay self-sacrifice of junior officers and non-commissioned officers; by the resource and cheerfulness in discomfort of the men of our Old Army, and their prompt answer to every call, confident in themselves and in each other.[1]

Dunn wanted to correct the popular notion of the war and the experience of the infantry, and in particular the impression of his battalion that Graves had created.

'Patsy' Pagan commanded the 1st Battalion The Gloucestershire Regiment on the Western Front, without a day's leave, from 1914 to 1918. The only times he was away from his beloved 28th were the occasions when he was wounded. Once, hearing of a German offensive, he discharged himself from hospital in his dressing gown to lead the battalion in defence. 'Service with a good infantry battalion in France,' he wrote, 'was the highest thing attainable during the years 1914 to 1918, and it is a pity that the life has generally been described by people whose outlook differed from that of the ordinary man.'[2] He went on to say that the good comradeship and enjoyment of life that existed, the courage, goodwill and cheerfulness of the men in the ranks, and the care for the troops on the part of the higher commanders and their staffs were the principal impressions left.

Hanbury-Sparrow's book is rather different in tone, but of particular interest, because the author was a regular officer in Dempsey's regiment, the Royal Berkshires, who fought with both its regular battalions in the course of the war. He wrote: 'The discipline of Aldershot is back once more. But yet it is no longer the same … instead of the regimental spirit it would be more accurate to speak henceforth of the regimental will.'[3]

As Dempsey prepared for his first battle with his new regiment, despite the casualties they had suffered, despite the loss of so many officers and the many times that the Battalion had had to be rebuilt with fresh drafts, the spirit among the officers and men of the Berkshires as they prepared for the battle to come, was undimmed. They would continue to do their duty, as they always had, and always would. The effect of the constant drain of casualties was to move officers around the Battalion as gaps appeared. In consequence, during his service in France, Dempsey served as company officer, company commander of different companies, acting adjutant, adjutant, and even – as opportunity offered – on the staff of brigade, division and corps.

The 1st Berkshires were not involved in the opening stages of the Somme battle, which were characterized by uneven gains and reverses. By 14 July, the British line formed a salient, the right side of which was threatened by Delville Wood. On 15 July, the South African Brigade attacked with great determination, securing almost the whole of the wood. In the artillery fire that the Germans called down to support their counter-attacks, the wood became a desolate landscape of shattered tree stumps and shell craters. It was now the turn of the British 2nd Division, and on 26 July the Berkshire's Commanding Officer, Lieutenant Colonel May, attended a conference at Brigade Headquarters at which it was announced that they would attack Delville Wood on the morning of 27 July. The plan was for the Battalion to be in reserve in the initial phase, with A Company detached to under command 23rd Battalion Royal Fusiliers, who were in the first wave with 1st Battalion King's Royal Rifle Corps. At 1700, May took his company commanders to view the ground over which they would attack, but as they returned to their men, gas shells from the German artillery began to fall. 'Slowly the gas clears. We remove our masks. Then it starts again in the valley. Scream – phut, scream – phut … Conditions are absolutely impossible. Twice have we put on our gas masks … within you is the almost unbearable tension of tight suppressed fear.'[4]

At 0200 on 27 July, the Battalion moved up to the southern edge of Delville Wood and lay down in their 'jumping-off formation' with B Company on the left, C Company centre, and D Company, in which Dempsey was serving under Lieutenant Reid, on the right. At 0510 the supporting artillery opened up on Longueval, and at 0610 on Delville Wood. An hour later, the artillery moved on to the northern part of the wood, and the Battalion advanced with its headquarters in the centre. After a temporary halt, the advance continued and by 0900 the Battalion had begun to dig in on its first objective, a trench system nicknamed South Street. The Germans kept up a heavy artillery fire on these positions throughout the day. Calls were received for assistance to the forward battalions, particularly the King's Royal Rifle Corps, and C Company was despatched to help. At 0500, the Battalion was ordered to withdraw to Mine Trench, but Dempsey's company was unable to comply at first, the enemy were so close, and only extricated with great difficulty after dark. The night was relatively quiet, but next day heavy artillery again made life extremely uncomfortable; at 1700 the depleted battalion was relieved and able to withdraw to the old British front line. Eight officers had become casualties, including D Company's commander, but Dempsey was unscathed.

On 2 August, reinforcements arrived, but as the Battalion moved up to relieve the Royal Fusiliers, their total strength was but 280 all ranks. A and D Companies amalgamated, as did C and B, transport drivers and drummers joined them, and on 4 August the Battalion was itself relieved and moved into billets behind the line. Dempsey was made up to acting captain and took temporary command of D Company from Reid. Dempsey's baptism of fire had been a hard one, but he had learned by experience the devastating effect of machine guns, two of which enfiladed the battalion from Longueval, despite supporting artillery fire.

He could now settle into the rhythm of his new life. In two and a half years in France, he moved from front line to support line, to rest and training, to frequent leaves. During quiet periods, of which there were many, even on the Somme, he could ride or walk with newly made friends on most days; he could attend the divisional concerts, of which there were many; he could occasionally take an evening pass to a town such as Amiens for a good meal; he could play sport. His diaries for these years are sparse, matter of fact, and filled with the minutiae of trench life, and of jolly times in the company of close comrades. Probably the closest of these was V.G. Stokes, also a regular officer, who was to retire as a brigadier. With him, Dempsey walked or rode every day on an Army horse, his favourite being Nigger, not a name that would be considered appropriate today.

After Delville Wood, the Berkshires saw little more action until November, when they moved into trenches near Serre. Dempsey was now commanding B Company. They were knee deep in mud, and the Battalion took thirty casualties before they were ordered into the attack next day. Half the Battalion was successful, capturing 200 yards of trench and fifty prisoners, but the other half was too weak for their task, and 150 casualties were sustained. Again, a long period out of the line followed, with the opportunity for rest, exercise, sport and training, and the integration into platoons and companies of reinforcements. Dempsey took his first home leave, and spent a few days at Crawley before visiting London to enjoy some of the shows that were playing to packed houses.

He was back in time for Christmas, which was spent in the time-honoured fashion of the British Army. A voluntary church service was held and, together with his fellow officers, Dempsey, now commanding A Company, served the men their Christmas dinner. Every effort had been made to give the Nissen huts a festive air and the Quartermaster, Captain Boshell, had provided ample fare – pork, beef and plum pudding, and a liberal supply of beer and cigarettes. The Commanding Officer went round the Battalion and addressed every man. At 1800 the Sergeants' Mess dined, and at 2000 the officers rounded off the day with their own dinner. The war diary noted that 'the spirit and discipline of the men was excellent.'[5]

In February 1917, Dempsey took over as Adjutant, a post he was to hold many times during his regimental service. The position of adjutant in peacetime is highly coveted; as the Commanding Officer's right-hand man on the 'A', or manning side, he is responsible for discipline, and for coordinating postings and promotions. He sets the standards for turnout and behaviour by which a battalion in barracks is judged. In war, he is the Commanding Officer's personal staff officer, running the day-to-day operations of Battalion Headquarters, and coordinating and disseminating tactical orders and instructions to and from brigade and company headquarters. He has to ensure that casualties are recorded, that next-of-kin details are regularly checked and relatives informed, in as sensitive way as conditions allow, of the death or injury of loved ones. With the Orderly Room staff, whom he commands, he must also ensure that soldiers' movements and qualifications are recorded meticulously, and that pay and allowances due are received promptly and in full. It is an extremely demanding post, made more so when large numbers of casualties are suffered.

There now began a three-month period which tested the Berkshires more severely than ever before. Attacks at Miraumont and Oppy Wood were so costly that by 1 May there were only enough men left to form two composite companies, and the Battalion was temporarily merged with 23rd Royal Fusiliers. One of the casualties was Dempsey's close friend, Stokes, who was shot through the head. Miraculously he survived and Dempsey was able to meet up with him in England when he took leave again in June. Together they enjoyed London.

Although it was soon resurrected, the Battalion was severely under strength for the next few months, during which it served in a quiet sector. The routine was to spend six days in the front line, six in support, six in the front line, and then six in reserve. Their numbers were such that they were excused much of the work on fatigue parties that was their usual lot, but the drainage and revetment of the posts and trenches and the sanitary conditions of the line were much improved.

It was during this quiet period that Miles again received disquieting news of Patrick. He had been posted to his regiment's First Battalion in France and gassed in a German counter-attack. Luckily Dempsey was able to meet him at the large base at Etaples, where Patrick was en route for England. As part of a scheme to prepare regular officers for service in the post-war Army, Dempsey was now attached to the staff of Headquarters II Corps for two months as an 'A' learner, understudying the officers who dealt with casualties, welfare, discipline and reinforcements – his job as adjutant writ large.

He returned to the command of A Company as poison gas was being increasingly employed by both sides. In October, gas operations were carried out on a large scale on the 2nd Division front. In the Berkshires' sector gas shells were fired from 4-inch Stokes mortars, and on their immediate left a gas cloud was released from 1,200 cylinders. The battalion war diary notes that the operation went off without a hitch and earned the congratulations of the Army Commander, but in the opinion of experts the wind was too strong for complete success. At the end of the month the Battalion was withdrawn to billets at Auchel. Over 300 reinforcements joined and for the first time in months they could train as a complete unit. New lessons were being absorbed from the ongoing battle of Ypres. Against their previous training and experience they had to learn that the 'continuous line of trenches' system must be abandoned, and fire and movement and 'the spirit of the bayonet' were emphasized. Dempsey again took leave in England, where he met up with Patrick and Stokes, both convalescing, both at the stage where they were able to enjoy life despite their wounds.

In November, the Berkshires had the opportunity to practise new techniques when they attacked at Bourlon Wood as part of the Cambrai offensive. Their experience of tanks in this, their first large-scale employment, was less than happy, and the attack was not a success. Tanks cooperated but were held up by a barricade and the infantry were forced back. Advancing again, small gains were made before the Germans put in a most determined counter-attack, supported by extremely heavy and accurate artillery fire. The Berkshires held on tenaciously and the line was never broken. It was a proud moment for the Regiment, which fortunately suffered comparatively few casualties. For Dempsey it was his first experience of a new form of warfare whose complexities he began to appreciate. His military education was now taken a stage further as he was attached to 99 Brigade as a 'G' or Operations staff learner for two months, then to the 2nd Division, then back to 99 Brigade.

By March, following the capitulation of Russia as a result of the Bolshevik Revolution, the Germans were able to switch huge numbers of troops from their eastern to their western front. Now outnumbering their opponents, the Germans were able to go over to the offensive. The British Army, starved of reinforcements by the Prime Minister, Lloyd George, was required to stretch its resources even thinner, as it took over more ground from the French. At this stage the Berkshires were at La Vacquerie, preparing for the anticipated offensive, and Dempsey was back with them, commanding D Company.

On 12 March, as part of the preliminary operations prior to their attack, the Germans put down a heavy mustard gas barrage on the Berkshires' sector. Dempsey, along with ten other officers and 250 soldiers, was wounded. The war diary notes that the bulk of these casualties were not serious, and few would have been evacuated to England had it not been necessary to clear the medical system to allow for the reception of casualties wounded in subsequent fighting. Dempsey's trench diary noted his progress as he passed from advanced dressing station to field ambulance, to casualty clearing section, base hospital and eventually to a hospital in the UK.

12 March. GASSED. ADS Villers Plouich. 100th FA Ruyaulcourt. CCS Ytres. Train from Ytres.

13 March. Arr, No. 10 BRC (Lady Murray's) Le Treport.[6]

He remained at Le Treport for a week, before his final stage to London, where he began his treatment at 12 Belgrave Square, where his mother visited him. Her relief at seeing him recovering, after the cumulative anxiety for the safety of the three brothers, must have been huge, the strain of the previous four years immense. Once the immediate uncertainties were removed, Dempsey was able to enjoy a leisurely three months of convalescence; golf, cricket and tennis were mixed with entertainment in the company of Stokes.

He was therefore away from the Battalion when, from 23 to 28 March it was in constant engagement, losing eighteen officers and 500 men. Although, after attending three medical boards, he was passed fit in June, the effect of the gas was such that Dempsey later had to have a lung removed. He returned to the Battalion, now in 99 Brigade, commanded by Brigadier General Edmund 'Tiny' Ironside, later to play an important part in his career. Ironside was a first-class commander who believed in thorough training and ensured that all officers and NCOs were fully versed in the latest techniques of infantry / tank cooperation. There was a lot to learn as infantrymen and tank commanders thought through the practicalities of working together.

In August the whole balance of the war changed as General Haig commanded the supremely successful advance that was to break the German Army. At Ayette, the Berkshires were ordered to play a major role in these offensive operations. But this time, battle procedure was carefully followed. Orders were given out on 18 August, rehearsals with the supporting tanks were carried out that day and the next, and a further day was spent in preparation before the Battalion moved off in lorries to form up for the first phase of the brigade plan. The Berkshires were to lead, with two companies up, supported by six Mark IV tanks.

Dempsey, now commanding A Company, was in the lead as the advance began at 0455. The morning was very misty and it was extremely difficult to keep direction, but all objectives were taken with little difficulty and the Battalion moved into reserve. On 22 August, they were warned that they would pass under command 6 Brigade and attack Ervillers the next morning. This was achieved, again with few casualties, and on 24 August, back under command of Ironside, they were ordered to attack high ground north of Maury. This time, ten Mark IVs were to be in support and cavalry was on hand to exploit success. Again, complete success was achieved, infantry and tanks working well together, and on 26 August the Battalion was relieved. They had every reason to be proud of their success. Supply arrangements worked well, the men were never short of ammunition, food or water, and all-arms cooperation had been remarkably good. Thorough training had paid off, and the Berkshires had taken all their objectives and a large numbers of prisoners.

In September, Dempsey went on local leave, and enjoyed a few weeks on the coast at Ambleteuse and Deauville, but was back as Adjutant in October, when, in a series of advances and attacks, the Battalion suffered over 300 casualties. On 11 November the Berkshires were at Escarmain. Dempsey's trench diary noted laconically:

> Armistice Signed.
> Cross country run in the morning.
> Celebrations.
> BGC and Robertson to dinner.[7]

The war was over and by Christmas the Battalion was in Germany, billeted at Arnoldsweiser as part of the Army of Occupation. They had earned many battle honours and added lustre to their name. But the cost had been heavy, especially for the regulars. There is a remarkable photograph in the regimental museum of the men of the 1st Battalion who went to France in 1914, and were still with it at war's end.

There are six men in the picture.

CHAPTER 3

'Orderly Room'

As the Berkshires settled into their peacetime routine, it was an opportunity for Dempsey to take stock. For a young man of just twenty-two years of age, he had much to be proud of. After a successful school career he had acquitted himself with distinction in the war, as both Adjutant and Company Commander. On 28 December 1918, he had been gazetted as included in Sir Douglas Haig's Despatch of 8 November – a Mention in Despatches or MID, denoted by an oak leaf on his Victory Medal – and in the Birthday Honours of 3 June 1919, he was gazetted as being awarded the Military Cross. Both awards were for distinguished service, rather than a specific act of gallantry, and there are no individual citations.

At a young age, Dempsey already had much first-hand experience of leadership, tactics and administration in battle. He had learned how good training and good battle procedure influenced performance. He had experience of other arms, including armour and artillery, under the most testing conditions. Most important of all, he knew what motivated men in battle – what it was that made them overcome their basic instinct to 'lie in a ditch until the shooting stops'.

Dempsey could also be proud of his family. All three brothers had done their bit, with two Military Crosses and four wounds between them. Above all, they had all survived. Dempsey, a regular officer almost continuously at the front for two and a half years, had had huge luck. The chapel at Sandhurst displays, on beautiful memorial tablets, the names of former cadets who fell in the Great War. The total for the Royal Berkshire Regiment is forty-four, of some eighty who served. Dempsey had survived odds of less than even. Of his Shrewsbury contemporaries in the cricket XI, in addition to Ellis, T. Onslow, 'an improving bat', was dead, killed in 1917 serving with the King's Shropshire Light Infantry. Of the twenty-two monitors, four had been killed.

However, the other two Salopians to pass into Sandhurst with him had both survived the war to win Military Crosses. Britain and the Empire had suffered grievously, but of the main protagonists it had come off the lightest. In comparison with German war dead of two million, and French of one and a third million, the United Kingdom figure of three quarters of a million killed is shocking, but comparatively light.

Dempsey was now a tried and trusted member of the Berkshire regimental family. He had been through the fire and emerged with his honour intact and his reputation high. Corporal Walter DCM MM, battalion stretcher bearer sergeant during the great advance of 1918, described him as a very brave man, loved and respected by all the old 1st Battalion. To 'Dimmer', as he was always known in the Regiment, such a tribute would have been worth more than any other. Another said: 'With Dimmer as Adjutant, no battalion could wish for more.'[1]

Dempsey's main task as Adjutant, now peace had come, was to oversee the demobilization of the 'hostilities only' members of the Battalion, and to grant leave to those who were staying in the Army. This was not an easy task. Units were visited by itinerant lecturers sent by Army or Corps to relieve the monotony. One of the subjects was 're-enlisting'; the Army realized that it needed men to garrison the Empire, which was expanding as administration followed conquest. The 1st Berkshires, as a regular battalion, was one of those called for this task.

In June, the 1st Battalion the Berkshire Regiment reformed at Chiseldon Camp in Wiltshire. Lieutenant Colonel Thornton was in command, Hanbury-Sparrow, now sporting a DSO and MC, was one of the company commanders, and Dempsey's close friend, Stokes, was also there. Dempsey was still Adjutant and could now find time to rekindle his love of sport, always a priority in the peacetime army. His forte was still cricket and over the next twenty years he played regularly at both regimental and county level, representing Sussex, which he regarded as his native county, as his duties allowed. He also played football and hockey in the Battalion, and became a most proficient horseman.

As Adjutant, it was Dempsey's responsibility to organize the next move, and in September the Battalion left Tilbury on the SS *Khyber* for Karachi, where they stayed for a fortnight before embarking on the *Elephanta* for Basra, thence via Nasiryeh to their duty station, south of Baghdad. They joined a force that numbered 60,000, the large majority from the Indian Army.

The situation in what was then called Mesopotamia was tense. When the British invaded the area in 1914 it formed three provinces of the Ottoman Empire, which had declared war as an ally of Germany. Ottoman rule was comparatively gentle and Turks occupied only the most senior positions in the administration. By 1918, after a serious but temporary reverse at Kut, Britain was in total control and had imposed a mixture of direct and indirect rule under martial law. They established and maintained lighting systems in the cities; they improved sanitation and hospital services; they ran the railways, and repaired and extended the road network; and they were involved in a host of commercial enterprises from steamers on the Tigris to farms.

It was the British intention that Feisal, the leader chosen by Lawrence, should become ruler of Syria and Lebanon. When this plan came to nothing, they promoted the idea that he should be king of a new country, Iraq, carved out of three former provinces of the Ottoman Empire. In April 1920, the League of Nations considered the future of the area and in May awarded a mandate – supervisory powers – to Britain. This was seen as a cost-effective solution to the British public. But Feisal's faction, who had expected immediate and complete independence, saw little for themselves in this arrangement. They also resented the large British and Indian Army presence in what was supposed to be a country at peace. In addition to the 53,000 uniformed military of the Indian Army, there were now 60,000 other Indian followers at Army headquarters and in various subordinate posts. This contrasted unfavourably in the people's minds with the previous regime in which 95 per cent of the Ottoman garrison was composed of local Arabs.

But numbers did not imply efficiency. Many of the best men, who had learned Arabic, had gone home. A complete breakdown in the administration seemed imminent. Although the British government announced that Mesopotamia was to be constituted an independent state under the guarantee of the League of Nations, with due regard to the rights, wishes and interests of all the communities of the country, their words fell on deaf ears. T.E. Lawrence was moved to observe that the Arabs had rebelled against the Turks, not because their rule was notably bad, but because they wanted independence.

The situation was made more precarious by the widespread practice of bearing arms, mainly among the rural tribes, and efforts were made to disarm them. By April, some 50,000 rifles had been collected – another cause for grievance – but there were still huge numbers in Arab hands when unrest broke out. Although Basra remained quiet, as did Baghdad – after a series of mass demonstrations – serious fighting started near the capital in July and spread to the lower Euphrates. The British garrison of Kufa was invested and a small force in Hilleh, south of Baghdad, was attacked, with the loss of twenty killed and 300 wounded. Eighty men of the Manchesters were taken prisoner and held for several months, and fighting continued for many weeks as supporters of the rebellion joined from farther afield. Rail and road communications were blocked. In August, Colonel Leachman, a widely respected political officer, and typical of the most effective of those who had taken on a quasi-civilian role, was murdered.

For a month after Leachman's death anarchy reigned, as the call for jihad went out. The Muntafiq rose in the south, the Dulaim tribes invested the garrison at Fallujah and another political officer, Captain Salmon, was murdered at Kufa. The British responded by concentrating their forces, where necessary fighting through road blocks and ambushes with armoured cars and air support. For the Berkshires it was a frustrating time as they performed a purely defensive role, but in August they were warned for a move to a completely different theatre of operations – Persia.

In 1918, as British troops moved to complete the occupation of Iraq, there was concern over the situation in its eastern neighbour, in particular the threat posed by the Bolsheviks. Persia had a weak central government and was unable to impose order in its north-west, in the region of the Caspian Sea. Britain's interests in the area, which were based on the security of India and the maintenance of her supplies of oil, were threatened. Troops were despatched to the area under the command of Major General L.C. Dunsterville, assumed by Kipling's biographer, Charles Carrington, to be the real-life hero of 'Stalky & Co'. The small force aimed to reach Baku and organize its defence against the Turks and Germans. But it had to battle first with the local Soviets in the port of Enzeli, and with a part nationalist, part bandit resistance movement in Gilan province, the Jangalis, under one Zuchik Khan. By the time they reached Baku, the Turks were already besieging the town. The Turks then launched an assault on Dunsterforce, which was forced to withdraw to Resht, closer to Tehran, leaving a small detachment at Enzeli.

This was the situation when the Great War ended, the Germans and Turks laid down their arms, and were replaced as the main threat by the Bolsheviks and the Jangalis. Two new factors now entered the equation. Twelve ex-British warships under General Denikin, the White (Anti-Bolshevik) Russian, commanded the waters of the Caspian, and a mix of locally based Persian forces were ranged loosely in an anti-Russian coalition. Among these were the 8,000 strong 'Cossack' cavalry division under White Russian officers, commanded by Colonel Starosselsky. Another, the gendarmerie, with Swedish advisers, was described by Dempsey as 'useless'. To add to the confusion, Simko was trying to carve a Kurdish kingdom out of the western part of Persian Azerbaijan, and the Bolsheviks had many sympathizers in the towns of the region.

A successor to Dunsterforce was created: North Persia Force, or Norperforce, initially under the command of Brigadier General Baterman-Champain, usually referred to as General Champain. Reporting to the GOC-in-C Mesopotamia, it was a self-contained mix of infantry, light armour and artillery, with supporting arms and a flight of RAF aircraft. Its task was to provide a defensive screen against any possible southward move by the Bolsheviks. Its headquarters were at Kazvin, south-west of the Caspian Sea, and by late 1919 it was established with a line of outposts centered on Enzeli, on the coast, and Zinjan on the road to Tabriz. Its Lines of Communication to Baghdad stretched 500 miles, only 300 of them over what could be described as roads.

In the spring of 1920 the security situation deteriorated rapidly. In western Azerbaijan, Simko resumed the offensive; in Tabriz, to their north west, Persian Azerbaijan declared independence; and a Bolshevik backed force from Baku started another revolt. One of the main platforms of nationalist agitation was the Anglo-Persian Agreement, signed in August 1919, but many of whose main clauses awaited implementation – among them the imposition of British Army officers on the Persian Army, including the

Cossacks. The treaty envisaged that a British officer was to be "Organiser-in-Chief" of the army, and a British officer was to command each of seven military areas. This was bound to offend Persian feelings and prevent the force being regarded as properly Persian. It was never fully implemented, and when the Bolsheviks occupied Enzeli in May 1920, forcing the small British garrison to withdraw, Norperforce was needed, not only to keep the Persians in check, but to prevent the Bolsheviks advancing on Tehran. It was to do this largely by bluff; it was not to hold Enzeli if seriously attacked, but to fall back on the nearest railhead.

In July, the Bolshevik-Jangali forces facing the British were increased to some 2,000, with artillery, and posts were pushed out in the direction of Menjil. Inevitably, clashes occurred with the Norperforce outposts on the road between Menjil and Resht. Although not serious, these threatening moves by the enemy were sufficient to cause the outpost line to be withdrawn further, and for Resht – rather precipitately – to be given up by the British, but garrisoned by the Cossacks. By August, the situation was critical, as the politicians in London squabbled over whether it was viable to keep a force in Persia at all.

In fact, the Berkshires were moved to join Norperforce, just as the Cabinet agreed in principle to retain a force for the time being. By an extraordinary coincidence, the Berkshires were to relieve the 1st Battalion Royal Irish Fusiliers, Patrick's old unit, and by 8 August they were ranged alongside them, together with the 2nd Battalion York and Lancaster Regiment, on the 'Outpost Line', running around Kazvin. The town was unprepossessing, and the camp, partly in huts, partly in tents, lay outside it.

At this stage Dempsey summed up the increasingly odd situation as follows:

> If we had been at war with Russia, and the commander had been given a free hand, there is no doubt that the matter could have been dealt with very quickly – and B.L. [Bolsheviks] kicked out of the country. But we were not at war with Russia, and the government had no intention of going to war with Russia. At the same time, Norperforce was charged with protecting Persia. But no offensive action was to be taken north of Menjil.[2]

Moreover, Champain was to act as he thought fit in assisting Persian troops in quelling any disorder in the region dominated by them. Dempsey noted, rather sarcastically, that in order to clear up the question of policy once and for all, Baghdad wired at the end of August: 'Don't let yourself get too entangled, and be careful not to run the risk of being cut off.'[3]

The situation had all the ingredients for a disaster; Champain was under instructions from the British minister at Tehran regarding his dealings with Cossacks and his attitude to the Bolsheviks; he was directly under command Headquarters Mesopotamia, 500 miles away in Baghdad, from whom he had to obtain permission to take any action; and to top it all, he was under notice that units could, and would, be taken from him to relieve the situation in Mesopotamia. At the end of August, matters descended to the level of farce when the Chestnut Troop, Royal Horse Artillery and the Guides (Indian) cavalry attached to Norperforce were ordered south. The order was countermanded, but only after they had already covered 30 miles of the journey. They returned, only to be ordered south again on 11 September, and for this order to be yet again countermanded after they had set off for the second time.

Dempsey's Orders for the Outpost Line noted that the enemy consisted of Jangalis and Persian and Russian Bolsheviks, together with 'parties of lawless malcontents'. It was the commander's intention to 'protect Kazvin with a lightly held outpost line, preparatory to ascertaining the enemy's intentions, and moving out to destroy him should he come within reach, or attack our forces'.[4] The Berkshires held the right sector, with the Irish Fusiliers in the centre, and the York and Lancasters on the left. Dempsey, as Adjutant, transposed the orders and issued the necessary coordinating points as they applied, noting that drinking water should be chlorinated. The heat at this time of year was excessive and Dempsey ordered that one *chagal*, or canvas water bag, should be issued per man. The Royal Irish Fusiliers were soon replaced by Gurkhas, and for the next two months affairs settled down into a routine, uninterrupted by any major alarms. Bolshevik subversion, particularly any directed at the Indian troops in the force, was a recurring preoccupation. A poster addressed to 'Indian Brethren' by the Indian Revolutionary Organisation, found at Menjil, captures the atmosphere. It begins:

> Congratulations! Through good luck you have secured another powerful ally of yours, the Soviet Russia which makes it certain that the problem of your freedom is about to be solved in no time. Continue and accelerate your struggle against the oppressors.'[5]

The atmosphere changed when a new commander took over from Champain. Major General Ironside had commanded the Berkshires in 99 Brigade in the closing stages of the war, and is thought to be the model for John Buchan's hero Richard Hannay. Known as 'Tiny' on account of his great height, Ironside had served in the Boer War, where his remarkable facility for languages made him an ideal choice for undercover military intelligence. After a very successful career in the war, he was promoted Major General at the unusually early age of thirty-nine. Not known for his sense of humour, he nonetheless liked to recount the story of how, when accompanying that 'most superior person', Lord Curzon of Kedlestone, on a visit to the Western

Front, they stopped to observe some soldiers bathing at a mobile bath unit. Lord Curzon then observed that he used to think that the lower classes had dark skin, all covered in hair, but he now saw that they did not.

Ironside was known for his courage and great physical strength and resourcefulness, and was picked to command Allied Troops in Archangel, Russia, in 1919, and Ismid, Turkey, in 1920. Neither of these campaigns had been successful and although no blame attached to Ironside – if anything his reputation was enhanced – it would not be surprising if he came to see himself as a bird of ill omen. He certainly came to be known as an expert in risky withdrawals and it was this, no doubt, that influenced his selection. The Cabinet's intention was that he should motivate the Persian forces, particularly the Cossack division under Starosselski, to the point where they could take over responsibility for both internal security and defence against external aggression. Norperforce could then go home.

Ironside assessed that his first priority was to get rid of the commander of the Cossacks and at the end of October, when Persian forces under Starosselski's command suffered a reverse in north Persia, Ironside seized on the opportunity. In an order to the commander of the outpost line, now known as Menjcol, from its headquarters location at Menjil, he began by saying that it had been decided to dismiss Starosselski, along with the Russian officers of the Persian Cossack Division. He was to be replaced by a Persian commander, who would be controlled by a British officer and staff.[6] Ironside did not envisage any trouble over this move and took a more offensive attitude, encouraging Menjcol to reoccupy Resht, with a reinforcement of Gurkhas and Deolis, and expressing his intention of bombing Enzeli as soon as possible.

The Shah grudgingly agreed to the dismissal of the Russian officers, but the Persian Cabinet was immediately replaced by one which feared the consequences on public opinion of replacing them by British officers. The scheme was in jeopardy, but Ironside took advantage of his knowledge of the situation at Resht. The true state of affairs there was known to Ironside through a wireless intercept unit, whose services were to prove critical. As the Cossacks prepared to withdraw, Ironside moved up to the head of the pass at Menjil and hatched his plot with Lieutenant Colonel Francis, commanding the Berkshires, an officer he considered first class. The Berkshires were deployed to cover the withdrawal of the Cossacks, while Military Police controlled their movement. As the Cossacks came through the pass, Starosselski left them to motor on to Tehran. His orders to the division to camp to the north of Kazvin were intercepted, and altered, to send them to a British-controlled camp at Aga Baba. There they were shepherded in by Gurkhas and the camp was picketed at night by the Guides to prevent any exit.

When Starosselski reached Tehran, he was told that he was no longer in command and that all Russian officers were to leave. A final attempt by him to countermand these instructions was again foiled by the intercept detachment and the Russian officers quietly handed over to the senior Persian ranks, under Surdar Homayun, a man of little military accomplishment.

The whole Anglo-Persian agreement was now in jeopardy, and only days after issuing his bullish instruction, Ironside was compelled to acknowledge that there was no hope of imposing British officers to replace the Russians, and that the unreformed Cossack Division were now beyond hope of speedy reorganization. He was also forced to pull in his horns and countermand his previous orders to attack Resht. Instead, Menjcol would be increased in size, with the Berkshires and 2nd Gurkhas forming the main defence. The fact that no action was now envisaged against Resht was to be kept quiet.

The men on the outpost line now turned their attention to preparing their accommodation for the oncoming winter. The Berkshires' headquarters was moved to Ganja, where they could set up a proper officers' mess. Dempsey enjoyed a final game of golf with Stokes and from then on his diary recorded snow every day. Despite the order not to engage in offensive action, the RAF continued to bomb Enzeli, and on 8 December one of their aeroplanes on such a mission made a forced landing between the two front lines. The pilot was killed, but the observer made it back to the British lines and a few days later two senior NCOs of the Guides cavalry, disguised as Persians, were able to inspect it. It was found to be intact, but impossible to recover.

Deep snow now began to hinder operations by both sides, but clashes continued, and the intercept unit proved its worth again and again, allowing the British to prepare for any enemy incursion. Shortly after Christmas had been celebrated in the usual style, a force of Russians who threatened the Gurkhas in the centre was fiercely counter-attacked. Nine enemy were left for dead and two prisoners together with two machine guns were taken. Opposite the Berkshires, a favourite enemy tactic was to move to a ridge overlooking their forward positions and open fire, retreating rapidly once the Guides were called forward. In one such incident, the Berkshires sent two companies by boat across the river on their front and dispersed the marauders, who appeared to be criminal rather than military.

The 21st of February was an eventful day. Hussan Khan of Shafti had sought shelter with the British, but, while seeking weapons and food from them, was found to be in communication with the Bolsheviks in Resht. A patrol of one and a half companies of Berkshires under Hanbury Sparrow was sent to apprehend Hussan, his brother Yusuf and his clerk. At dawn they had the village surrounded and the Berkshires closed in. They were met by accurate fire but pressed on and soon had the village under control. A search was made, resulting in the capture of the clerk, two machine guns and several rifles. Hussan Khan had fled and crossed over to the Russians, but in a follow-up operation Yusuf was captured by the Gurkhas.

On 22 February intelligence was received that the Bolsheviks would attack on 3 March, but although this was later revised as bad weather affected their operations, Dempsey noted in his diary: 'Ironside warned that we should have trouble with snipers on the way down.'[7]

Meanwhile Reza Khan, a protégé of Ironside, had taken command of the Cossack Division, and was leading his men in a march on the capital, forcing the Premier to step down. Now that Persian officers had replaced Russians, Ironside considered that the Cossacks were the compromise solution to the protection of Persia. Any attempt to impose the terms of the Anglo-Persian Treaty was now seen to be dead, and the Cabinet made a final decision to withdraw Norperforce. By the beginning of April, the snows were beginning to melt and, as Cossacks took over their positions, the Berkshires began their withdrawal. They had first to repair the flood-damaged roads, working night and day to cut new tracks through the hills.

Dempsey noted: '2nd line transport with Aveline moved towards Menjil as the bridge was beginning to go.'[8] Indeed, as they approached, they saw that the river, swollen by melted snow, had forced the piers out of position. They hurried across, passing stores from hand to hand so as to avoid the risk from lorries using the weakened structure, and two days later Dempsey's diary takes up the tale: 'Battalion and Menjcol moved to Menjil – leaving Colonel Huddleston and Persian Cossacks in possession. Whole road flooded and bridge going; last troops crossed bridge after dark – distance only 11 miles. Spent night at Post House. Pouring rain.'[9]

By 16 April they were safely in Kazvin. On 21 April they began the move by march stages back to Himaidi on the outskirts of Baghdad. Here they found that the camp was largely tented, and cuts in the construction budget meant that there was no local labour for building. In the time-honoured fashion of British soldiers, the Battalion turned to self help and erected a suitable barracks. But the effects of the climate were being felt. The regimental magazine remarked:

> There has been a certain amount of sickness and during the hottest part of the summer some deaths unfortunately occurred, but when we remember what a contrast there is between Mesopotamia freak temperatures of 125 degrees in the shade, and the snows and ice of the last winter in the snowy heights of Persia, it is not remarkable that the less virile constitutions have needed little persuasion.[10]

In August the Regiment provided a band and Guard of Honour for the ceremony marking the accession of King Feisal to the throne of Iraq. Back in Persia, Reza Khan mounted the coup that was eventually to lead to his installation as Shah in 1925. The Pahlavi dynasty was to sit on the Peacock Throne until its overthrow sixty years later.

The wheel had come full circle for the Berkshires and for Dempsey. He had experienced a volatile security situation in Iraq and an extremely complex politico-military one in Persia. As the Adjutant of one of only a small number of major units in the force, he was privy to all the effects of the government's weak and vacillating policy, and the difficulties caused by the attempt to micro-manage a campaign from afar. He would have been well aware of the potential ramifications of the smallest action, in a situation in which the deeds of a section, or even of one man, could have far-reaching consequences. From small actors on the huge stage of the Great War, the Berkshires had become major players on a small one. Dempsey was being noticed as a highly competent officer, calm and capable, a 'safe pair of hands'. One of those to get to know him well was Ironside, whose opinion from the 1918 offensive would have been reinforced by the four months in which they had been at close quarters. 'Tiny' Ironside rose to become Chief of the Imperial General Staff, professional head of the British Army. His good opinion was not earned lightly and was the more valuable for that. A brother officer later wrote of Dempsey at that time:

> As Adjutant, both in war and peace, he set a standard which could well serve as a model for such an appointment. The experience he gained then, including the handling of a greater variety of Commanding Officers than falls to the lot of most Adjutants, probably did much to further his future career.'[11]

Dempsey added another arrow to his quiver in Persia. He took up Pelmanism, the system of scientifically training the mind invented by William Joseph Ennever. It was intended to expand mental powers in many directions and remove tendencies to indolence and inefficiency. The course progressed from removing any inferiority complex, and the setting of goals in life, through concentration and mental control, to self-expression and good judgement in business and affairs. In other words, this was not just memory tricks – although Dempsey could and would perform astonishing feats of memory with a pack of cards, such as finding cards 'blind' from a pack he had looked at once – it was a whole system of life-enhancing skills. The knack of perfect recall is useful in any walk of life, but in the Army it gives commanders an extra edge to address anyone, of any rank, by their name. For Dempsey, who had a fascination with maps, there was an extra dimension – he could recall every feature of a map, and describe the ground it covered in great detail, after a short study. But the significance of Dempsey's study of Pelmanism goes beyond this. At the age of twenty-four, when his peers would normally be occupied with enjoying life to the full, he was deliberately embarking on a course of training his mind to fit him for a serious study of his profession. Dempsey's old history master later remarked that he was not particularly inclined to study while at Shrewsbury; from the time of his involvement in Persia that would change.

Chapter 4

'Officers'

The next eight years were, for Dempsey, an opportunity to practise peacetime soldiering in a way that he had so far been denied by war and the campaigns in Iraq and Persia. At the end of 1921 the Berkshires were posted to Bareilly in India. Having organized the move with practised efficiency, Dempsey handed over as Adjutant and was given command of C Company, a rifle company of about 100 men. There were many advantages to service in India for a British unit. It was always kept at its full establishment strength, if necessary at the expense of those units – in this case the 2nd Battalion – back in Britain. An officer could live on his pay, and, for a single captain, life as very comfortable. As well as his own officers' mess, there was a local club where he could meet other military men and civilian employees of government and business. There was ample leave, short periods on local leave and very long leaves back home.

For the great majority of the time, Bareilly was a favoured station, and one of the most popular postings in India. Situated in northern India, on the Ramganga River, it is within sight of the Himalayas rising majestically to the north. The climate varied from the extremes of the summer, which included the monsoon season, to cool winters. However, the rainfall was moderate, and the annual training cycle of army units, both British and Indian, was adjusted to allow for seasonal changes. Most of the more strenuous training was carried out in the cold weather. In the heat of the summer as many as possible moved to the cooler climate of the hill areas. There was abundant game and the Bareilly Tent Club was famed for its addiction to pig-sticking. Riding was cheap and most officers kept at least one horse. Dempsey was a keen horseman, if a little heavy in the saddle.

The C Company 'scribe' noted soon after Dempsey took over that he was a keen and capable sportsman, and a great acquisition to the company. In the spring of 1922, Dempsey went home for the first time for almost three years for a long leave. Before he left, he had time to top the battalion batting averages and to guide his company to first place in the inter-company athletics, tug-of-war and cross-country shooting. A second home leave followed in early 1923 and later in the year the 'scribe' recorded his heartfelt appreciation of Dempsey's time as company commander:

> Capt M C Dempsey MC, our Company Commander, has left us and gone back to 'Dear Old Blighty' to take up an appointment at the Royal Military College Sandhurst. We all deeply regret his departure because he was such an enthusiastic sportsman and always had a keen interest in everything that took place in the company. Our thoughts go with him and we all – from the bottom of our hearts – wish him the very best of luck in his new home, and sincerely hope that one day he will return to us once more.[1]

The Sandhurst to which Dempsey returned in August 1923 was unchanged physically from the establishment he had left in early 1915. However, the urgency of preparing young men to meet the demands of trench warfare had been replaced by a gentler rhythm. Although the first few weeks were still taken at a frenetic pace as drill sergeants honed their charges to a standard fit to 'pass off the square' – that is, to be seen in public in uniform – thereafter life settled down to a two-year course in which there was considerable free time. All the cadets followed the same syllabus for the first year, studying the principles of geography, the Empire and its history, civics and French. There was the opportunity in the second year to diversify into other languages, science or other subjects of their choice.

For Dempsey, this was a prestige appointment. An officer on the staff of the College was selected by his regiment with care, for not only did he represent its face to the rest of the Army, he was also its talent spotter.

For the next few years, Dempsey was able to see much of his family. A relative described how 'Jim, Pat and Miles were grown men with well launched careers, and I was much in awe of them'. She went on to say:

> Needless to say they took little notice of me. That was when they – Pat and Miles – were living with their mother in Crawley. Jim, the elder brother, was already the Black Sheep, and Aunt Katherine, looking around and lowering her voice, would tell me 'Well Jim – now don't tell anyone I told you this – but he's travelling around England recuperating from an overdose of LIQUOR in one of those canal boats.' Pat and Miles when I visited their mother avoided the subject of their brother, as did she, and I was cautioned not to mention him when I visited. Pat and Miles were confirmed bachelors, tremendously correct, and they paid little heed to me. I was Miles' slavish admirer as a schoolgirl and it continued into adolescence and

until I realised he had no interest in me, and we were totally unsuited to one another.[2]

Jim, who married soon after the war, was indeed a problem brother, and his erratic behaviour is summed up by another relative, with whom he was lodging, after leaving his wife: 'I am afraid events have moved quickly since I saw you last Saturday. I am very unwilling to turn Jim out, but I felt I ought to tell you I have told him that I feel this friendship is a danger to him and most undignified on both sides and so I have asked him to leave if it continues.'[3]

For the four years that Dempsey was at Sandhurst, he commanded No. 1 Platoon of No. 1 Company. Initially his company commander was Lieutenant Colonel N. Robinson, but he was replaced by an officer who was to play a major part in Dempsey's career. Later to become General Sir Richard O'Connor, Dick, as he was always known, was seven years older than Dempsey. Commissioned into the Cameronians, the ferocious Lowland regiment which was wont to strike fear as much into friendly as enemy hearts, he had won an outstanding reputation in the Great War. In 1917, at the age of twenty-eight, he was promoted Lieutenant Colonel and commanded an infantry battalion of the Honourable Artillery Company (an anomaly that is only explicable by reference to that unit's long and illustrious history as the Territorial Army's most prestigious regiment). He took them to the Italian front and captured the island of Grave di Papadopopoli on the Piave River, then held by the Austrians. By the end of the war he had been awarded the DSO and bar and MC, and was held in awe by those beneath him. He was an inspiration to Dempsey, who became a lifelong friend.

A fellow platoon commander in No. 1 Company was A.H. Gatehouse, of the Royal Tank Corps. Originally in the Royal Northumberland Fusiliers, Gatehouse saw the tanks as the coming war winner and transferred to the fledgling corps at the end of the war. He was later to command the Mechanisation Experimental Establishment and become one of the Army's foremost exponents of armoured warfare, retiring as a major general soon after the Second World War. One year older than Dempsey, Gatehouse was the perfect foil for his emerging views on tactical doctrine.

The College Adjutant, at that time one of the most prestigious appointments for a major in the British Army, was Major 'Boy' Browning DSO, Grenadier Guards, also destined for the highest ranks. Always immaculately turned out, it is said that, at the end of a rehearsal for the Sovereign's Parade – the final parade marking a cadet's passing out – he rode his horse up the steps of Old College to protect his uniform from a passing rain shower, thus instituting one of the most treasured of Sandhurst's traditions. He too was to become a general and play a major role in Dempsey's later career.

The years passed pleasantly, and Dempsey was able to play much first-class cricket, representing the Regimental Depot and playing regularly for Berkshire, the county in which Sandhurst is situated, as well as for Sussex. He also had the opportunity to travel and began the series of journeys around Europe which were such a feature of his life between the wars. His first trip was to Germany, Poland and Danzig, then a city state of unusual status. In 1925, with three fellow officers from the College, he spent six weeks travelling around Scandinavia. They stayed for a few days in Tallinn, capital of Esthonia (as it was then spelt), a city of intrigue and adventure, where the intelligence services of the Western world carried out their espionage activities against Bolshevik Russia. It was there that Arthur Ransome, author of *Swallows and Amazons*, lived with Evgenia Shelepina, Trotsky's private secretary, and spied for at least one side, and possibly both. In 1926, Italy was Dempsey's destination, and in 1927, France. But he was also working hard to prepare for the future, and he studied for and passed the Staff College examination.

The semi-official guide of that time to Camberley – so called to distinguish it from the Military College whose grounds it shares – recommended that an officer serious about trying for entry should do five and a half months' ground work, then study for three and a half to five hours every day. It recommended sixty-seven published works as essential study, and another twenty-seven as desirable. Many hopefuls paid to be coached by crammers for the entrance examination, which consisted of:

Training for War and Military History	4,000 marks
Organisation and Administration	2,000 marks
Imperial Organisation	2,000 marks
Optional Subject	1,000 marks

The optional subjects ranged from French, German or Russian to the history of Europe, India or the USA, and science. In 1926, out of 440 officers who took the exam, twenty-two passed. Dempsey's phenomenal memory had got him through.

But passing the exam did not guarantee entry to Camberley. A prospective student had to show good service in the field, three years as adjutant and good service on the staff or as an instructor for two years. Dempsey had fulfilled all these requirements; now he had to wait for a vacancy.

In 1927, he returned to regimental duty, not this time to the 1st Battalion, but to the 2nd, stationed at Wiesbaden. Under the reforms of the late nineteenth century, regiments of foot were linked. Thus, the 49th Foot became 1st Battalion the Royal Berkshire Regiment, and the 66th Foot became the 2nd

Battalion. All members of the Regiment wore the same cap badge, wherever they were serving, and officers and NCOs were held on a common seniority roll. However, one battalion would normally be stationed in India and the other in either the United Kingdom, or, at this time, in the Rhine Army of Occupation. Thus Dempsey came to serve, for the only time in his career, with the 66th, or 2nd Berkshires. After a course at the Small Arms Wing at Hythe, Dempsey took over B Company and was soon involved in sport, captaining the company hockey team to victory, and playing cricket for the Battalion. Although his main skill was as a batsman, he could bowl when required, and took a hat-trick in one inter-company match.

He took the opportunity afforded by his posting to travel, often by bicycle, in Europe, and it was from this time that his wanderings took on a more serious purpose. For the next few years he visited not only the battlefields of the past, but the likely scenes of combat in any future conflict. Each area was studied on the map, visited, annotations made and then locked away in his extraordinary memory; every contour, every wood, every defile, every potential field of fire or obstacle was marked and remembered. It was the labour of a highly professional practitioner of the art of war.

Whatever the limitations and discouragement, Dempsey put his heart and soul into his soldiering. A brother officer wrote of his time at regimental duty:

> He had in those days as a comparatively junior officer the necessary qualifications for success, in a little greater measure than his colleagues. Professional knowledge, physical courage, determination, imperturbability and charm, among other assets…were already maturing in the subaltern and captain. Although, as is now so clear in retrospect he was always learning and studying and taking his profession seriously, his approach to regimental life was human and social and earned him the affection and respect of all ranks.[4]

In January 1930, Dempsey joined the Staff College for its two-year course. Although still a captain, he was now recognized as a potential senior officer. His outlook had to move upwards from the affairs of his company of 100 or so men, to grand strategy, international affairs and the part that Britain might play in any future war. The Army, like the other two services, was viewed by the public with a jaundiced eye. Its very existence seemed indecent to public opinion, in the prevailing climate of belief in disarmament and the League of Nations. A strong tide of pacifism flowed not only against war itself, but against soldiers.

Despite the depressing lack of support from either the nation or its leaders, the Army pressed ahead with considering how to fight a well-equipped

European army. It tried to assimilate the lessons of the Great War, while attempting to predict how developments in weapon technology might affect the modern battlefield. The General Staff accepted that a relatively small but highly professional army with the most modern weapons offered the ideal way to avoid a repetition of the static warfare and high casualties of the previous conflict. Mobility, quickness and activity were to be achieved from the outset. Prompted by the ideas of Liddell Hart and Major General Fuller, the Experimental Mechanised Force was established in 1927. However, lack of funding led to its disbandment in 1929, and from this time innovation and the development of tactical doctrine were left largely to the Staff College. As Dempsey began his course, he knew that he had to think deeply about his profession, against a backdrop of financial stringency and alienation from the public. Britain was fortunate that it possessed soldiers such as he and his fellow students, who were prepared to press ahead against so much discouragement.

The course in 1930 was divided into two divisions, the Junior Division of sixty students in their first year, and the Senior Division, of the same number, in their second year. They and their instructors, known as Directing Staff, or DS, were some of the brightest talents in the Army and numbered several who were to play vitally important roles in the coming war. It was an environment in which to notice and be noticed. The DS in Dempsey's first year included Colonel (later Field Marshal) 'Jumbo' Wilson, who was to be Commander-in-Chief Middle East and represent the British Chiefs of Staff in Washington; Lieutenant Colonel George Giffard, destined to become, by the end of the war, the senior general in the Army; Lieutenant Colonel (later Lieutenant General) J.G.W. Clark; Lieutenant Colonel (later Lieutenant General) James Gammell; and the RAF exchange DS, Wing Commander (later Air Marshal) Leigh-Mallory, who was to work closely with Dempsey in North-West Europe.

In the Senior Division were Captain (later General) George Erskine, who entered several years below the average age of thirty-four; Captain (later Lieutenant General) H. Lumsden; Captain (later General) Neil Ritchie, destined, like Erskine, to be Dempsey's subordinate; and the Royal Navy exchange student, Commander (later Admiral) Troubridge, another fortunate acquaintance for Dempsey. Fellow students in the Junior Division were Captain (later General) 'Strafer' Gott; Captain (later General) G.F. Hopkinson; Dempsey's old school fellow, G.F. Maclean of the Argyles; and Maurice Chilton, who was to become Dempsey's Chief of Staff in North-West Europe.

In the next year, Major General John Dill, one of the Army's foremost officers, took over as Commandant. Loved by all who knew him for his sincerity and endearing warm heartedness, he influenced a generation of officers who were to hold high office in the war. As Field Marshal, he was British representative to the American Chiefs of Staff when he died suddenly in November 1944. New DS to arrive were A.E. Percival and Jackie Smyth VC, both to become generals, both to end their careers in failure in the Far East; and Squadron Leader John Slessor, a future air marshal and Chief of Air Staff. Into the Junior Division came Captain Brian Horrocks, later to serve as corps commander under Dempsey; Pete Rees, who was to win fame as a divisional commander in Burma; and F.E.W. Simpson, N.C.D. Brownjohn, S.C. Kirkman and C.G.C. Nicholson, all destined to retire as full generals.

In this stimulating environment, students were expected to work and play hard. In the first year, the main requirement was the production of clear, detailed and accurate appreciations, orders, briefs and discussion papers. The emphasis was on mechanized warfare, fast movement and communication by the developing means of voice radio and telegraphy. Perfection was demanded, and red ink was used liberally to flay the idle or sloppy. Every tactical scheme was studied in the syndicate room, then on the ground, where students bicycled from stand to stand. Other work carried out indoors included syndicate discussions, in which students were forced to defend their views under fierce probing, and telephone battles, in which students adopted the roles of staffs at different levels of command.

There were also visits to big industrial firms, such as the Morris Motor Works at Cowley, and to the Army's own schools of instruction, for example the Small Arms School at Hythe and the Royal Engineers at Chatham. There were talks by visiting lecturers such as Sir Maurice Hankey, a week was spent on mountain warfare in north Wales, and there was a Staff Tour of four days. During the tour, selected students acted as divisional commanders, with complete staffs under them drafting and issuing the appropriate operation orders and administrative instructions.

In the second year, the operations studied moved up to corps and army level when scenarios could even include imaginary cabinet discussion of a possible operation to sharpen the political sensibilities of the students. The highlight was the Foreign Tour, in which a group of students and one member of the Directing Staff studied, on the ground, a battle of relevance to the army of the 1930s. They concentrated on the lessons to be drawn, and the differences that modern weapons and communications could make to the forces of both sides.

Dempsey's chosen topic was the Battle of Gumbinnen and preparation for the study started in the January of his Senior Division year. With Dempsey were Captains Barclay of the Cameronians, Maurice Chilton, Bury of the 17th/21st Lancers, and Lucas, a brother officer in the Berkshires. Their DS supervisor was Lieutenant Colonel A. G. Paterson DSO MC. Each of them was given a portion of the battle to work up and was then required to expound his findings at a series of meetings. By the end of March the bulk of the report had been written in outline, so that by the time they started the tour they were thoroughly familiar with the project. Dempsey showed his remarkable flair for maps by preparing and annotating the ones used in the final report.

A light-hearted account of the tour appeared in the college magazine for 1931. 'The syndicate met at Liverpool Street Station,' it began, 'with ten suitcases, besides one registered, and a mass of coats.'[5] Passing through Berlin for briefing by the Air Attaché, they moved on to Insterburg, in East Prussia, where they met their liaison officer from the German Army, Hauptmann Anton-Reichard Hermann Friedrich Maria Freiherr von Bechtolsheim. An artilleryman, von Bechtolsheim had fought with distinction throughout the war on the Western Front. In 1930 he was detached to spend two months with the British Army, and, apart from his challenging title and forenames, was an excellent choice to accompany the small group. With him they moved on to Gumbinnen, then a small town close to the Lithuanian border; today known as Gusev, it lies within the borders of Russia. In August 1914, it was the scene of an initial German success by I Corps at Stalluponen, followed by a rare defeat on that front for the German Army, when a premature and over-ambitious attack by von Prittwitz's Eighth Army led to a humiliating rout.

Dempsey's group set out its reasons for studying these operations:

They are of a mobile nature similar to the type of warfare for which the British Army of today is training.

In view of the professional nature and high standard of training of our Regular Army, the operations of the German Eighth Army are of special interest to British officers.

The campaign lends itself to speculation as to what might have been the outcome had one or both sides possessed modern armaments – as we know them in the British Army today.[6]

The first day was spent on a general survey of the battlefield south of Gumbinnen, the second on a study of the actions of one of the German divisions, and the third studying those of a Russian cavalry division. On the fourth day, the party split, Paterson, Barclay and Chilton visiting Stalluponen, and Dempsey, Bury and Lucas accompanying von Bechtolsheim to Lotzen, in the area of the Massurian Lakes.

According to the *Owl Pie* account, it was only by great exertion that Dempsey's party avoided entering Lithunia, which would have been embarrassing. Their host left them that evening and the group's opinion of von Bechtholsheim, who was to become Military Attaché in London in 1939, was summed up as: 'He had been most charming, tactful and helpful, and we were very sorry to see him go. If he is typical of the present-day German officer they are a wonderful body of men.'[7]

It is pleasing to relate that their judgment was well founded. In the Second World War, after taking part in the invasion of France and the Low Countries, von Bechtolsheim served on the Eastern Front, and ended the war as Commander of LXXI Corps in Norway. Held prisoner in Britain, he was unaffected by any charges of wrongdoing and in the 1950s moved to America where he worked on the US Army's Foreign Study Program.

Among the syndicate's conclusions, the effect of inadequate communications on one of the Russian cavalry divisions was highlighted. It was, they said, almost incredible that Oranofski, the commander, was out of touch, with the result that he could take no part in the battle at a critical moment. In considering the probable influence of modern weapons, had they then been available, the study focussed immediately on Armoured Fighting Vehicles, or tanks. Declaring that the ground was suitable for their employment, and with the proviso that suitable precautions would have to be taken to camouflage their concentration area against air reconnaissance, it then took up the critical question of how they should be handled. Interestingly, in view of Dempsey's later handling of armour, they concluded that they would have been best used in great strength on a limited front. This enlightened approach was continued on a more pedestrian level as they considered the use of machine guns and smoke – all good stuff, but not the war-winning weapons that tanks potentially were. They concluded with the sensible view that it was impossible to overestimate the effect that an efficient air force would have had.

Camberley was not all study. Dempsey was, as usual, prominent on the cricket field, with a good first season as the mainstay of a useful batting side. Playing with him was Troubridge, the sailor, later to work with Dempsey in the invasion of Sicily. In his senior year Dempsey captained the College XI, but although he played one magnificent innings against the Old Wykehamists, he was out rather unluckily on several occasions. On horseback he excelled in the point-to-point, just pipping 'Strafer' Gott to the post in the heavyweight class of the Infantry Challenge Cup. His sporting career was summed up in the college magazine:

> We don't want a man who plays cricket like Dimmer,
> In between innings he's a heavyweight winner.

Although he was remembered as rather reserved and difficult to get to know, renowned as a cricketer and horseman rather than for any military genius,

Dempsey left Camberley at the end of 1931 a better-educated and a wiser man. Montgomery was to claim in his memoirs that Dempsey had been one of his students at Staff College. Since Montgomery ceased to instruct there in early 1929, the great man's memory appears, on this occasion, to have been at fault. A likely explanation lies in the coincidence that O'Connor moved, in 1927, from instructing at the RMC to instructing at the Staff College. Although the two establishments were always referred to as Sandhurst and Camberley respectively, they actually shared the same grounds. It is most likely that, as a great friend of O'Connor, Dempsey would have been introduced to the rising star, who would, many years later, confuse the connection.

Dempsey's first staff job was not in the operational field at all. Still a captain, like most of his fellows, he could only aspire to a Grade III post. While his fellow Berkshire, Lucas, went as Staff Captain to the 4th Division, Dempsey was posted to the Military Secretary's department. The work of the Military Secretary, or MS as he is universally known, is little understood outside military circles. Put simply, he oversees the careers of all officers, their postings, their promotions, and their honours and rewards. His powers of patronage are immense, but not unhindered. He and his small staff work through a series of boards, composed of senior officers summoned for the occasion, sitting at regular intervals throughout the year. In 1932, there was but one – the Selection Board, composed of the Chief of the Imperial General Staff, the Adjutant General, and the General Officers Commanding in Chief of Aldershot, Eastern and Southern Commands.

The Military Secretary's staff was very small, but of very high calibre. Below Major General G.S. Clive, who had a distinguished record in the Great War, his Deputy, Colonel, acting Brigadier, F.S.G. Piggott was an extremely bright officer in the Royal Engineers. Highly decorated in the war, he was Military Attaché in Tokyo twice in the inter-war years, and Chief Staff Officer Intelligence at the War Office. He retired as Major General, as did his assistant, Major Sir Colin Jardine Bt, who was to become Gort's Military Secretary in the BEF. Dempsey's predecessor was Captain Gordon McMillan of McMillan, while his successor was his acquaintance from Camberley, Brian Horrocks. Both of these officers were to achieve high rank and distinction in the Second World War.

Dempsey's branch, MS2, was responsible for the careers of all officers of lieutenant colonel rank and below, and he therefore had access to their annual confidential reports. As well as commenting on an officer's intelligence, tactical ability, leadership and application, such reports were expected to give an indication of their subject's future potential, not only for promotion, but employment. Some officers are better at command than administration or staff work, and some are the opposite. A rare few, of whom Dempsey himself is a prime example, are stars in both fields. Although the staff officers of the department are equipped with every possible aid to easy reference – in Dempsey's time a series of large box-like card indexes containing each officer's 'book' – a good memory is a huge advantage, and Dempsey's extraordinary powers of recall would have impressed his superiors and any officer with whom he had to deal. He would also, through his time there, have remembered all the officers of any standing, their qualifications, strengths and weaknesses, their postings and their foibles. He would come to know, and be known by, everyone who mattered.

Dempsey continued his racing and hunting interests and in Banker he found the ideal horse to combine both. Riding him in the Inter-Regimental race at the East Kent Point-to-Point against The Buffs, he was leading by a distance four fences from home and would have won comfortably when his saddle slipped and he was thrown on the flat. He continued to ride Banker for the next few years, until he was replaced by Teddy, who saw him through to the outbreak of war.

Promotion to major came in late 1932, but escape from the Military Secretary's department did not come until the beginning of 1934 when he handed over to Horrocks, on his appointment as Brigade Major of 5 Infantry Brigade at Aldershot. Although he was now thirty-seven and by today's standards old for such an appointment, it must be remembered that promotion between the wars was excessively slow, and Dempsey was up with his peers.

CHAPTER 5

'Alarm (for Troops to Turn out under Arms)'

The year in which Dempsey took up his appointment in Aldershot marked the nadir in the British Army's fortunes between the wars. In 1919 it was the best-trained, best-equipped and best-led army in the world, but in the years since, things had changed. Although the 'Ten-Year Rule' was abandoned in 1932 and rearmament was discussed, very little was done. In 1933 the Chiefs of Staff, in their annual review, placed on record their concerns at German rearmament, and in 1934 the Defence Requirements Committee of the Committee for Imperial Defence warned that the Empire could not be safeguarded against the possible threat posed by Germany and Japan. The Army's budget had been reduced from £43.5 million in 1923 to £36 million in 1932, and only a marginal increase was approved for 1935.

Against this background, it is remarkable that the Army pressed on, as best it could, with modernisation. An obvious problem in attempting to shape and train itself for the future was the lack of an agreed national strategy and role for the Army in a general war. Its primary task was seen as imperial policing; its possible contribution to Allied operations in Europe was fourth in the list of priorities, and largely undefined. It was partly helped, partly hindered by the influence of two men of great, but uncertain, vision, Fuller and Liddell Hart.

Reflecting the mood of many of his contemporaries, Dempsey now began to think seriously about his future. He asked his old company commander and friend from Sandhurst days, Dick O'Connor, to come down to Aldershot. He put to him the question that was troubling him: should he stay or go? O'Connor's advice was uncompromising: stay. Dempsey's career was saved and a great soldier's talents were preserved for the nation. O'Connor did a signal service to Britain, as well as to Dempsey, with his sound advice.

Although the Experimental Mechanised Force was no more, the Army pressed ahead as best it could with a series of trials. The manoeuvres between

1927 and 1931 of mixed and wholly armoured formations, communicating by radio, set the standard which the larger European armies would not emulate for several years. Despite the technical problems, an impressive demonstration was carried out on Salisbury Plain at the end of this period, when a brigade of tanks moved through dense fog with total precision, relying only on radio for command and control.

Because Salisbury Plain was the obvious arena for these trials, Aldershot Command, which was regarded as likely to form the basis of any future expeditionary force – whatever official government policy might be – oversaw them. During Dempsey's time in 5 Brigade, he was fortunate to serve under some of the best and most radically minded senior officers in the Army. His brigade commander was Brigadier Victor Fortune, of the Black Watch and Seaforths, later to command the 51st Highland Division in their gallant stand at St Valery. His incarceration was to rob the Army of one of its brightest talents. The Brigade belonged to the 2nd Division, commanded initially by 'Jumbo' Wilson, and then by Archie Wavell, both of them destined to become Commander-in-Chief Middle East. Above them, in turn, was General Jock Burnett-Stuart, described by Montgomery as the most brilliant general in the Army.

The emphasis on training was intense. In 1934, 6 and 7 Brigades were selected to test the new infantry organization, one feature of which was to concentrate the Vickers medium machine gun and the infantry anti-tank gun into specialist battalions, small detachments of which would be 'penny packeted' as the operational situation required. In the 2nd Division manoeuvres that year, 5 Brigade played a key role, holding the right flank of a position south of the Basingstoke Canal. The Division was to fall back from the line of the River Thames from Wallingford to Chertsey – a foretaste of what was to come six years later. The need for concealment was emphasised, and aerial photography was employed to drive the lesson home.

The following year, *The Times* reported that the training season for the Army would include major operations for Aldershot Command, with mobility and mechanization constituting a dominant note. The mechanization referred to was based on the use of the Carden-Lloyd carrier, the forerunner of the Bren carrier.

Second Division's exercises also included some I – infantry – tanks, one of the less happy results of Fuller's and Liddell Hart's teaching. They were slow and cumbersome and designed to be spread thinly to boost the firepower of the infantry, the very opposite, in fact, of what armour was supposed to be employed for.

In 1935, a sapper, Francis Nosworthy, took over 5 Brigade, and was in command when they participated in a major exercise which was popularly known as the 'CIGS Stakes'. The Brigade, consisting of the King's Own, East

Yorks, Worcesters and Cameron Highlanders, formed part of the 'Eastland' force, under Aldershot Command, pitted against 'Westland', consisting of Eastern and Southern Command. The start time was brought forward by six hours, which passed some of 'Eastland' by, and in the course of the manoeuvres, General Sir Cyril Deverell, commanding Eastern Command, artfully concealed a division on the southern flank of General Sir John Gathorne-Hardy's corps. Dempsey produced the detailed orders for the deployment of his brigade, as part of the 2nd Division, between Petersfield and Alresford. On 19 September, they captured Overton, and by the third day of the exercise they were in a good position on the flank of 1 Guards Brigade, advancing towards Laverstoke and Winchester. In the opinion of the umpires, the two brigades would have overwhelmed 12 Brigade of 'Westland'.

However, while they attacked north, Deverell struck a decisive blow from his concealed division that was accepted by the umpires as completely successful. Summing up, the CIGS, Montgomery-Massingberd, stated that in his opinion Gathorne-Hardy had shown a rather over-defensive attitude, whereas Deverell had had a definite plan and stuck to it One month later Deverell's appointment as CIGS was announced. Nosworthy, also, came out well, and was to command a corps and then West Africa Command during the war.

In 1936 Dempsey again handed over to Horrocks, and after a posting, immediately cancelled, to the 2nd Battalion in Egypt, and another, also cancelled, to the staff of Aldershot Command, he reported to 1st Berkshires at Shorncliffe for what was to be a foreshortened tour of regimental duty. Having earned his spurs as a rifle company commander, it was appropriate that, as a senior member of the Battalion, he should take over Headquarters Wing, as it was then known.

As well as Battalion Headquarters, the Company in those days contained the infantry's specialists. The Signal Section trained its men in laying line and operating the telephone system used, in those pre-radio days, to communicate with the rifle companies in the field. Number 2 Group was the Anti-Tank defence of the unit. In theory it was equipped with the Boyes anti-tank rifle, but financial stringency resulted in these vital – if inadequate – weapons being represented by wooden mock-ups. In place of the Carden-Lloyd carriers that should have carried their notional guns, they were equipped with Morris trucks, unarmoured and lacking cross-country mobility. Number 3 Group was the Mortar Section, equipped at that stage with just two 3-inch mortars; if they had been allowed to, they could have fired a 10lb high-explosive projectile 4,000 yards, but they did not because none were available for training. Number 4 Group was the battalion transport, slowly mechanizing, and the Band and Drums (double-hatted as anti-aircraft defence without anti-aircraft guns), made up the remainder. The full establishment numbered some 300 men, and the command, at a time of the introduction of new weapons and tactics, should have been one of the most challenging and interesting in the Army. In practice, as a result of poor recruiting (itself a function of the pitiful pay that government stringency forced on the services), and the need to find drafts for foreign service (the government's priority), the numbers required to train on the – non-existent – equipment were hopelessly inadequate. A popular cry of the time ran:

'How many men for company drill today, Sergeant Major?'

'Twelve Sir!'

It is interesting to note that the Battalion took its own imaginative steps, to remedy this state of affairs. In early 1936, it invited twenty unemployed young men to stay and sample life in the Regiment at first hand. Not one of them enlisted.

The Battalion served in 10 Infantry Brigade, commanded by Brigadier Willen, and a major commitment each year was to provide men for the Aldershot Military Tattoo, which took up the better part of the summer. The remainder of the training year was spent on range work, route marches – over four days in August they covered 75 miles – and higher-level manoeuvres. Sport figured prominently and in a match against 22 Field Regiment RA, Dempsey was top scorer for the battalion with 40 not out. There was also much emphasis on Regimental (as distinct from Battalion) affairs, and Dempsey featured prominently at the At Home Day and Garden Party held at the Depot.

Shortly after Dempsey returned to the 1st Battalion, the Regiment was not a little perturbed to learn that a stranger, Lieutenant Colonel Eric Miles, of the King's Own Scottish Borderers, was to take command. Miles had won a DSO and MC in the war, and was a highly competent officer who went on to command a division in Iraq and North Africa. But not only was he not a Berkshire, he was from a regiment of Lowland Scots, as different from the gentle-natured men of his new command as chalk from cheese. It was a challenge to which Dempsey, who soon became Battalion Second-in-Command, rose with tact and charm. It helped that as a bachelor he lived in the Officers' Mess, where he could restrain any hot-headed youngsters, always the slowest to accept any break with tradition. Later in life, Eric Miles was to become Colonel of his old regiment, his tenure of command of the Berkshires was successful, and much of the credit for this is due to Dempsey, whose time then was remembered by one of the subalterns:

On the soldiering side I shall always remember his complete understanding of the map. Many times I have seen him study a map, then fold it up and describe in detail exactly what the ground actually looked like. He had that art of seeing in his mind's eye the details on paper, and interpreting them on the ground.

On the human side he was kindness itself to all in the regiment, whatever his rank or length of service. He understood the problems of even the most junior. He was the sort of man we could all go to without fear or trepidation.[1]

At one stage the officer was worried that he was being asked to play too much cricket. The Senior Subaltern advised him to go and see 'Dimmer'. His advice was typical – of course he should play, and Dempsey would square things with the Adjutant and Commanding Officer.

In 1937, the Military Secretary's Department, in consultation with the Colonel of the Royal Berkshire Regiment, decreed that Dempsey was to fulfil every officer's dream – command of the 1st Battalion of his own regiment. He was to take over in February 1938, but it is never considered wise for an officer to assume command of a unit from within its own ranks, so a spell away was called for. After consultation with MS the perfect solution for a bachelor was found in attendance at the two-month Senior Officers' Course at Sheerness, followed by a short tour with the Defence Forces of the Union of South Africa. Although officially filling a Grade 2 staff officer post, what he actually did was to join the staff of the Union's Officer Training College at Roberts Heights, Pretoria. Dempsey thoroughly enjoyed his time there and became imbued with a love of Africa which was to find further expression in later years.

In January 1938, Dempsey returned to Shorncliffe to take over from Miles. The Regimental journal noted with satisfaction and perhaps some relief: 'He is too well known in the Battalion for anyone to doubt that his period of command will be happy and prosperous, and we join with his many friends outside the Battalion and Regiment in wishing him a very successful tour.'[2]

He faced again the challenges he had come to know so well a year before. Dwindling numbers of men had to train on new equipment which was either lacking or for which the appropriate ammunition could not be provided. But the war clouds were gathering and slowly things began to change. The new light machine gun, the Bren, was introduced; the full inventory of fifty-seven vehicles was built up, so that some riflemen could be carried in lorries instead of marching; the new Carrier Platoon was introduced into the establishment – albeit with trucks representing the non-existent carriers; and officers and senior NCOs spent more and more time learning the new tactics on TEWTs – tactical exercises without troops (which was as well, because there were not many of them with which to exercise).

The Munich Crisis came, the Berkshires were put on four-hours notice to move and dug trenches around the old Martello towers on the Kent cliffs and beaches. The crisis passed, but the nation had been put on alert and, in a sign of the new times, drafts of reservists began to report in for ten days of training at a time.

In October 1938 Dempsey moved the Battalion to its new station, Blackdown Camp. The Commander of the 4th Division, Major General D.G. Johnson VC, bade them farewell: 'It is with a feeling of sincere regret that I have to say goodbye to your battalion. During your tour of service in this division, the battalion has shown itself a model battalion of British infantry. The traditional efficiency of your regiment has not only been upheld, but enhanced.'[3]

The Berkshires were now in 6 Infantry Brigade, under Brigadier Ponsonby. The Brigade Major was Vyvyan Evelegh of the Duke of Cornwall's Light Infantry, who was later to serve under Dempsey in Italy. The camp was new and, as 1938 became 1939, the tempo increased. The Carrier Platoon actually received some carriers and a Pioneer Platoon was formed, to enable the Battalion to carry out its own minelaying and mine clearance, demolitions, watermanship and wiring. The announcement that the Territorial Army was to double in size was quickly followed by a series of intensive cadres to train the new part-time volunteers that flooded in.

As the war clouds gathered, Dempsey hunted when he could on Teddy. In early 1939 he was out with the Crawley and Horsham, and his Hunting Journal records his last meet prior to the coming conflict: 'Meet – Frindon Green. Cold wind from North. Scent poor. Hacked from Washington. A good ride. Hunted in the hills – v. small field – good going – cold, but very pleasant. I stopped at 1.30 and hacked back to Washington.'[4]

As a lieutenant colonel, it was time for Dempsey to heed the old army maxim: 'Subalterns may not marry, captains may marry, majors should marry, colonels must marry.' But, although a confident social mixer with a pleasant singing voice and a gift for playing the piano, he remained a resolute bachelor. A contemporary records his views: 'He was a dedicated soldier and maintained that one could never be a really good soldier and be married. One could not have two loyalties or always be looking over one's shoulder.'[5]

On 22 August, the Berkshires, along with the rest of the Army, were mobilized. This time it was for real, and as reservists and mobilization stores flooded in, the mood of the nation changed. Soldiers who had been accustomed to being regarded by the British public as beneath notice, found to their pleasurable surprise that they were now rather popular. Unfortunately, years of underfunding and neglect by successive governments could not be remedied so quickly, and although Dempsey could say in his welcoming talk to reservists who had rejoined the colours, 'We've got the men, we've got the weapons, and we've got the guts to use them', the fact was that the Battalion was still woefully short of the sinews of war. Dempsey now faced a crisis – he was ordered to report to an infantry division as GSO1 Operations. The moment for which all his service had prepared him – command of his battalion in war – was about to slip from his grasp. Appalled, he rang the Military Secretary's branch. 'What about this general staff job they have given me? I want to stay with my battalion.' He was granted an interview with General Sir John Dill, his Commandant from Camberley, and a man he revered. Dill cancelled the posting order and Dempsey remained with the Berkshires.

They crossed to France in the middle of September, and as they moved up to their position at Berin, on the Belgian border, it began to rain, and seemed to go on like that for the next few months. Dempsey, however, was not one to allow himself or his soldiers to be depressed. A newspaper article later recalled of this time: 'He could do anything with his men, and in turn would do anything for them. He even organised beagles during the "phoney war" period.'

In November 1939, halfway through the 'phoney war' period, Dempsey received the most significant advancement of his career. After only twenty-one months as a lieutenant colonel, all of them in command, he was promoted to colonel, acting brigadier, and placed in command of 13 Infantry Brigade. In considering whether his strength lay more in command or on the staff, this move shows quite clearly that he was regarded primarily as an outstanding leader. In the general shake-up of the BEF over this period, there was ample opportunity to employ his considerable talents as a staff officer, but he was chosen for a crucial promotion on the command side. It was a mark of signal confidence by the leadership of the BEF, which was to be amply justified in the months ahead.

CHAPTER 6

'Retire or Troops Right About Wheel'

Dempsey took command of 13 Infantry Brigade in November. His predecessor, Brigadier Willcox, took up a staff appointment, prior to assuming command of the 42nd Division, to which Dempsey later followed him. The Brigade Major, Bullen-Smith, was a huge, highly competent Scot, who was later to rise to major general and again serve under Dempsey. The Brigade was made up of the second, regular battalions of three famous regiments, the Inniskilling Fusiliers, the Wiltshires and the Cameronians. The Brigade, together with 17 Brigade, commanded by Monty Stopford, was part of the 5th Division, commanded by Major General Franklyn, a highly professional soldier, with a good staff. All the ingredients were present for an easy handover and a smooth ride in command for Dempsey.

However, not all was well with the Brigade. Through no fault of their own, they had spent the time since they arrived in France in the rear base area of Nantes, at the mouth of the Loire. There they had been involved in an endless round of administrative and guard duties. Very little training had been done and there had been no opportunity to test battalion and company commanders. Dempsey's arrival coincided with a change in the deployment of the Division, spelled out by Franklyn to all the senior officers on 5 December. It was to move from GHQ reserve to under command II Corps, commanded by Lieutenant General Brooke (later to become CIGS and Lord Alanbrooke); a week later he visited the Brigade and spoke to each of Dempsey's battalion commanders. They were ordered to take up a position on the extreme left of the BEF, on the border with Belgium, where they spent Christmas. Dempsey visited every unit in the Brigade on Christmas Day and over the next few months of the 'phoney war' he became a frequent visitor, as did Franklin and Brooke.

A company commander in the Brigade remembered him well:

Tall and slim and always immaculate he looked very young to be commanding a brigade. He was immensely popular with his own staff and also with the troops. During the very severe winter of 1939-40 in France he spent a good deal of his time visiting forward companies of the brigade who were – on frozen ground which could only be penetrated by pneumatic drills – trying to construct defensive positions, ie trenches, sandbag and concrete pill boxes against the expected German attack. He was always a very welcome visitor. His immense charm, friendliness, quiet air of unmistakable authority and knowledge acted as a tonic at the time producing not only affection for him but also tremendous confidence in his ability as a commander.

It always seemed to be snowing when he arrived at my company – owing to the urgency of the situation work in the open carried on just the same – and, maybe a small point but always commented on by the troops, was that as they were not wearing overcoats neither was he. He acquired as the war went on a reputation for unruffled composure whatever the circumstances, including being under fire.[1]

The tempo now quickened. A series of exercises took place, involving much night work and long moves, infantry/tank cooperation and all the phases of war, including the hasty occupation of a new defensive position, and withdrawal. Older officers made way for younger – in the case of the Wiltshires their commanding officer, Lieutenant Colonel Oliphant, was replaced by an officer from the Inniskillings. A new brigade major, Captain Rock, replaced Bullen-Smith, and at the beginning of May he gave instructions for a move to Amiens, preparatory to the Brigade being deployed to operations in Norway. This was a false start, however, the orders were cancelled and on 7 May, with no immediate prospect of action, Dempsey left his headquarters to go on leave, his place being taken temporarily by Lieutenant Colonel Moore of the Wiltshires. His plan was to join Patrick – who had been called up on the outbreak of war and was serving on the military administrative staff attached to the RAF's Advanced Air Striking Force in France – at home with their mother.

The Allied plan was for the Belgians to hold the Albert Canal, while British and French formations moved to occupy defensive positions on the River Dyle. The weakness of this plan was obvious, and occasioned by the Belgian government's refusal to allow any cooperation with, let alone movement forward of, Allied troops on Belgian territory until the country was invaded. The initiative was thus passed to the invader and the BEF had to move forward a long distance to new positions, while uncertain of the enemy's progress. In fact the Belgians were by no means ready when the Germans invaded on 10 May, and their positions at Maastricht and in the

Ardennes were soon overrun. The 5th Division was now placed back under GHQ as Gort's reserve. Patrick described the effect of these momentous events in a letter to their mother:

> We live in rather troubling times, don't we, but we all feel that if the Germans can be held soon, as they will be, the war may not last long. I am afraid my leave will be postponed, but I hope not for too long. I was very sorry to hear that Miles's leave was cut short.[2]

As soon as the news broke, Dempsey returned to the Brigade and, while the BEF occupied the Dyle positions, 13 Brigade moved to a position near Hal, on the site of the Battle of Waterloo, south of Brussels. As was inevitable in the early days of war, there were muddles and false alarms, and much initial anxiety regarding the use of aircraft by the Germans, who seemed to have a free run. At one stage the 4th and 7th Royal Tank Regiments, less their Brigade Headquarters, were sent to Hal to stem a supposed breakthrough by German armour. Having set off and driven most of the 9 miles to Hal, they were met by Dempsey. He told them he had not asked for any tanks and there were no Germans in the vicinity. His own brigade was itself having teething problems, but soon sorted itself out under the calming influence of its commander, and successfully enabled the 48th Division to fall back through its position, screened by the 12th Lancers in their armoured cars.

The Brigade was now in defensive positions on the River Senne and Charleroi Canal, with the Inniskillings and Cameronians forward. Streams of refugees poured over the few bridges that had not been blown, adding to the problem of movement, and on 17 May orders were given for the demolition of the remaining crossing points. As the Germans closed up and made contact with the forward battalions, two companies of Inniskillings went astray and got caught up in the rush of refugees. Dempsey visited each battalion headquarters. Completely unruffled, good humoured and totally in command of the situation, he radiated a sense of quiet determination and optimism.

On 18 May, the Brigade was ordered to move west; reconnaissance and harbour parties had already left when just before midnight the move was cancelled. Instead they moved to cross the River Dendre at Lessines. Again, refugees clogged the roads, as did the BEF's own vehicles and equipment, but despite the difficulties the Brigade got across and the bridges were blown by the afternoon of 19 May. That evening orders came for a further withdrawal and by the next day they were concentrated south of Lille.

Events at the operational level now forced an entirely new plan on Gort. German armour was heading for Abbeville and the Channel coast, and the BEF was in danger of being cut off to the south. A hasty defence line was organized from Arras to the sea. The 5th Division was to take the 50th Division and 1 Army Tank Brigade under command and form Frankforce. Their mission was to hold the southern end of the defensive pocket and deliver the only major counter-attack of the campaign, the action at Arras.

Lt Birkett Smith, commanding a machine-gun platoon of the Cheshires, attached to the 50th Division, happened to pass through Lens as Dempsey was holding his Orders Group there in a farm courtyard. As artillery shells exploded all around them, Dempsey proceeded to give out his orders for the next phase. His totally unruffled demeanour and calm, clear delivery made a deep impression on the young officer, who was to work for Dempsey later in the war.[3]

Meanwhile, on 21 May, 13 Brigade was to take over the positions held by the French mechanized corps, so that they in turn could take part in the action at Arras. They dug in on the River Scarpe, the 4-mile long frontage determining that the brigade was stretched thinly, with no depth. A rifle company commander in the Brigade remembers Dempsey;

Shortly after dawn he arrived at my company. We were overlooked by the Germans on the high ground on the other side and had been shelled all night. He arrived alone, immaculate as ever, and to my dismay wearing his brigadier's uniform hat – the red band of which to my jaundiced eye appeared to shine like a beacon for all – including the Germans – to see!

In the centre of my position was a bridge over the river which had been very inefficiently blown up, and was covered in French anti-tank mines, some exploded some not. I had given orders that no one was to go near it!

Quite unperturbed, with his red hat glowing in the sunshine, he led me to the centre of the bridge where we were joined by two hungry French dogs – who immediately started a fight amid the mines – where, balancing on the rubble, he gave me precise and detailed orders to establish a small bridgehead on the high ground across the river as a prelude to what the history books now refer to as the British counter-attack at Arras! Saying he was going to nip back to lead up the reserve battalion he then left – plus red hat – to my great relief. This again may seem a small matter but at the time the effect on the troops' morale was considerable.[4]

Dempsey had decided to give himself some depth by pushing forward of the river at Roueux, with a view to passing the Cameronians through to take up a position on the high ground beyond at Monchy-le-Preux. The situation at first looked favourable. One company of the Wiltshires managed to cross by pontoon bridge, only to find itself cut off. The only radios in the Battalion were on the rear link to Brigade Headquarters, and it was not possible to get a telephone cable – the normal method of controlling companies – across, so Second Lieutenant Chivers twice swam the river to report the situation. At this stage the Brigade lost its Anti-tank Company and the Cameronians to 17 Brigade, itself in danger of being cut off by 50th Panzer Division.

The situation was now becoming critical. With three German Panzer divisions pressing in from the south-west and within striking distance of the road on the line Arras-Bethune, an infantry division investing the town itself, and another coming up from the south, Arras was in danger of being cut off. As the German infantry and engineers moved forward with their assault boats in front of 13 Brigade, they were cut to pieces by 91st Field Regiment Royal Artillery in support, and the machine guns of the 9th Battalion The Manchester Regiment. But the Germans kept up the pressure and the Wiltshires were forced back to a position of all-round defence with Brigade Headquarters at Gavrelle.

Communication with battalions was now difficult due to radio vehicles being knocked out, and it was with great difficulty that Dempsey's men fought their way out and began to move. The Inniskillings, in danger of being outflanked, charged with their carriers and wheeled transport over a ploughed field and their German foe. Eventually 13 Brigade was in position on the Biache-Gavrelle road, with their flank 'in the air', when orders for the withdrawal eventually came.

By 25 May, they were near Lille and, along with the other remaining brigade of 5th Division and the newly arrived 143 Brigade, they were then ordered to take up position on the Ypres-Commine Canal. On 26 May, they started digging in, and for the next three days, the safe evacuation of the BEF rested in the hands of the 5th Division, now in II Corps under command of Brooke. It was not an ideal defensive position. The canal itself was a poor obstacle, dry for much of its length, and a covered approach for the enemy was provided by a railway line running to its east.

Dempsey's brigade at first held their 2-mile sector of the canal with the Cameronians, now back under command, and Inniskillings forward, but soon Dempsey was compelled to move the Wiltshires forward to reinforce the Brigade's centre. This enabled the Inniskillings, who were in danger of being outflanked, to adjust the left of their position. As Lieutenant Colonel Moore of the Wiltshires was moving round the new company positions, Dempsey arrived at Battalion Headquarters. The Adjutant, Captain George Woolnough, described what happened:

> I told Brigadier Dempsey that the CO was forward, and his response was to tell me to listen carefully. 'This position is vital to the whole of

the BEF. If we fail, the BEF is finished. It MUST be held.' I was under no illusions what this meant, and as soon as the CO returned I passed on the message. We held, the brigade held, and the BEF was saved.[5]

On 26 May, the Brigade, in common with the rest of the BEF, went on to half rations. Although this measure had serious implications – as much psychological as physical – in practice most units managed to supplement their rations by living off the well-stocked countryside. Everyone in the Brigade was desperately tired and overworked minds began to take counsel of their fears. 'One company had been overrun ... the Germans had broken through here ... a company had been wiped out there ...' Dempsey's calm, unhurried, reassuring presence ensured that such fears were soon dispelled, and with strong artillery support the line was held.

The Brigade now underwent its stiffest test of the whole campaign. Initial probes by the Germans took time to build up, but as they got in between the forward battalions and his flank with 143 Brigade was threatened, Dempsey was forced to withdraw the Brigade to slightly higher ground to the rear, just forward of the Messines Ridge of Great War fame. In the confusion, some of the Cameronians went too far back and had to be brought forward again. Spelt out simply, this sounds simple, but the opposite is the case. To rally exhausted, hungry and battle-shocked men as darkness came on, in a desperately confused situation, called for all the Regiment's leadership. The Commanding Officer, Lieutenant Colonel Gilmore, by force of personality and personal example, saved the situation. Having directed supporting artillery to break up the attacking Germans, he mustered a scratch force of cooks and bottle washers, and led them in a bayonet charge that routed the enemy.

Poor communications now caused another setback. Orders for the withdrawal took a long time to reach the Inniskillings. Because the brigade radio net was hardly functioning, they were not aware that the Cameronians had moved, and so they delayed their own move too long. The Germans followed up hard and the Commanding Officer and most of Battalion Headquarters were captured. Dempsey was now forced to pull back right onto the Messines Ridge. Fortunately Brooke, in command of II Corps, was alive to the danger and ordered Montgomery, who had his 3rd Division well in hand, to extend his line. In a brilliant night move, which only an exceptionally well-trained formation could have carried out, 3rd Division completed the task. This in turn enabled 10 Brigade of 4th Division to come in behind the ridge, and a spirited attack by extra battalions placed under 5th Division's command helped ease the pressure.

On 28 May, as the Belgian Army surrendered, orders came for 13 Brigade to withdraw to another canal position near Loo. The move went through Poperinghe, which became a choke point, and the long lines of soft-skinned transport became an easy target for German aircraft. The Wiltshires were further discomfited by taking a wrong turning in the middle of the night. As they retraced their steps, the weary men could have been forgiven for losing heart. They did not. Discipline held and the depleted battalion, with what was left of 13 Brigade, eventually got through.

On 29 May, all vehicles and equipment except personal weapons having been discarded, the Brigade marched into the Dunkirk perimeter. There, Dempsey ordered them to form a composite battalion under the command of Lieutenant Colonel Moore. It would consist of Battalion Headquarters and two companies of the Wiltshires, total strength 175, two companies of Cameronians and one of Inniskillings.

Dempsey and his men had done all that had been asked of them, and more. Out of some 3,000 in the Brigade who moved up to Waterloo at the start of the campaign, less than 500 were still with it when it was evacuated from Dunkirk three weeks later. During that time they had carried out withdrawal after withdrawal, fought several running battles, been under almost continuous artillery and air attack, and moved hundreds of miles. Most difficult to endure was the fact that they were always on the defensive, not the offensive – and through no fault of theirs. Man for man they were confident that they could fight the Germans on their terms and hold their own. It was not 13 Brigade, nor the 5th Division, nor even the BEF that had been defeated, but their allies. Once the Dutch capitulated, the French offered little resistance in the centre and no coordinated plan for an Allied counterstroke could be carried through, the BEF, tiny by comparison with its French ally, was unable to influence events at theatre level. Gort, by his morally courageous decision to withdraw the BEF, enabled Britain to fight on alone.

Back in England, Dempsey was awarded the DSO for his handling of his brigade. Major General Franklyn's citation read as follows:

> An outstanding Commander, who, throughout the operations in Flanders set a fine example of enthusiasm and disregard of danger. On several occasions he restored doubtful situations by his personal interventions, particularly on the YPRES-COMMINES Canal.
>
> Under the most difficult circumstances he remained cool, cheerful and completely efficient.[6]

After a few weeks leave, he was posted as Brigadier General Staff (Operations) to Headquarters VII Corps. He had arrived with the Canadians.

The story of Canada's approach to the Second World War is an exaggerated mirror image of Britain's. In March 1939, only months before the outbreak of war, Canadian statesmen of more than one party declared their belief that Dominion expeditionary forces were unlikely to be required in a future war. Her defences were organized accordingly. When Germany invaded Poland and Canada declared war, her Permanent Force (Regular Army) numbered just over 4,000. Her Non-Permanent Active Militia (Territorial Army) had an enrolled strength of 51,000. The entire Canadian mechanized force consisted of twelve Bren carriers, one artillery tractor and two British light tanks. The expansion of this force to half a million of the Empire's finest fighting troops by the end of the war was a major industrial and logistic challenge. The rapid promotions required to fill the new establishments, and the formation from meagre resources of new headquarters, inevitably resulted in some officers being promoted beyond their ability and headquarters being staffed by officers learning on the job. In late 1939, the first elements of a Canadian division landed in England and by February 1940 there were 25,000, forming the large part of Headquarters VII Corps, its ancillary units and 1st Canadian Division. 2nd Canadian Division began to arrive in mid-1940, and by the end of the year I Canadian Corps was formed. In the meantime, those Canadian troops who had arrived were caught up – but not gainfully employed – in the events of the spring. Their part consisted mainly of waiting in the wings; and on the one occasion when the Canadians in any numbers did actually manage to get onto the stage, the curtain was suddenly rung down before they could play the role for which they had been intended.

When Germany invaded Norway, an ideal theatre for the employment of Canadian troops seemed to beckon, and a small force, composed of picked units and individuals, was rapidly assembled. They never got further than an embarkation port in Scotland. Only two Canadians reached Norway, private soldiers from a Saskatchewan regiment who had volunteered as interpreters. They saw a little fighting, but are said to have complained that the English of the North Country soldiers they worked with was more difficult to understand than that of the Norwegians!

When the Germans invaded France and the Low Countries, the 1st Canadian Division was one of the few formations in the United Kingdom with reasonable equipment and training – everything else was 'in the shop window' with the BEF. The Division was put on short notice at once and on 23 May was given the task of restoring the BEF's communications with the Channel ports. They prepared for embarkation, while the Divisional Commander, General McNaughton, moved to France to assess the situation. With a small party he visited Calais and Dunkirk, discussed the state of affairs with those on the spot and reported back to London. It was then decided to stand them down and Canadian soldiers, who had already boarded transports, were disembarked and moved back to Aldershot.

Another disappointment awaited them in June, when Lieutenant General Sir Alan Brooke was appointed to command a 'new BEF' to fight alongside the French. Again, troops embarked and a Canadian infantry brigade landed at Brest on 14 June, before entraining for the move to the expected area of operations. The next day, the orders for the move were reversed, and the Brigade moved the 200 miles back to St Malo, where they again embarked for Britain. It had been one more bitterly disappointing experience for the Dominion troops, who by now were translating CASF as 'Canadians Almost Saw France'.

As Dempsey joined them, the Canadians could have been forgiven for feeling resentful at the way they had been treated. General Dill, soon to hand over as CIGS, wrote at length to General McNaughton, commander Canadian Forces in Britain, apologizing for the muddle. The Canadians, however, did not waver. Their spirit was magnificent and it was Dempsey's task, as the Corps Commander's right-hand man, to harness that spirit in shaping the formation into a battle-ready entity. It called for a first-class professional who could exert tact and charm with a steely determination to get the job done. Dempsey, who combined these characteristics with invaluable recent battlefield experience, was a perfect choice, and one of his Canadian staff officers remarked to a visitor that he was a splendid officer, with whom he was very glad of the opportunity to serve.

As summer changed to autumn, the Canadians were on constant alert to repel the invasion that was expected at any moment. This limited the amount of time that could be devoted to training, but by early September the 2nd Canadian Division was formed, and at the end of the year I Canadian Corps was established. A small number of British Army officers were retained in key posts and at the beginning of 1941, the new formation held its first high-level exercise. Dempsey had identified that the greatest problem facing the Canadians was developing the ability to move great masses of men and directing them in action.

The move of Montgomery's 3rd Division on the night of 27/28 May, recounted earlier, involved one of the most difficult manoeuvres in war – to withdraw from the line, embus and move along small roads only a few thousand yards in rear of a front line which might break at any moment under German pressure. This would have been a difficult operation at any time, but owing to the congestion on the roads it looked almost impossible. Clear orders, good staff work and battle procedure, and discipline, combined to make sure that it worked perfectly. This was the benchmark against which Dempsey judged the Canadians. Not unnaturally, they fell short initially of this high standard.

Exercise FOX was conducted by I Canadian Corps from 11 to 13 February 1941, with Corps Headquarters, 1st Canadian Division and a large proportion of Corps Troops (units such as artillery, engineers, signals and logistics which came directly under Corps command and were not allocated to a division). The objects of the exercise were to practise units and formations in a road move to a concentration area; an advance to gain contact with hostile forces; and the issue of orders and deployment for an attack.

Great emphasis was laid on traffic control and communication. In the debrief that followed, the Corps Commander began by saying that the exercise had shaken the complacency of everyone participating, from himself down to the lowest private soldier. Quite simply, battle procedure and traffic control had been inadequate, largely due to poor and untimely orders, and the failure of units to keep to the instructions of the staffs. These shortcomings would be rectified and it was now Dempsey's task to do so.

A similar exercise, DOG, conducted from 26 to 28 February, involved a similar order of battle to FOX, but in this case the newly formed 2nd Canadian Division took the place of the 1st. The general idea, based on their war role at the time, was for the Canadians, who formed part of GHQ Reserve, to move forward from their concentration area around Leatherhead in Surrey to reinforce forward units of the Home Guard repelling an attempted German invasion. Again, similar errors were identified and, not surprisingly, these appeared at all levels, from brigade down. The new staffs of 2nd Division were learning on the job and mistakes were part of the learning process.

In April, fate played a part in Dempsey's career when Brooke visited the Canadians as they were conducting an exercise for 1st Canadian Division, directed by Corps Headquarters. McNaughton was ill and the normally retiring Dempsey had to front the headquarters. Although Brooke noted that the Canadians had a lot to learn, the visit reinforced his favourable first impressions of Dempsey, gained in France with II Corps, and at the selection board for three new divisional commanders the following month, he pushed for Dempsey to be given one of the vacancies.

The Canadians did learn, and learn well. In action in Italy and in North-West Europe, the Canadian fighting man proved himself the equal of any on the Allied side, and commanders and staffs had mastered their art so that these magnificent men were sent into action smoothly and efficiently. A lot of the credit for this must go to Dempsey and the other British officers on loan during the formative period. A report issued just as Dempsey concluded his year's attachment to I Canadian Corps noted that he and another British brigadier were both regarded as unusually able soldiers. Not only was Dempsey exceptionally competent, but he was also possessed of a patient temperament which made him agreeable to work for, though it did not prevent him getting things done. The report concluded that it seemed that the British had assigned very able officers to serve with the Canadians.

Dempsey had now proved his fitness for high command. He had done exceptionally well under testing conditions in Belgium and France, where his performance had been observed at close quarters by Brooke and Montgomery, among others; he had shown his outstanding ability as a staff officer with the Canadians; and he had demonstrated his ability to work harmoniously with allies – a quality that was going to become more and more valuable as the war progressed. His star was now rising and in June 1941 he was promoted acting Major General and appointed to command the 46th Division. In a little over three years he had advanced from major to major general; from instructor in a small college in an imperial outpost to command of 15,000 men.

CHAPTER 7

'Draw Swords'

The 46th Division, to which Dempsey was appointed in June 1941, had had an unfortunate war. A Territorial formation, it recruited from the Midlands and Yorkshire, and had gone to France as part of the original BEF as a 'pioneer' or labour unit. It had no artillery and much of the supporting infrastructure of a proper fighting division was lacking. It spent the period of the 'phoney war' on keeping open the BEF's Lines of Communication, and other basic tasks. It was not fit for modern war. When the German Panzers broke through the Ardennes, it was employed initially in a defensive position at Seclin; on 26 May it moved to the Canal Line and then into the Dunkirk perimeter, before evacuation to the United Kingdom. Glory had quite definitely passed the Division by.

The Divisional Commander, Major General Curtis, left soon after and the Division then suffered several changes in command in short order. Dempsey's predecessor, Major General Wimberley, was a Highlander through and through, whose ambition was to command his fellow Scots. He later commanded 51st Highland Division with great distinction, but 46th Division was not for him and he was only with them for one month. Dempsey did not stay for much longer. After four months, in which the Division trained for mountain warfare, he moved on. Sadly, his successor was only in command for one month before he too, moved on. It was an unfortunate but inevitable fact of life that at that stage of the war good generals were in short supply, and were posted more for the benefit of their own professional improvement, and that of the few top formations, than for the benefit of less ready formations. Their turn would come and it is pleasing to record that 46th Division acquitted itself most honourably in the later years of the war.

It was during this period that Brooke, initially as C-in-C Southern Command, and then Home Forces, was shaping the future army. Crisscrossing the country with enormous energy, he swept like an avenging angel through its senior ranks, sacking or moving those not up to his exacting standard. Green ('too old and lacking in drive'), Le Fanu ('did not think much of him'), Gotto ('a queer specimen'), Haining ('quite useless'), Morgan ('very disappointed') and Creagh ('not up to it') joined the ranks of twenty or so brigadiers and generals whose careers were cut short. Fortunately for Dempsey, Brooke's inspection of his division at Feltwell aerodrome passed off well, as 'a good show', and the fall from grace of Creagh, whom Brooke had originally accepted with reluctance, provided an opportunity for his advancement.

Dempsey was now to command the 42nd Division, a first-line Territorial formation, recruiting from Lancashire and Manchester, comprising 125, 126 and 127 Infantry Brigades. In August 1940, the decision had been taken to form seven armoured divisions, soon raised to ten, by August 1941. The 42nd Division had been chosen for this purpose and it was Dempsey's task to convert his command into an armoured division, with the brigades becoming 10 and 11 Armoured and 42 Support Group. This involved the majority of the infantry re-roling as armoured soldiers, a huge task in which almost every man in the Division had to go on a specialist course of one sort or another, while at the same time brigade and divisional headquarters had to be trained and exercised in the new tactics of armoured warfare.

Dempsey – and his division – now faced further frustrations arising from the change in composition of armoured divisions decreed six months after he took command. One of the armoured brigades was replaced by an infantry brigade and the Support Group was abolished, with the artillery being placed under command of the Commander Royal Artillery and his staff at Divisional Headquarters; 10 and 11 Armoured Brigades left to become Army Tank Brigades; and 30 Armoured and 71 Infantry Brigades joined the Division. The experience was not a happy one for the Division, which was disbanded shortly after, with many of the tank units re-converting to infantry. Old soldiers may be reminded of the famous words attributed to the Roman, Petronius Gaius Arbiter:

> We trained hard. But it seemed that every time we were beginning to form up into teams we would be reorganised. I was to learn later in life that we tend to meet any new situation by reorganising; and a wonderful method it can be for creating an illusion of progress while producing confusion, inefficiency, and demoralisation.

For Dempsey, his time in command of an armoured division was critical to his future. It not only gave him ample opportunity to show his genius for organization, it gave him invaluable insights and experience in the art of armoured warfare. Perhaps most importantly, it took him to the renewed notice of Brooke, who again made a successful visit to the Division, and of Montgomery, now commanding South-East Army. Montgomery's ideas on generalship and the handling of formations at what is nowadays called the operational level were expressed forcibly and often. He took a particular interest in the armoured divisions, punching home the need for flexibility in regrouping and 'balance', and the need to concentrate armour. He summed it up as concentration, control, simplicity. The leader must be well forward; if he wished to discuss operations with his subordinate commanders, he should go forward to them, not bring them back to him. But the higher formation commander must give himself time to think ahead, and that meant having a good night's sleep, a clear head and strong nerves, so as not to be diverted by momentary events.

The morale of his soldiers was Montgomery's overriding concern. High morale required good, hard, realistic training by young, fit leaders who were totally on top of their job, and who would never spend their soldiers' lives wastefully. He spent about one third of his working hours in considering the merits and faults of all the senior officers in his command, forever making notes on personalities in a little black book. If a commander passed scrutiny, he was a 'Monty man' for the rest of his career. One such was Dempsey, who passed the test in every respect, and who had, in addition, a quality which appealed deeply to Montgomery – a proper sense of religious truth. The impact of Alington of Shrewsbury was making itself felt at a critical time in Britain's fortunes.

In late 1942, Montgomery requested that Dempsey take command of XIII Corps in North Africa, in place of Horrocks, who had been wounded. This vital promotion now marked Dempsey as one of the fastest rising stars in the Army, with six promotions in four years: a phenomenal rate of progress, and undoubtedly due to his affinity to Montgomery. Their paths were now to march side by side and it is perhaps appropriate at this stage to consider their relationship. Montgomery, the consummate professional, was one of the greatest battlefield soldiers that Britain has produced. To quote General 'Pete' Pyman, an outstanding officer from a later generation:

> Montgomery was the best field commander I ever knew during the whole of my military service. He was the complete soldier, with a capacity to outfight the enemy which put him in a class of his own … He led the British, Canadian and at times American divisions with unerring skill … he made it possible for us to do a tremendous amount with what we had … woe betide the man who tries to belittle the achievements on the battlefield of our Monty.[1]

Montgomery was, perhaps, the first very senior officer to appreciate the importance of building confidence between himself and a largely conscript army – and between himself and the British public. By constant exposure and certain flamboyant little tricks such as wearing two badges, he became an instantly recognizable figure. To some, these methods were distasteful, but they worked. He built a feeling of complete confidence, of invincibility, of fellowship, and of trust. In assessing military leaders, those of an academic mind are inclined to neglect the importance of leadership – as opposed to management – in those they study, and, too often, criticize. An eminent Staff College lecturer summed it up admirably:

> To learn that Napoleon in 1796 with 20,000 men beat combined forces of 30,000 by something called 'economy of force' or 'operating on interior lines' is a mere waste of time. If you can understand how a young, unknown man inspired a half-starved, ragged, rather Bolshie crowd; how he filled their bellies; how he out-marched, outwitted, out-bluffed and defeated men who had studied war all their lives and waged it according to the textbooks of the time, you will have learned something worth knowing. But you won't get it from crammers' books.

But with Montgomery's enormous virtues came faults: an inability to admit he was ever wrong, or to see other points of view; he was insubordinate, insensitive and difficult. As a senior commander in a coalition of many nationalities, these faults became serious obstacles to Allied progress, and were shortly to involve him and Dempsey in a major crisis. In particular, Montgomery rubbed up the Americans the wrong way, sometimes going out of his way to make disparaging comments about their fitness as soldiers. Initially, he had much to be disparaging about, for the American Army that arrived in North Africa in 1942 was badly trained and badly led. The fiasco at the Kasserine Pass, where an inadequate divisional commander failed to rally his demoralized and outwitted troops, seemed to confirm this viewpoint. Moreover, their commander, Eisenhower, was a total novice on the battlefield. But the Americans learned fast and Eisenhower showed his greatness, not as a battlefield commander, but as a 'manager' of a grand alliance.

Dempsey, as we have noted, shared Montgomery's views on battlefield command, and their tactical concepts were in harmony, as were their underlying beliefs and integrity of character. Outwardly, the two presented a complete contrast. Dempsey was quiet, restrained, modest and averse to publicity. His personal staff officers were devoted to him and his subordinate commanders trusted his judgement implicitly, but he never attempted to foster any sort of personality cult. He was always immaculately turned out and his soul would have revolted at the idea of employing the sort of showmanship that characterized Montgomery. A major asset to Montgomery was Dempsey's charm and his ability to work harmoniously with others, at whatever level, of whatever service or nationality. He could talk to the Royal Navy and the RAF and the Americans and the Canadians without upsetting them, and this ability was to be sorely needed.

Although Dempsey was now a lieutenant general and commander of a corps, that corps existed only in name. Unlike divisions and brigades, which by and large retain their composition unchanged, corps are created and their formations added or subtracted, entirely as the operational situation dictates. Thus, when Dempsey took over XIII Corps, he inherited a headquarters and staff, but virtually nothing else. The campaign in North Africa was drawing to a close and Montgomery, looking ahead with the clarity of vision and purpose which was one of his hallmarks, was turning his attention to the next objective, Sicily.

At the Casablanca Conference in January 1943, the Allies agreed that, once the Axis forces were driven out of Tunisia and Tripolitania, where they were now being squeezed from two directions following the TORCH landings, the war should be carried to what Churchill fondly described as 'the soft underbelly' of Europe. Plans were then set in hand to effect this. In London the Joint Planning Staff had produced an outline appreciation for an invasion of Sicily, which was adopted at Casablanca. The problem was that the plan had been cobbled together hastily by staff officers without input from a commander. Although it looked impressive, and its multiplicity of staff tables and other annexes gave it the appearance of deep study, it was, as its authors themselves acknowledged, not a viable operational document for waging a campaign.

The plan, with all its faults, was then taken and worked on by the Allied planning staff in Algiers, known, from the number of their hotel room, as Task Force 141. They were headed by Major General Gairdner, an officer of great tact and charm, but lacking experience of high command, and definitely not a 'Monty man'. He insisted that the plan, which envisaged an American landing on the north coast, aimed at capturing Palermo, and a British landing on the south-east, aimed at Syracuse, must be adhered to. The plan attempted to reconcile the Navy's requirement for ports to offload the tonnages required by the armies once ashore, with their own and the RAF's demands that the complex of airfields at Gela, on the south-west side of the island, be captured immediately.

Dempsey was, in his own words, 'hauled up from Syria ... and Alex said to me "I want you to plan the Sicily landings. You'll find it all in the file."'[2] Dempsey was appointed Chief of Staff to the Eastern Task Force Headquarters, named Force 545, based in Cairo, a post he filled for some months until Freddy de Guingand, Montgomery's brilliant and affable Chief of Staff, could be spared to take over. De Guingand was full of praise for Dempsey, whom he described as highly intelligent, human and easy to get on with – an ideal commander for such a difficult campaign. Dempsey then concentrated on the planning for his own XIII Corps. A happy coincidence for him was that his old cricketing friend from Camberley, Rear Admiral Troubridge, commanded Force 'A', the naval support for his Corps.

Dempsey wrote to brother Patrick: 'I am doing a lot of travelling over my scattered command, and got back yesterday from a four day trip; air and car.' He was obviously constrained in what he could say about the operational situation and in this letter, as in the dozens that he exchanged with Patrick over the next two and a half years, he wrote mainly about his great passion – horses and their breeding:

> Yes, it was hard luck about the foal. She was a very attractive little beast – and had clearly been 'done' very well at Stanley House. Matt seemed to like her very much – and he is a good judge. I was not optimistic when I last saw her – and Dines gave me the news on the 'phone the day I left London. I would welcome all the news you can give me on Trireme and Mussel Bay.[3]

While the commanders who would have to put the invasion plan into effect were busy fighting the campaign that was to result in the surrender of the Axis forces in North Africa, Dempsey soon realized it was faulty, with 'disconnected landings each aimed at grabbing an airfield'.[4] On 13 March, accompanied by Admiral Ramsay, the commander of the naval forces for the Eastern Task Force, Dempsey presented the plan to Montgomery. Although, according to Dempsey, Montgomery said he was fighting a battle and could not be interrupted, he took Dempsey's point and expressed his objections with his usual force, demanding that the plan be recast. He was convinced that the Italians, who made up the bulk of Sicily's garrison, would strenuously resist the invasion of their homeland – the division of forces envisaged would therefore be unwise and could even lead to disaster. A secondary problem was that the British did not have the forces required to take out the Gela complex and would need to borrow an American formation.

Dempsey went on to Algiers and, despite being greeted initially with a certain amount of *froideur*, at a meeting on 18 March formally spelled out his and Montgomery's objections. In the absence of firm direction from Alexander, who was briefed by Dempsey and Gairdner, the planners were left to drift. As the date for the operation came closer, Montgomery's impatience grew, and at the critical AFHQ conference on 2 May he took the unorthodox approach of buttonholing Bedell Smith, Eisenhower's Chief of Staff, in the cloakroom. He put to him his objections and suggested that the only way to accommodate all the requirements of the interested parties was to switch the entire American effort from the north to the south-west. This would concentrate the land forces, while ensuring that the airfields at Gela were an immediate objective. Bedell Smith agreed and persuaded Eisenhower to adopt the plan. Dempsey was full of admiration for the way Montgomery had handled the situation and considered it his finest hour, but he also considered that the diminution of Tedder's input was the start of the bad blood between him and Montgomery.

The utmost tact was now called for, to avoid the impression that Montgomery had steamrollered everyone. It was not apparent, indeed Montgomery himself seemed to assume that Eighth Army under his command was to lead the invasion, with the Americans under Patton in a secondary role providing flank protection, while the British headed north to take Messina. To be fair to Montgomery, the British contribution far outweighed the American. The Royal Navy was committing a total of 1,614 different craft, including over 300 major and 700 minor landing craft, compared to the 945 craft, with 190 major and 510 minor landing craft of the Americans. The British and Empire land forces totalled 115,000 against the 66,000 Americans. But American *amour propre* had to be massaged and Eisenhower achieved this with his usual tact. A helpful factor in deciding the argument was that the recently introduced DUKW amphibian vehicle allowed large tonnages to be brought ashore over open beaches, and their insertion into the plan allowed Palermo to be abandoned as a primary objective without excessive loss of face.

The Axis garrison of Sicily, prior to the invasion, consisted of two German divisions, with a strong concentration of anti-aircraft guns around Messina, four Italian divisions totalling 60,000 men and five static Italian coastal divisions of about 40,000 low-quality troops with inadequate equipment. In addition there were a large number of administrative and other forces that brought the combined Axis total to over 300,000 men. The problem for the Axis was that they were unsure what would be the Allies' next objective after North Africa. Although geographical proximity pointed to Sicily, it was not the only possibility, and the Allies determined to keep their plans secure until the last possible moment. To district the Allies from Sicily, a brilliant deception plan, MINCEMEAT, was put in place, designed to convince the Germans that the Allies were aiming elsewhere. The story, portrayed in *The Man Who Never Was*, is well known. Although the Germans took steps to overhaul their plans for the defence of Sicily, no reinforcements were sent there until the invasion had begun.

The Eighth Army objectives were to capture the port of Syracuse and the landing grounds around Pachino, establish a front along the line Syracuse–Pozzalo–Ragusa, and make contact with Patton's Seventh Army. They were then to push rapidly forward to capture Catania and the Gerbini airfields. Dempsey's XIII Corps would land three brigades between Avola and Cassabile. Once the beachhead was secure they were to push hard to take Syracuse, Augusta, Catania and the Gerbini airfields on the western edge of the Catania plain. Naval, air and airborne forces would support the assault by containing and disrupting the enemy's reserves.

Under Dempsey's command for the invasion was the 5th Division, which had just arrived in the theatre from Syria, staging briefly at Port Said before joining the invasion fleet. It was commanded by Major General Berney-Ficklin. Apart from a spell on the Saar front during the 'phoney war' of 1940, he had seen no active service in the war so far, and was inclined to be slow and cautious. Dempsey's old brigade, 13, was still in the Division, its composition unchanged, and now commanded by a respected Territorial, Brigadier L.M. Campbell VC. They were joined by the 50th (Northumbrian) Division, commanded by Major General Sidney Kirkman, a gunner who had impressed Montgomery by his handling of artillery in the Western Desert, and a contemporary of Dempsey at Camberley. The 50th had also just arrived from Syria. Under command for the invasion phase was the 1st Airborne Division under Major General Hopkinson. The Division consisted of an airlanding brigade, which came to battle in Horsa and Waco gliders piloted by the Glider Pilot Regiment, and a Parachute Brigade. The independent 4th Armoured Brigade, commanded by Brigadier Currie, consisting of the County of London Yeomanry and 44th Royal Tank Regiment, gave the Corps tank support.

In the weeks leading up to the invasion, the plans were rehearsed and war-gamed, beaches were reconnoitred closely and in detail, and Dempsey's two assault divisions trained for their landings. They relied entirely on their naval counterparts to ensure that they hit the right beaches at the right time for the tide, and the rehearsals engendered confidence between soldier and sailor. The logistic plan called for XIII Corps to be self-sufficient for seven days; their 4,300 vehicles and 191 tanks required 11,700 tons of supplies. Very detailed briefings, including the use of models of the landing areas, were carried out down to every level, and in 44 Armoured Brigade every vehicle was issued thirty-seven different maps. Dempsey also had the opportunity to become acquainted with a type of unit until then unfamiliar to him – Special Forces. On 13 May, he visited the Special Raiding Squadron on the coast of northern Palestine, but he had not been properly briefed and addressed them in what they regarded as a rather patronizing fashion, as if they were green troops. As the men were marched off, their commander, Paddy Mayne, whispered in Dempsey's ear. The men were called back and Dempsey made a handsome apology. 'Those bloody fools back at HQ will one day tell me who I am talking to and stop me making a bloody fool of myself,' he said. He then watched a training demonstration and stayed the night, and after watching further demonstrations the next day, briefed them on a forthcoming operation. It was to be the start of a very long and happy association.

The preparations for the largest combined operation in the history of warfare to date were, for the most part, thorough and comprehensive. Only in one area were preparations and training less than comprehensive and that was in the airlift for 1st Airborne Division. The objective of the airlanding brigade, in the very opening phase of the invasion, was to capture the Ponte Grande Bridge, which had to be in XIII Corps' possession if they were to break out of the bridgehead and head north. The plan for its capture, LADBROKE, was explained to the Brigade, its Glider Pilot Regiment members and their affiliated towing aircraft crews on 1 April. They therefore had over three months to prepare, but the American pilots of the 51st USAAF Troop Carrier Wing, towing 100 gliders behind their C-47s, were not ready. Their navigational skills were so poor that each group of five towing aircraft depended on one leader to find the way; if their formation broke up, four of the five were lost.

At Taormina, on the evening of 9 July, the men of the South Staffordshire Regiment loaded up their gliders, which were lifted into the night sky. As they approached their target, heavy anti-aircraft fire from Italian ground batteries forced many of the pilots to take evasive action, breaking up the formations. The inexperienced pilots now showed not only their lack of training, but their resolution. Some cast off their gliders while still over the sea, some turned tail, and some became totally disorientated and headed for anywhere but Sicily. Of the 147 gliders, half went down in the sea, drowning those aboard; fifty-nine landed over a 25-mile area and played no part in the operation, and just twelve, towed by experienced RAF pilots, landed on or near the objective.

Fortunately, two young officers who did arrive on target showed outstanding initiative. Lieutenant Louis Withers, with the twenty-six men of his platoon of South Staffords, was joined by a Royal Engineers lieutenant, who organized the removal of the demolition charges attached to the stone pillars of the bridge. Withers, with five men, swam the canal and successfully attacked the pillbox guarding the north end of the bridge as the rest of the platoon attacked from the south. The Ponte Grande Bridge was now in their possession, and during the night they were joined by other airborne soldiers and Glider Pilot Regiment NCOs. By daybreak on 10 July, shortly after the leading wave of landing craft hit the beaches to their south, the little garrison numbered eighty-seven men. Other brave actions by the airborne soldiers included the attack by the Deputy Brigade Commander, Colonel O.L. Jones, on the coastal battery in Syracuse harbour, which resulted in the capture of five guns.

In a supporting action, described by Dempsey as a brilliant operation, brilliantly planned and brilliantly carried out, the Special Raiding Squadron landed at Cape Murro de Porco, with orders to take and destroy a coastal battery. In fact they took out three batteries and captured 450 prisoners. It was this operation that Dempsey had himself briefed them on during his visit in May.

The following morning the Italians counter-attacked on the Ponte Grande Bridge. A strong force, supported by mortars and armoured cars, attempted to dislodge the tiny garrison. After seven hours of intense fighting they numbered fifteen men able to fight, but their ammunition was exhausted. They threw their weapons in the canal and surrendered, only to be freed shortly after by a patrol from the 2nd Battalion Northampton Regiment, while advance elements of 2nd Battalion Royal Scots Fusiliers rushed the bridge with their Bren carriers and recaptured it. The exploit saved Dempsey seven days and he was quick to express his appreciation to Hopkinson and his men.

H-Hour for the beach assault was 0245 on 10 July. For some hours before this, heavy winds had made the sea very rough and many of the troops who had been at sea for what seemed an age became very seasick. Landing craft slowed and began to straggle, and ships lost their place in the convoy, but the timetable was just about adhered to. Fortunately, although Hitler had already been alerted and ordered reinforcements to be prepared to move from southern France, tactical surprise was complete and there was virtually no resistance. This was as well as a number of units had been landed on the wrong beaches, much to the fury of Kirkman, commanding the 50th Division. Some coastal batteries started firing, but were soon silenced by naval gunfire. By 1000 hours, XIII Corps had taken Cassibile and Casanuova, and gained a footing in Avila and Noto, and by nightfall the 5th Division had occupied the plateau overlooking Cassibile, taken Syracuse with its port undamaged, and held the Ponte Grande Bridge They had not had everything their own way, though. The County of London Yeomanry, supporting the Northamptons as they approached Syracuse, were ambushed by Panzer Grenadiers from the Hermann Goering Division and lost five Shermans.

As D-Day drew to a close, XIII Corps could be satisfied with their achievements thus far. Despite some failings in the support received from the other services, the soldiers had achieved all their objectives. Dempsey now urged them to press on as quickly as possible to Augusta, the next port up the coast to the north. Kirkman needed no persuasion and was determined to capitalize on the lack of serious opposition. He urged his brigade commanders to push their men as hard as they could. The ground they marched over was the ground that they would have had to fight for if they had not pressed on. Marching was what they had to do, for much of their transport had been lost to bombing, and what was left was not high on the priority list for unloading. So far, resistance had been light, and they had yet to meet the Germans in any numbers. This was now to change.

On 12 July, as 5th Division were approaching Augusta, they ran into the Hermann Goering Division and for the first time had a hard fight on their hands. With the help of naval gunfire support, they forced their way through and took the town that night. It was now the turn of 50th Division and on 13 July, Dempsey and Montgomery met Kirkman to brief him on the next phase, the capture of Catania, which was expected to fall by 16 July. The key to the capture of Catania was the crossing of the Simeto River, the plan being that Hopkinson's Airborne Brigade would capture the Primasole Bridge that night to enable 50th Division to cross. In a subsidiary operation, No. 3 (Army) Commando would land from the sea and capture the bridge over the Lentini River, south of the Simeto. The plan required 50th Division to advance 30 miles in less than twenty-four hours – feasible against little opposition, but not so easy if the Germans got in the way. At the same time, 5th Division would push up along the coast north of Augusta and join up with 50th Division at Calentini.

The airborne operational plan was for 1 Parachute Brigade to jump onto dropping zones around the Primasole Bridge, followed three hours later by a small glider-borne party with ten guns. The operation was cursed with similar misfortune to the one four nights earlier, and for the same reasons. The force of 1,900 parachutists embarked in 126 American Dakotas, while the guns were loaded into gliders towed by RAF Halifaxes and Albermarles. As the air fleet passed over the armada of ships below, nervous naval gunners opened fire, causing aircraft to veer off course, and the tight formations were broken up. Some aircraft dropped their loads haphazardly, from the interior of Sicily to southern Italy, and many returned to base without attempting to complete their mission. Lieutenant Colonel Pearson, commanding 1st Battalion Parachute Regiment, whose task it was to seize the bridge itself in a *coup de main*, was asleep when he was awakened by his Dakota lurching as it avoided the flak. He pushed his way into the cockpit to find the terrified American pilot determined to return to base, while his co-pilot held his head in his hands and cried. Pearson drew his pistol and under threat of being shot, the pilot turned and dropped Pearson and his men. Twelve officers and 283 men, out of nearly 2,000, were dropped near enough to their target to be of use.

The bridge was soon taken by Captain Rann and fifty men of the 1st Battalion and Brigadier Lathbury organized its defence as best he could. At 0630, troops of the German 1st Parachute Division, supported by heavy mortars, attacked from the west. The attack was beaten off by extremely accurate fire from the 6-inch guns of HMS *Mauritius*, lying offshore for the purpose. Wave after wave of Messerschmitts then dived in to the attack and further ground attacks followed. By evening, the garrison had suffered serious casualties and was withdrawn to the southern bank of the river. From here they could cover the bridge with fire, and prevent the Germans replacing the charges and blowing it.

Meanwhile, No. 3 Commando was in action to their south. On 13 July, their commanding officer, Lieutenant Colonel Durnford-Slater, had been summoned by Dempsey to meet him on the quay at Syracuse. There he heard that he and his men were to be put ashore that night from HMS *Prince Albert* in the Bay of Agnone. From there they were to march across country to seize the Ponte dei Malati, spanning the Lentini River, and hold it until relieved by 50th Division from the south. Again, it would have been a reasonable undertaking against minimal opposition, but, in the event of things not turning out as planned, Dempsey added that if 50th Division were not with them by first light, No. 3 Commando were to move off and hide up for the day. In the event they did meet opposition from highly determined Germans and the commandos only reached the bridge after a series of running battles. Once there, they chased off the Italian defenders and removed the demolition charges, but daylight brought increasing attacks and, like the paratroopers further north, they were finally forced off the bridge. Breaking into small parties they carried on the fight in the scrub-covered gullies as they tried to get back to the British lines. Their efforts were rewarded when, in the late afternoon, the 5th Battalion East Yorkshire Regiment became the first troops of 50th Division to break through, and captured the bridge intact. Dempsey was effusive in his praise for the men of No. 3 Commando, calling them the finest body of soldiers he had seen anywhere. A plaque was commissioned to commemorate their feat of arms on the 'No. 3 Commando Bridge'.

The 50th Division were pressing hard and by that evening they had taken the towns of Lentini and Calentini, and the Durham Light Infantry, supported by a squadron of tanks, had linked up with the remnants of 1st Airborne Division south of the Primasole Bridge. The next day, assaults by the Durhams and 44th Royal Tank Regiment in the morning and in the afternoon both failed. In the early hours of 15 July, the Durhams crossed by a ford a mile upstream and finally took the bridge. However, they were unable to break out of a tight perimeter on the north side and it was only when the Germans withdrew to a better defensive line that the Durhams were relieved by 168 Brigade. The contrast was clear between the relatively easy-going Italian defenders and the brave, skilful German parachute troops. Dempsey's XIII Corps had now begun to slow down. Mount Etna, to their north between them and Messina, presented an impassable obstacle. Between the slopes of the volcano and the sea the only coast road squeezed through a series of very narrow defiles and was easy for the defenders to block.

On 16 July, Dempsey came forward to the Primasole position with Montgomery. A tentative plan was hatched for an amphibious operation to capture Catania from the sea, but the difficulties of exploiting further north were so evident that the plan was abandoned. It was undoubtedly the right decision and was endorsed as such by Eisenhower in his memoirs. A headlong push up the coast was only ever going to be successful against the sort of feeble resistance offered by the Italians. Once the Germans were in play, the rules of the game changed and the two commanders only needed a short time to view the scene of utter devastation at Primasole, described by seasoned veterans as some of the bitterest fighting they ever experienced, to realize that a change in effort was needed.

The main weight of Eighth Army's advance was now switched to XXX Corps on the western side of Mount Etna, giving XIII Corps a chance to rest and regroup. They had been marching and fighting at a terrific pace – when the tank crews of the County of London Yeomanry at the Primasole Bridge were stood down, many were so drunk with weariness that they fell asleep immediately wherever they hit the ground; one man was found asleep draped over a small bush.

On 25 July, Mussolini was overthrown, and 1 August was fixed as the date for the resumption of the offensive. It was at this stage that Dempsey, in consultation with Montgomery, decided that Berney Ficklen was too tired to continue in command of the 5th Division, and Gerry Bucknell, who had been a student under Montgomery at Staff College, took over. On 5 August, the Germans evacuated Catania to fall back on the natural defensive line anchored on Mount Etna; XIII Corps moved in and then on to Aci Castello, 8 miles to the north. For the next week they followed as the retreating Germans stubbornly and skilfully used demolitions, mines, road blocks, booby traps and ambushes to slow their advance on the very restricted front. Such was the difficulty presented by this combination of terrain strongly suited to the defence, and the aggressive and skilful character of the defenders, that a Canadian tunnelling unit was urgently flown out from Britain – in four days they had bored a tunnel right through the rock and reopened the road.

A daring plan to bypass the coastal strip was set in motion by Dempsey, in tandem with Troubridge's sailors. A task force based on No. 2 (Army) Commando, commanded by Lieutenant Colonel Jack Churchill, a squadron of tanks, a battery of guns and anti-tank guns, and a company of Royal Engineers was embarked under the command of Brigadier Currie, commander of 4th Armoured Brigade. Sailing up the coast by moonlight on the night of 15 August, they disembarked with little opposition at Scaletta, just 7 miles south of Messina. Forming themselves into a column they pressed northwards, bypassing demolitions and lifting mines on the small bridges. By the next morning they had linked up with the Americans in the outskirts of Messina, where they received an ecstatic welcome from the inhabitants. Regrettably, neither the American advance along the north coast, nor the British from the south, had been fast enough to prevent some 40,000 German troops withdrawing in good order in a brilliantly organized evacuation across the Straits of Messina to the Italian mainland.

Dempsey was able to relax for a few days, and wrote to Patrick:

It's rather lovely in 'Cicely' these days. I have put my HQ on a most delightful hill – with a grand view of Etna and the sea – and although I am very full of work, I manage to get a bathe most days. Most things are unobtainable, but lemons, figs, grapes and almonds are in good supply – also Marsala![5]

The Sicily campaign was over. It had brought mixed fortunes and lessons had been learned the hard way. The determination and skill in defence of their German adversaries, linked to the difficult terrain, was to be encountered again and again in the coming campaign in Italy. Much experience had been gained in combined operations, of great benefit to staffs planning similar operations in Italy and, in the greatest undertaking of its type ever, OVERLORD, the invasion of Europe. Although mistakes had been made, such as the low priority in the load tables of troop transport, XIII Corps' logistic requirements had mostly been met adequately, and the DUKW in particular had proved its value. Where mistakes had been made – notably in the training of aircrew for airborne operations and naval landing parties – they would be rectified. The tank, so long the dominant weapon in North Africa, had demonstrated its shortcomings in the denser countryside of Sicily, and infantry would be the dominant arm in Italy. The advantages and shortcomings of air power had been relearned and the importance of close liaison, including co-location, where possible, of air and ground commanders emphasized.

Unfortunately, relationships at the higher levels had not prospered, and Montgomery was now an object of suspicion to the Americans and dislike to the RAF. Dempsey had done well and he was now an established corps commander, albeit still in Montgomery's shade. He had also acquired a new nickname. Known always in his regiment as 'Dimmer', to friends as 'Bimbo' and to the wider army as 'Emsy Dempsey Emsy' from the initials before and after his name, he now picked up the soubriquet of 'Lucky' from the coincidence of his having commanded 13 Brigade and XIII Corps. He had two experienced formations under his command, with trusted commanders, as he contemplated the next campaign, the invasion of Italy.

CHAPTER 8

'Head of Column Change Direction Half Right'

The invasion of the Italian mainland was to be conducted in two phases separated by five days and 200 miles. Initial landings were to be made by Dempsey's XIII Corps on the toe of Italy – BAYTOWN – followed by a major amphibious assault by the Fifth Army on Salerno, just south of Naples on the south-west coast – AVALANCHE. The strategic purpose of BAYTOWN was never clear. Its operational aims were laid down by Alexander as being, first, to enable the Navy to use the Straits of Messina, and second, in the event of the enemy withdrawing, to follow up and engage them with such force as could be made available. The greater the extent to which they could be engaged in the southern tip of Italy, the more assistance would be given to AVALANCHE.

In the event, BAYTOWN developed into an initial advance against light opposition, a link-up with AVALANCHE and then a slow slogging match against determined enemy resistance, in terrain and weather that favoured the defender. Many of the troops involved had been in almost continuous action for three or four years, and were growing tired and slow. Dempsey was therefore pleased to be allocated the 1st Canadian Division to replace 50th Division in XIII Corps. The Canadians had fought well in the Sicily campaign, but were relatively fresh; Dempsey knew and liked the Canadians from his time with them in 1940/41, and they knew and liked him; and their commander, Guy Simonds, was one of the best and brightest of the Allies' commanders and a personal friend.

Although negotiations for their surrender were under way, the Italians were still, in theory, enemy combatants, and the Germans had shown themselves to be highly skilled in defence. Reconnaissance parties had been landed on the mainland, but with little result. Lacking definite intelligence of enemy dispositions, Dempsey refused to cross the Messina Straits unless adequate assault craft were provided, which could not be before 3 September. This view was put forward at a major conference on 23 August, prompting a hot response from Cunningham, the peppery Naval Commander-in-Chief. Cunningham immediately flew to Sicily, and saw Dempsey and Admiral McGrigor. After he had been put in the picture, Dempsey reported to Montgomery that he had never seen such a change in any man, and that Cunningham was almost servile in his assurances that he would do anything the Army wanted.

Whereas valuable lessons had been learned from HUSKY, by comparison Operation BAYTOWN was more complicated for all three services, with only three weeks for preparations. Air operations, involving 4,500 sorties, with 6,500 tons of bombs to be dropped on the mainland, had to begin at once, as did the loading of ships with stores, the dumping of ammunition for the preliminary bombardment, the sweeping of mines and the preparation of forward airstrips.

On 3 September, under a massive bombardment from fifteen warships and every artillery piece that could be brought to bear, Dempsey's 5th and 1st Canadian Divisions crossed the Messina Straits in 300 landing craft and ferries. There was no opposition. The German 29th Panzer Grenadier Division had been in the area, but had withdrawn two days earlier. By nightfall the line San Stefano–Scilla had been reached, and that night commandos landed at Bagnara and got in behind the German rearguard. The plan now was for the Canadians to cross the mountains immediately and work their way up the east coast, while the 5th Division continued to advance up the west side, aided by further landings, until they linked up with Fifth Army from Salerno. The Italian capitulation was expected to coincide with the Salerno landings, but there was little expectation that it would change the balance of effective forces. Although the lead elements of the 5th Division soon linked up with a force of commandos who had been landed ahead of them, forward movement was now hindered by demolitions, which meant that movement was only possible by foot.

By noon on 6 September, Gioia Tauro had been captured and the Canadians had been switched to the southern coast road to try to speed up the advance. Dempsey now sent 13 Brigade by sea to Palmi, from where they marched all night through the mountains. He then sent 231 Brigade Group, commanded by Roy Urquhart, round by sea to land at Pizzo. As they approached the beaches, they came under fire from 29th Panzer Grenadier Division, which was pulling back on the coast road just inland. The operation was almost a disaster, due mainly to the naval force being untrained in combined operations, so units were put down on the wrong beaches and were widely scattered. The landing craft, escorted only by a monitor and two gunboats, came under fire from artillery and dive-bombers. A Landing Ship Tank (LST) caught fire and was beached, at which point the ramp went down and mobile guns rushed ashore. Fighting continued around Pizzo all day and it was only the overland advance of the 5th Division which saved 231 Brigade Group from being overrun. During the night the Germans slipped away. Dempsey was not impressed by the performance of Urquhart, whom he was to meet again in the Arnhem operation.

By 10 September, XIII Corps had reached Catanzaro, an advance of 100 miles in seven days, a very creditable achievement. They had faced great difficulties in getting the fighting vehicles and essential supply echelons forward over the damaged and mined roads. By this stage, the situation on the Salerno front was grave and Dempsey was being urged to push on as fast as possible, to maintain pressure on the Germans and relieve Fifth Army. But logistic factors, more than enemy resistance, now hindered him. The Salerno operation had priority for maintenance, administrative transport was limited and the two roads for forward resupply of the divisions were not good. Nevertheless, he pushed ahead with light forces and captured Crotone with the Canadians on the 11th. The plan now was for the 5th Division to concentrate at Castrovillari, and the Canadians at Spezzano and Rossano, but this would take four or five days.

On 14 September, 13 Brigade from the 5th Division, which had been taken in landing craft 100 miles up the coast, reached Sapri, and the following day, when extra ferries and road transport were provided, their patrols pushed forward to Vallo. They soon linked up with Americans from the Fifth Army and with 1st Canadian Division, coming up on their right. Taking advantage of naval and air superiority, Dempsey now used sea landings to capture Auletta with the 5th Division, and a composite unit of Canadians, 'Boforce', headed off at speed towards Potenza, which was taken by 3 Canadian Infantry Brigade on 19 September. In seventeen days, XIII Corps had advanced 300 miles despite the formidable difficulties of terrain and the never-ending series of demolitions, mines, booby traps and every sort of obstacle by which the enemy could slow their progress. Dempsey congratulated both divisions on their determined and speedy progress, and took the opportunity to send birthday greetings to Patrick, now a major in the RASC Record Office:

> Many happy returns! I wrote to you last on August 29th. Since then I have been so busily engaged in capturing Italy that there really has been little time to write. We are all very well – Italy being so constucted that one can generally get a bathe! I recently added five Italian divisions to the Corps – but have now managed to palm them off onto someone further back![1]

But the supply lines were now very stretched and struggling to meet the urgent operational demands of forward units, at the same time as the – very differently configured – requirements of depots and bases further to the rear. Dempsey now gave orders to Simonds for the next phase.

On 22 September, the 1st Canadian Division, in conjunction with 1st Airborne Division, which had earlier been landed at Taranto, closed in on Altamura. It then took under command 4th Armoured Brigade and, as the Germans withdrew, pressed on to Canosa. Brigadier John Currie's plan to attack Foggia, the next objective, was based on two mixed columns, 'Bakerforce' on the right and 'Cameronforce' on the left. The River Cervaro was defended in strength, but the defenders were cleared out and the Germans abandoned Foggia on 27 September. 4th Armoured Brigade pressed on to Lucera, where the 56th Reconnaissance Regiment freed scores of Allied prisoners of war. When the County of London Yeomanry (the Sharpshooters) lost some tank and scout car crews outside San Severe, the locals gave them a splendid funeral, with thousands lining the route of the procession.

By 1 October, XIII Corps had cleared the whole of the Gargno peninsular, and the advance was resumed. The Sharpshooters and the 5th Northamptons of 11 Infantry Brigade forded the Fortore and moved on to take Serracapriola. Most of the bridges had been destroyed and the Sharpshooters took one of the two remaining to occupy the ridge south of the town, while the Northamptons took the other and attacked the town through the thick cover of some olive groves. But the tanks had covered 200 miles and on 5 October the whole of 4 Brigade was concentrated at Lucera for intensive maintenance.

While the 5th Division was given an opportunity to rest and send some men to Bari for local leave, the 78th Division was grouped under XIII Corps. Commanded by Vyvyan Evelegh, whom Dempsey knew as his Brigade Major from his time in command of the Berkshires, the Division had fought under First Army in North Africa, Sicily and landed at Bari under V Corps. It was to take the lead on the right, with the Canadians on the left. Supporting them were 4th Armoured and 1 Canadian Tank Brigades. The Biferno was the next obstacle and the Germans were known to be taking up positions along it. The 78th Division were tasked with advancing straight up the coast road, with the objective of taking the port of Termoli, just north of the river, while the Canadians headed for Campobasso and Vinchiaturo, 40 miles inland. The latter now took under command the 1st Airlanding Light Regiment, which was fortuitously equipped with the 75mm pack howitzer. This versatile weapon could be stripped down into six loads, to be carried by mule or other means. It was to prove invaluable in the difficult going ahead.

The advance up the coast road was slow and, added to the usual problems caused by demolitions, German aircraft were now in action, harrying the long columns of men and supplies. Dempsey's answer, once more, was to use the sea. An amphibious force based on No. 3 Commando, 40 Royal Marine Commando and the Special Raiding Squadron under Paddy Mayne, sailed on 2 October in order to outflank the opposition. Despite the grounding of a number of landing craft on a sand bar, complete surprise was achieved, resulting in the capture of Termoli, with its harbour undamaged. The leading brigade of the 78th Division reached the Biferno in the morning, waded across and got some anti-tank guns over on rafts to reinforce the commandos. A light bridge was quickly erected, and a reconnaissance regiment and a regiment of field artillery soon joined them, along with Dempsey's tactical headquarters. He wanted to be at the critical point. During the next night 36 Infantry Brigade was landed, but the force still lacked tanks.

It was now obvious that the Germans were preparing a strong counter-attack; with no immediate possibility of a bridge strong enough for armour being constructed, and artillery ammunition severely limited, the situation looked critical. To add to the defenders' problems, torrential rain now swept away the light bridge and obstructed the siting of anti-tank guns. Fortunately, due to communication problems, the German attack was badly coordinated, but they were able to direct very accurate artillery fire, and a gallant night action by the Argyles, in which they lost five officers and 150 other ranks, failed to improve the situation. Although six tanks managed to cross the Biferno by an improvised ford, four were knocked out almost immediately. The RAF and USAAF provided magnificent support, flying Spitfire and P40 sorties. Finally, on the afternoon of 5 October, the unceasing efforts of the Royal Engineers, who had been working for twenty-four hours in pouring rain, were successful, and a Bailey bridge strong enough for the tanks was in position. The Sharpshooters crossed, sending one squadron to support 11 Infantry Brigade, while the rest of the Regiment headed for Difesne Grande to take on the tanks threatening 36 Brigade.

This marked the turning point and that evening men of 38 (Irish) Brigade came ashore in the harbour. As the garrison of Termoli built up, Evelegh mounted a counter-attack of his own to the south, using Canadian tanks and the Buffs, and the Irish Brigade then attacked from Termoli. By nightfall, Termoli was firmly in British hands and the road north was open. The Sharpshooters of 4th Armoured Brigade had performed heroically, but they had taken twenty-seven casualties, and only eleven tanks remained in a battle-worthy condition. The 78th Division had performed splendidly and Dempsey was quick to congratulate them, mentioning especially 12th Canadian Army Tank Regiment.

Dempsey also made a special point of congratulating the men of the Special Raiding Squadron. He impressed on them that the Termoli operation had completely upset the Germans' schedule and the balance of their forces by introducing a threat to the north of Rome. As a result the enemy were obliged to bring to the east coast the 16th Panzer Division which was in reserve in the Naples area. They had orders to recapture Termoli at all costs and drive the British into the sea, orders they were unable to carry out; not only that, the pressure on the American Fifth Army was eased, enabling them to advance. Then, in a speech which tells as much about Dempsey as it does about his audience, he gave six reasons why he thought they were so successful, and hoped they would bear them in mind when training newcomers:

> I have never met a unit in which I had such confidence as I have in yours ... First of all, you take your training seriously. That is one thing that has always impressed me about you. Secondly, you are well-disciplined. Unlike some who undertake this specialised and highly dangerous job, you maintain a high standard of discipline and cleanliness which is good to see. Thirdly, you are physically fit ... Fourthly you are completely confident in your abilities ... Fifthly, despite that confidence you plan carefully. Last of all, you have the right spirit, which I hope you will pass on to those who will join you in the future.[2]

Dempsey also found time to write to Patrick:

> We have covered a very considerable distance, and with the constant moves, and long motor drives (and air trips in light aircraft) which I make, I have found little time to write letters. We did a pretty good one in the last week: you may have read about a substantial incident at a place (rather attractive) called Termoli. I will tell you all about it one day. One of the lesser results is that the German formation commander's Alsatian is lying outside my caravan as I write this; and he himself is in the bag! They did not like it a bit, and took vigorous – but quite futile – action to deal with it.
>
> I have been out of England ten months now; it seems much less. The first two were interesting travelling: the next five were hard and monotonous planning: the last three have been quite first class. It is such a joy to work under a man like BLM – and the soldiers have been wonderful.[3]

While the 78th Division was struggling at Termoli, the Canadians moved through Foggia and Lucera, their advance guard hitting the enemy in the foothills at Motta di Montecorvino. At the same time, 2 Canadian Infantry

Brigade had been tasked with left-flank protection and prepared to attack towards Vinchiaturo. The Canadians, who by this stage had suffered 200 casualties in the campaign, realized that from now on, fighting would revert to the style they had known in Sicily, where ground was a more obstinate enemy than the Germans. They were faced by the 1st German Parachute Division as they pushed on through San Marco and Colletorte to the Fortore River. 3 Brigade now passed through and the Royal 22e regiment – the famous Van Doos – attempted to obtain a foothold on the west bank of the river, above a demolished thirteen-span bridge. They were driven back by heavy fire from the 15th Panzer Grenadiers, but the next day the West Nova Scotias, with the support of the whole of the divisional artillery, crossed further south and took the high ground overlooking it. The Canadian artillery now found that they were unable to bring their guns forward and the 1st Airlanding Regiment came into its own. The 48th Highlanders, tasked to take Torella, were halted by heavy mortar and artillery fire. The only way to get artillery forward was to dismantle the 75s and carry them on tanks, along with their crews. The same method was used to support the 5th Division's attack on Rionero.

Relying on mules more and more for resupply, the Canadians eventually took Campobasso on 14 October. Meanwhile the 5th Division was brought forward to fill the gap that was opening between the 78th and 1st Canadian Divisions, and captured Casacalenda and Vinchiaturo.

The Germans now withdrew back behind the River Trigno, giving XIII Corps an opportunity to pause and consolidate. Particular attention was paid to resting and relaxing the soldiers. Cinemas and troop concerts entertained them, and mobile bath units and extra warm clothing were provided. On 8 October, Dempsey had attended a major conference at Eighth Army Headquarters. With the winter closing in rapidly, the need to press on while movement was still possible was imperative. Headquarters V Corps, recently arrived in theatre, would take back the 78th Division at the end of the month, and, with the 8th Indian Division under command, would press on up the coast road. Meanwhile, on 28 October, XIII Corps, with its two original divisions, 5th and 1st Canadian, would resume the offensive inland, as a diversion. At this stage, Guy Simonds handed over command of 1st Canadian Division to Major General Vokes, the newly promoted former commander of 2 Canadian Infantry Brigade. Simonds took over an armoured division in preparation for his promotion to Corps Commander, when he would again serve with Dempsey.

As the Germans retreated behind the Trigno, the problems facing the Allies became acute. The enemy had a series of naturally strong and well-prepared positions behind them, to which they could withdraw, and the weather was closing in. The roads were poor enough at the best of times, but now virtually every bridge and culvert had been blown, heavy rain made the rivers rise and fill every track and rivulet with gushing water, and the temperature dropped. Mules were increasingly employed for transport, but for the troops, each day turned in to a struggle against the elements, sapping morale and dulling their aggressive spirit. By this stage, even de Guingand, Chief of Staff to Montgomery, was beginning to wonder if it was worth it, and Alanbrooke, CIGS, was complaining that the American preoccupation with re-entering North-West Europe was rendering it impossible to gather the full fruits of the Mediterranean strategy.

Dempsey wrote to Patrick:

> I think I told you last time something of my latest seaborne venture at Termoli. It was a great success, and we have captured more than one German document showing what a great operation it was. Since then we have gone rather rapidly from summer to winter condition. It has been extremely cold in the mountains, with long rainstorms, and clouds 'on the ground'. This naturally delays everything – and prevents us getting full value from our air.[4]

Dempsey's Corps began the renewed offensive well, with his old 13 Brigade in the van. Despite a postponement of thirty-six hours, a difficult night attack on Cantalupo, led by 2nd Wiltshires, was successful. Dempsey visited each battalion in the Brigade and congratulate them. They then occupied Isernia after another night march. Between 12 and 22 November, 3 Canadian Infantry Brigade carried out an independent operation supported by artillery. The Brigade covered the frontage that would normally be allocated to a division, the aim of their operation being to protect the engineers who were working on the lateral road towards the coast, as part of the preparation for the crossing of the Sangro further east. The operation was a complete success and again earned Dempsey's congratulations.

By 19 November, the Trigno had been crossed, but as they closed up to the Sangro, Dempsey's men were very tired. They were allotted the task of making a feint towards the area of Alfredena to Castel di Sangro. Extensive and aggressive patrolling masked their true intentions and dummies simulated growing administrative installations, engineer parks and ammunition dumps. The Canadians were tasked with infiltration and bridging tasks, which continued to the end of the month, when they passed under command of V Corps, while the 78th Division came back to XIII Corps, to be held in reserve. The swollen state of the Sangro made it unlikely that the enemy would attempt to cross and the 5th Division settled into an outpost line on the south bank, from which they patrolled extensively.

Their major enemy now was the *Tellermine*, encountered with increasing frequency in various guises.

Orsogna was allocated to Dempsey as his next objective. On 23 December, the 5th Division took Arielli, but were still short of the hill village, which was a natural fortress. The weather by now was severe and the Division's main dressing station was cut off by snowdrifts for a week. Battle casualty replacements were not enough to replace the dead and wounded, and units were dangerously below strength. In early January, the 5th Division was transferred from XIII to X Corps and Dempsey said goodbye to the veteran formation. After hard fighting with the BEF, the Division had spent two years in Britain, before taking part in the invasion of Madagascar, followed by periods of time in India, Iraq, Persia, Syria and Palestine, before, as part of XIII Corps, fighting throughout the Sicily and Italy campaigns. Their commander, Gerry Bucknall, left them for command of a corps, to be replaced by Major General Gregson-Ellis. In the 78th Division, Major General Charles Keightley had taken over from Evelegh and, with XIII Corps now having under command just one division, and in a quiet role, it was time for Dempsey himself to say goodbye.

In his year commanding a corps, Dempsey had shown drive and flexibility. He had also gained huge experience in combined operations. As he was fond of emphasizing in later years, he had directed or planned a dozen such missions, the large majority amphibious. As a result he had extensive experience of working with many of the unconventional forces, such as the Commandos and the Special Raiding Squadron, of which there were a plethora in the Mediterranean. Many senior officers had serious reservations about the value of such units. They tended to attract the high-quality young leaders who took such high casualties and were now so badly needed in more conventional units. But Dempsey recognized their worth and his words to the Special Raiding Squadron, quoted earlier, have entered Special Forces' folklore. But while he welcomed innovation, while retaining the very best of the old-fashioned military virtues, not all his ideas on their employment were accepted. A particular bone of contention was Dempsey's principle that Special Forces should not be deployed further forward of the main army than twelve to twenty-four hours to link-up. This principle was to be relaxed, to great benefit, in North-West Europe.

As a senior officer in a coalition, Dempsey had gained experience of working with other nationalities and had reinforced his strong links with the Canadians. He had also worked with the other services – happily, with his friend Troubridge and with the Royal Navy; less happily, at least initially, with the RAF. Dempsey's opposite number in this service was Harry Broadhurst, an extremely brave and colourful character. After combat experience as a fighter pilot in the Battle of Britain, and in North Africa and Sicily, he became the youngest Air Marshal in a 'young' service. His relations with Dempsey developed serious strains during the fighting in Italy, as a result of several errors of coordination by the staff of Headquarters XIII Corps. In one incident, Dempsey addressed a furious message to Broadhurst after his troops came under air attack by their own side. In fact, the Bomb Line – the coordinating line forward of which it was safe for supporting aircraft to strike – had not been updated by his own staff. It was a serious mistake, which earned Dempsey a stinging rebuke from Montgomery. Dempsey apologized handsomely, Broadhurst accepted that the apology was a tribute to Dempsey's fairness, and a partnership and close personal friendship developed which was to be of huge importance in the campaign in Europe.

Dempsey and Montgomery had now worked so long together that he was totally in tune with his commander's tactical thinking and had his entire confidence. Thus it was that, shortly after he arrived back in Britain to begin the planning for the invasion of Europe, Montgomery requested Alanbrooke to appoint Dempsey to command the British Second Army within his 21st Army Group. De Guingand made the point in his memoirs that Montgomery chose his higher commanders from those he knew, from those who were in many cases brought on under him. They therefore knew his form and accepted it. They always knew he was there to be leant on, he took the utmost pains to nurse them into their command and give them the benefit of his experience.

Certainly, Montgomery would have been impressed by Dempsey's cool handling of 13 Brigade in 1940, his command of two different divisions in England, and his successful running of XIII Corps in Sicily and Italy. He was later asked how he rated Dempsey as a general – was he a '*bon general ordinaire*' or was he in the sparse ranks of the truly great commanders. Tellingly, although he rated Leese, Dempsey's fellow army commander, as the former, for Dempsey he reserved the highest accolade: 'A *grand chef*? Yes.' Alanbrooke, with the same background knowledge, albeit at second hand for the most part, agreed.

It was an extraordinary promotion for Dempsey. From major in 1938, he had, in six years, risen through lieutenant colonel commanding a battalion, colonel, brigade command, command of a division, then a corps, now of an army. It was unprecedented and could have given rise to the sort of jealousy and intrigue that Montgomery attracted. That it did not says much for Dempsey's lack of flamboyance, his transparent honesty and integrity, his unwillingness to court publicity, his willingness to accept and apologize for his own failings and his concern always to praise others.

Horrocks, who knew him well from Camberley days and was soon to serve under him as a corps commander, described him as one of the ablest soldiers in the British Army. He was very shrewd, he never flapped, but, vitally, Horrocks then went on to say that he doubted whether anyone else could have worked so harmoniously and successfully with Montgomery. The two were complementary – Montgomery the extrovert, who loved the headlines, Dempsey the introvert, who shunned publicity but got on with the job efficiently and without any fuss. Montgomery was not at his best with Allies; Dempsey went out of his way to iron out the friction caused by the other's tactlessness.

Guy Simonds remembered later:

> I served with him when I was commanding 1 Canadian Division in Sicily, and under his command in 13 Corps we crossed the Straits of Messina and advanced through Southern Italy. I have met few people in my lifetime who carried the high responsibilities borne by Miles, and yet were so universally liked, respected and admired by all who came in contact with him. His great professional abilities and his clear, quick and decisive mind were balanced by such integrity and honesty of purpose as to win universal respect and affection.[5]

Dempsey would have his staff dazzled by his ability to remember everything on a map and then to visualize a battlefield even though he had never actually seen it. Although Dempsey deserved this promotion on his own merits, he had not been the first choice. Montgomery initially proposed, with typical lack of political acumen, that Leese should command Second Army, and Dempsey should command the fledgling First Canadian Army, on the grounds that he had worked with them and was highly popular with the Canadians. Luck had also played a part. If his company commander from Sandhurst, Dick O'Connor, had not been captured in North Africa at the height of his reputation as the victor of the initial campaign against the Italians; if his rival in the point-to-point at Camberley, 'Strafer' Gott, not been killed in an air crash; if Horrocks had not been wounded; if Leese had not had to remain in Italy to take over Eighth Army; if Anderson had impressed more as Commander First Army in North Africa … there are a myriad of possibilities, but perhaps the important point to bear in mind is Napoleon's adage: 'But is he lucky?' Dempsey was lucky, but generals make their own luck, and as he prepared for the greatest combined operation in history, Dempsey could reflect that his whole life had been a fitting preparation for the most important task that he was ever to undertake.

CHAPTER 9

'Front'

By January 1944, planning for OVERLORD, the invasion of North-West Europe, had been proceeding for over a year. In March 1943, Lieutenant General Frederick Morgan had been appointed Chief of Staff to the Supreme Allied Commander, COSSAC, and charged with planning the Second Front. He was introduced to the post by Brooke, CIGS, with the words 'It won't work but you must bloody well make it.' His problem was that he did not, at that stage, have a Supreme Commander to direct the plan, and as Montgomery and Dempsey, with their experience of combined operations were to say many times, therein lay disaster.

Based on an extensive appreciation of the possible options, Morgan recommended landing three divisions in the area of Caen. Neither he nor his staff had huge confidence in the plan, but Morgan was quite unprepared for the withering criticism it received when it was presented to Montgomery on 3 January. It was too restricted and the planners were directed to reshape it into a new plan embodying a five-divisional assault, flanked by airborne landings, on a 50-mile front from the Cherbourg peninsula to the River Orne. That Montgomery was right and that his rapid recasting of the plan had averted a disaster, there can be no doubt. But he had put noses out of joint, foremost among them Morgan's.

Two armies were to be committed – the Americans on the right, and Dempsey's Second Army on the left. From the first, Montgomery laid down that the task of Second Army was to operate to the south, to prevent any interference with the American Army from the east. He explained this to the senior officers involved on 13 January, at which date Anderson was still the nominal commander designate of Second Army. Dempsey arrived later in the month to take over and on 11 February, attended Montgomery' second briefing for commanders. He and Bradley, his opposite number commanding the American landings, left the briefing quite clear that Montgomery's plan was to hold on the left (with the British) and break out on the right (with the Americans). All five divisions had to be got ashore, with supporting weapons and tanks, on the first tide, following a heavy air bombardment.

That afternoon, Dempsey and Bradley crawled around on the floor, spreading out the maps, and, as far as Dempsey was concerned, looking at the Normandy terrain seriously for the first time. Montgomery stressed the fact that after the immediate reserves had been drawn in all German reserves would arrive at the battle front from the east and south-east; thus to get across to the American sector of the bridgehead they would have to pass across the British front around Caen. Dempsey was very clear:

> It was my job to make sure that they didn't move across, that they were kept fully occupied fighting us in the Caen sector. Monty also stressed that whatever happened my left flank had to be kept absolutely secure. The Eastern wall along the Orne must be held otherwise the whole bridgehead could be rolled up from that flank. He never wavered in his determination to pursue this policy.[1]

Setting up his headquarters on 26 January at Ashley Gardens in London, Dempsey and his Chief of Staff, Maurice Chilton, could now begin detailed planning, building on the mass of data available and their first-hand experience of mounting amphibious operations. Engaged with them were Rear Admiral Vian, commanding the Eastern Naval Task Force, and Harry Broadhurst, continuing the happy association with 83 Group.

Their first consideration had to be the enemy. Dempsey was concerned with three main questions: what preparations had the enemy made to the beaches to make them impassable to an invader; what would be the strength and tactics of the enemy during the assault; and what would be the likely build-up of enemy forces, particularly Panzer (armoured) units, against his three beachheads.

By June 1944, the Germans had fifty-eight divisions in France, sixteen of which covered Normandy and Brittany. They included nine Panzer divisions and one Panzer Grenadier division. The strength and calibre of the divisions varied; static coastal defence divisions could contain as few as 6,000 men of varying quality and morale, while Panzer divisions could be as strong as 20,000 fanatical and well-trained soldiers. The defences of the 'Atlantic Wall' had been developing for several years. In Dempsey's sector, which stretched from Port-en-Bassin, his junction point with the Americans, to the Orne-Dives river system, there was a system of linear defences based on a string of strongpoints manned by coastal defence troops. The gun emplacements were of concrete and armour, protected by extensive minefields, wire entanglements and a variety of obstacles including walls insurmountable by tanks. On the beaches themselves, and at varying distances from the shoreline, there were underwater obstacles designed to impede landing craft and armed with impact charges. Behind the fortified gun emplacements mobile field and heavy artillery batteries could bring fire to bear on any part of the shore.

Fortunately for the Allies, the German tactics for repelling invasion were an unhappy compromise between the desire to put everything in 'the shop window', with the aim of preventing any landing in strength developing, and the need to hold mobile forces back to counter-attack in strength once the Allies' objectives were clear. In the event, three Panzer divisions were to remain under Hitler's personal command as a strategic reserve, and three only were allotted to Army Group B, responsible for covering Dempsey's objectives. An absolutely critical factor in Dempsey's appreciation was, therefore, how quickly these formations could arrive on his front. Key to this was the Allied deception plan, Fortitude North, which convinced Hitler, both before and for weeks after D-Day, that the main Allied landings would take place in the Pas de Calais and that the assault of 6 June would be a diversion. Nevertheless, in May the German High Command moved the 91st Division, together with a parachute regiment, to the Cherbourg peninsula, 21st Panzer Division to just south of Caen, and Panzer Lehr, the strongest formation in the German Army, to Chartres.

Dempsey's intelligence staff assessed that Second Army would be opposed by the 716th and 352nd Divisions on the beaches, and that 12th SS and 21st Panzer Divisions were located close enough to the beachhead to pose an immediate threat to the landings. Dempsey's 'Balance Sheet'[2] clearly showed how he expected the opposition to build up on Second Army's front – the two panzer divisions on D+1, another panzer and one infantry division on D+2, one panzer and two parachute divisions on D+4, and a further infantry division on D+5. They presumed that the combined air and sea assault would provoke immediate counter-attacks right down to the beaches. Should these fail, more organized attacks were expected to be launched about D+4 or D+5, by which time the Germans would have up to six Panzer divisions available. By D+6, it was anticipated that the Allies as a whole could face twenty divisions, including eight Panzer formations, but how they were deployed and what proportion of that total would actually face Second Army would depend on the Germans' perception of where the main threat lay. Bearing in mind Montgomery's forceful assessment at his first planning meeting with Dempsey, it had to be assumed – and it was indeed Montgomery's impression – that the majority or all of them would fall on Second Army.

Dempsey's plan for the assault on D-Day was to put ashore an airborne division and three infantry divisions, with supporting armour. They would be followed on D+1 by an armoured division, an infantry division on D+2, an armoured division on D+3, and an infantry division on each of the next three days. His 'Balance Sheet' showed that by D+6 he expected to have nine British and Canadian divisions with 1,200 tanks to face a possible twelve German divisions with 1,140 tanks. An uncertain factor was the speed at which the enemy would be able to concentrate his mobile and armoured divisions for counter-attack. It was important, therefore, to watch the situation carefully, and not let the main bodies become so stretched that they would be unable to hold out against determined counter-attack. On the other hand, they must maintain the initiative seized by their initial assault. Montgomery's idea was to push forward an armoured brigade group from each army as soon as possible, to take and hold an area ahead of the main force, from which a larger area could be dominated. Although Montgomery made it clear that he was prepared to risk the total loss of these brigade groups, it is not clear how realistic he thought this concept was; but in the *bocage* country of Normandy it was of doubtful reality.

In the same way that an army corps has no fixed organization, an army has no fixed allocation of army corps under it. Divisions by and large retain the same grouping indefinitely – and thereby attain an identity and ethos not possible at higher levels – but beyond that formations are allocated and then switched as the operational situation, and the battle worthiness of their formations dictate. Second Army was allocated five corps for the initial phase of OVERLORD. I Corps would land on the furthest left beach, SWORD, with the 3rd Division, and on the next to it, JUNO, with 3rd Canadian Division. The Corps Commander, John Crocker, was regarded as an officer of outstanding ability. After winning a DSO and MC in the Great War, he left the Army for the law, only to return and join the newly-formed Royal Tank Corps. In the 1920s and 1930s, along with others such as Broad, he developed armoured tactics in great depth, with little encouragement or materiel. A taciturn officer, while Liddell Hart and Fuller let the world know their views, Crocker quietly and steadily worked for the benefit of the Army and the Tank Corps, and was placed in command of IX Corps in March 1943. The same age as Dempsey, his career suffered a setback when he was injured at a weapon demonstration, but he recovered to take command of I Corps in time for the invasion.

To the right of Crocker, XXX Corps was to land 50th (Northumbrian) Division on GOLD beach. The Corps Commander was Gerard Corfield Bucknall, who had served under Dempsey in Sicily and Italy. Two years older than Dempsey, he had won a reputation for bravery in the Great War, in which he had taken command of his battalion of the Middlesex at the age of twenty-two during the Somme battles. He was old to be commanding a corps and a question mark hung over him.

Following up was VIII Corps commanded by Richard O'Connor, Dempsey's company commander and senior at Sandhurst. He had had the bad misfortune to be captured in North Africa, but had escaped from a POW camp in Italy and reached the Allied lines. Considerably older than Dempsey, his age was against him, but Montgomery had backed him, initially suggesting that O'Connor should take over Eighth Army when Montgomery left it at the end of 1943.

Commanding XII Corps was Guy Ritchie, slightly younger than Dempsey, but his senior in experience, having been Commander Eighth Army in November 1941. Tall, impressive looking and a man of strong character, he saw through the successful CRUSADER offensive, but after a series of defeats he was relieved in June 1942. Brooke was convinced he had been hard done by and that he would do well in the less demanding role of corps commander.

Finally, Dempsey had operational command of British Airborne Troops, commanded by 'Boy Browning', the College Adjutant at Sandhurst during Dempsey's time as an instructor. The same age as Dempsey, Browning had commanded an airborne division at the time Dempsey was also experiencing two-star command.

In age, experience and seniority, therefore, Dempsey's five subordinates for OVERLORD were his equals or seniors, and any one of them could, with some justification, have challenged his authority or even claimed his position. It is a remarkable tribute to his character and powers of leadership, as well as to the loyalty and team spirit of his formation commanders, that no such problem ever seemed remotely likely. It is true that at times they dealt directly with Montgomery, or he with them, in a way that defied normal military convention. But that was Montgomery's way; everyone knew it and accepted it. If it helped to win battles, which it did, so be it.

Montgomery considered it an important part of his duties as a leader to train and bring on his formation commanders, and went through this process with Dempsey, as he had others. As D-Day approached, he put out a series of operational directives, aimed at getting everyone 'on board'. One concerned the pace of build-up of Allied Forces, and a reminder of the need for 'balance' so as to maintain momentum, and not get stuck as was the experience at Anzio in the Italian campaign. Montgomery went on to say that in France there would be no possibility of flanking operations of the sort that Dempsey had initiated so successfully in Sicily and Italy. Instead they would use airborne forces, and he then went on to lay down principles for their employment, the foremost of which was to coordinate their employment so closely with the main force that they were mutually supporting. Second Army was to employ 6th Airborne Division to secure their left flank and for certain special tasks, and at one stage was also allocated an American airborne division to take Caen. This was withdrawn

MR. M. C. DEMPSEY (Captain, Shrewsbury XI).

The Schools.

1. Captain of the School XI, 1914.
(*Dempsey Family Collection*)

2. Cricket at Shrewsbury. (*Dempsey Family Collection*)

3. MD as a schoolboy at Shrewsbury.
(*Dempsey Family Collection*)

4. The Somme 1916. MD with V.G. Stokes.
(*Dempsey Family Collection*)

5. The Somme 1916. Royal Berkshire
wounded. (*Rifles Wardrobe Museum*)

5. The Somme 1918. Royal Berkshires attack at Ayette. (*Rifles Wardrobe Museum*)

. Survivors. Officers of 1st Royal Berkshires, November 1918. (*Rifles Wardrobe Museum*)

8. NW Persia, MD at Gangah, 1921.
(*Dempsey Family Collection*)

9. NW Persia, 1921.
Cossacks. (*Dempsey Family Collection*)

10. Bareilly. Royal
Berkshires on the march.
(*Rifles Wardrobe Museum*)

11. Bareilly. MD (second left) with brother officers. (*Dempsey Family Collection*)

12. Bareilly. Royal Berkshire officers. MD middle row, four from end. (*Rifles Wardrobe Museum*)

13. RMC Sandhurst. O'Connor (front left) and MD (four rows back). (*Dempsey Family Collection*)

14. Estonia, 1925. MD (rear right) and brother officers. (*Dempsey Family Collection*)

15. Staff College, 1931. Foreign Tour. MD (rear right) with his study group. (*Dempsey Family Collection*)

16. Staff College, 1931. MD out with the Drag. (*Dempsey Family Collection*)

17. South Africa, 1937. MD (far left) with fellow instructors. (*Dempsey Family Collection*)

18. South Africa, 1937. MD (far right) on a flight to Northern Rhodesia. (*Dempsey Family Collection*)

19. Commander 13 Brigade, 1939. MD with Stanley Oliver, War Minister, inspecting a guard of honour. (*Rifles Wardrobe Museum*)

20. North Africa, 1943. MD and Monty study the ground. (*Dempsey Family Collection*)

21. Italy, 1943. MD with Guy Simonds. (*Dempsey Family Collection*)

22. Italy, 1943. MD with members of his staff. (*Dempsey Family Collection*)

23. Normandy, 1944. MD with Crocker and Bucknall. (*Dempsey Family Collection*)

24. Ike, Monty, Patton, Bradley, three Corps Commanders and MD. (*Dempsey Family Collection*)

25. Holland 1944. MD with the King and Monty. (*Dempsey Family Collection*)

26. AVM Harry Broadhurst with MD. (*Dempsey Family Collection*)

27. MD with Boyle, 83 Group. (*Dempsey Family Collection*)

28. MD with his pilot, Oliver Murphy, and his 'whizzer'. (*Dempsey Family Collection*)

29. MD and his 'whizzer'. (*Dempsey Family Collection*)

30. Rhine Crossing, 1945. (*Dempsey Family Collection*)

32. Peace. MD meets the Russians. (*Dempsey Family Collection*)

31. After the Rhine crossing, MD with Churchill and Monty. (*Rifles Wardrobe Museum*)

33. Singapore. MD with Alanbrooke. (*Dempsey Family Collection*)

34. Dutch East Indies, 1945. MD with Christison and Dutch Commanders. (*Dempsey Family Collection*)

35. Dutch East Indies, 1946. MD with Monty Stopford. (*Dempsey Family Collection*)

36. Racing, Highlander Stakes. Paul Maxwell the jockey. (*Dempsey Family Collection*)

37. MD and Tuppenny, on their wedding day. (*Dempsey Family Collection*)

38. Colonel of the Regiment. The King inspects at Brock Barracks, accompanied by MD, 1948. (*Dempsey Family Collection*)

when Bradley made a stronger case for taking them on his flank, a decision that Dempsey was to regret.

A further directive dealt with the assault and the problem of beach obstacles. These were to be cleared when above water, which led to different H-Hours for different beaches, dependent on the times of optimum tide height. A major difficulty that became apparent only three days before D-Day was that one line of rocks was 3½ feet higher than anticipated, leading to some frantic staff work to change timings. An option was for a special force of engineers to land ahead of the main assault purely to work on these obstacles, but Montgomery was against this idea. The assault had therefore to contain tanks right up with the infantry, and other specialist armoured vehicles to deal with both the defences and anticipated difficult going. A remarkable man, Major General Percy Hobart came up with the answers. An early pioneer of armoured warfare, Hobart was a difficult man to work with, but inspired in his advancement of ingenious and unconventional armoured fighting vehicles, known as 'funnies'. None of them was actually a new idea, but Hobart's genius lay in adopting, adapting and pushing through the production of a series of inventions, some of which had been tried in battle, but all of which were imperfect in engineering or application. They fell into two categories: those developed for the purpose of getting armour or infantry from ship to shore; and those intended to overcome obstacles.

The most important of all were the DD, Duplex Drive or 'Donald Duck', tanks so called because they could drive on land or water and could, therefore, with careful coordination, hit the shore at the same time as the infantry, and give vital fire support on to pillboxes and other strongpoints during the time of the infantry's maximum vulnerability. The tank hull had a deck built round its middle on which was fitted a collapsible canvas screen that encircled the entire vehicle and, when filled with compressed air, enabled the vehicle to float. It could be driven at sea by two propellers at up to 4 knots; once on land and the screen was discarded it became a normal tank. Since the screen supported some 30 tons of tank, it was a hazardous operation to launch it from its Landing Craft Tank (LCT) when any sort of sea was running, and inevitably the further out it was launched, the lower the chances of it reaching shore. This factor became of vital importance during the landings.

The flail tank, a converted Sherman Crab, had a rotating drum attached, from which chains beat the ground as it turned, detonating any mines in its path; the Crocodile, a converted Churchill tank, had a flame-thrower instead of a gun, designed to take out pillboxes or armoured gun casements; other adaptations were tanks carrying fascines – bundles of wooden poles for crossing gaps – and tanks with a bridge attached, which could be put in place over a small gap without the crew exposing themselves to fire. Finally, there was the Armoured Vehicle Royal Engineers (AVRE), also based on a Churchill, with a specialized gun which fired an enormous explosive charge a short distance to demolish an obstacle or a hard defensive position.

These were weapons of huge tactical significance and Dempsey adopted them with enthusiasm. The Americans were less enthusiastic and suffered accordingly.

On 20 March, Montgomery addressed Dempsey and all his senior commanders. Setting out the philosophy of command that he expected to be applied throughout Second Army, he emphasized the things that he considered really mattered, among them thorough and realistic training of their soldiers related to their specific tasks. This was able to progress hand in hand with the development of detailed operational plans for each component of the whole. In a series of work-up exercises, FABIUS II to IV, Second Army trained at Littlehampton, Bracklesham and Hayling Island. Amphibious training was carried out in the Moray Firth by the 3rd Division, and at Studland Bay by the 3rd Canadian and 50th Divisions. This included the waterproofing of vehicles and equipment, the elaborate organization and vital work of the Beach Organisation, and the treatment and evacuation of wounded from shore to ship.

A matter of great importance at the operational level was the relationship between the ground and air forces. Montgomery stressed the importance of the two arms operating closely together, with appropriate staffs liaising closely, and headquarters being collocated. He hammered home the point that without the help of the air, the land battle could not be won, and that airmen placed in support of ground forces must realize that their 'sole job is to win the land battle'. As a statement of intent it was unexceptionable, but it masked a deep problem, based partly on strategy, partly on personalities, which was to have serious consequences for Montgomery and Dempsey as the campaign developed. At its heart was the question of whether air power, assisted by ground forces, could win the war; or whether ground forces, assisted by air power could do so.

The Chief of the Air Staff, Air Marshal Portal, had a good relationship with Brooke, and was happy to make the distinction between strategic use of air power – primarily the RAF and USAF Bomber Forces – and its tactical use. But Air Marshal Tedder, Deputy to the Supreme Allied Commander, Eisenhower, was not only convinced that Army plans must be dictated by air considerations, notably shaping operations to make the capture of airfields a priority, he also possessed a deep dislike of Montgomery. This feeling was shared by 'Maori' Coningham, the Commander of 2nd Tactical Air Force, opposite number to Montgomery as Commander 21st Army Group. Air

Marshal Leigh-Mallory, Coningham's superior as Commander Allied Air Forces, did not; indeed, as a former instructor at the Army Staff College, he had a good understanding of, and sympathy with, the Army. Supporting Dempsey's Second Army was Air Vice-Marshal Harry Broadhurst's 83 Group, and here the relationship was excellent. Broadhurst was to recall later that the two never made a move without talking to each other. However, their seniors' feuds placed an extra burden on both of them. Broadhurst felt that Coningham's personal and vehement anti-Montgomery attitude was adversely affecting air operations and resented being placed in the middle of a personal squabble, while on Dempsey's shoulders was increasingly placed the responsibility of smoothing relations with the RAF, and actually making it all work.

On 7 April, Montgomery, appointed overall ground force commander for the first phase, assembled all the senior Allied commanders, of all services, who were to take part in OVERLORD. He made it clear that Dempsey's Second Army on the eastern flank would seize the key centre of Caen 'as early as Second Army can manage', pivoting on it to form a powerful shield, while Bradley's First American Army broke out to occupy the Cherbourg Peninsula. Patton's Third US Army would then come ashore, clear Brittany and cover Bradley's southern flank while he broke out towards Paris. There could be no doubt what Montgomery's strategy was, indeed Bradley himself acknowledged in his memoirs that the plan was for Second Army to draw the enemy reserves on to their front, while the Americans were to make the breakout. He acknowledged that, in terms of national pride, 'this British decoy mission became a sacrificial one' as they pinned down the Germans, but that it was 'a logical division of labors', since it was towards Caen that the German reserves would move.[3]

Clear it may have been, yet misunderstanding of this strategy – wilful or otherwise – was to be a recurring cause of tension, not to Montgomery's subordinates, who understood it and carried it through, but to those such as Morgan, Tedder and Coningham, who wished Montgomery ill. One contentious point concerned the phase lines for the development of the bridgehead which were drawn on the map for the briefing. Although intended to be purely notional and unrelated to the actual chronological development of the battle, they were later to be seized upon as evidence that Second Army had somehow failed to execute the master plan.

There was, however, one concrete aspect of the plan that affected Second Army in its mission of taking and holding Caen as the hinge on which the Allied forces were to pivot. It had originally been intended that Dempsey's flank would rest on the River Dives, thus presenting this river, and the marshy ground that lay between it and the Orne, as a natural obstacle to protect his left. Because of a shortage of landing craft, and because as previously alluded to, the American airborne division that was to have secured this area could not in the end be allocated, the flank was to rest on the Orne. Second Army was to assault to the west of the River Orne, and to develop operations to the south and south-east in order to secure airfield sites, and to protect the eastern flank of First American Army. In its subsequent operations it was to pivot on its left at Caen and offer a strong front against enemy movement towards the lodgement area from the east. Once sufficient formations were ashore, First Canadian Army would form on its left, taking I Corps under command, and ultimately capturing Le Havre.

This was to restrict Dempsey's room to manoeuvre around Caen and delay its capture, originally planned for D-Day, for over a month. This was not fully appreciated as Dempsey followed with his presentation, setting out the Second Army plan, in which he still had Caen earmarked as an objective to be taken on D-Day. He was followed by Crocker and Bucknall, commanding the two corps that were to make the initial landings. Bucknall made a poor impression and rambled on over his allotted time. Brooke noted that he was very weak and in his opinion quite unfit to command a corps.

Another factor was again emphasized to Dempsey. The supply of British manpower was beginning to dry up and it was estimated that by the end of 1944 the British Army would be 60,000 men short, of which 40,000 would be infantry. Dempsey now had to consider every operation in terms of its likely impact on his infantry. It was becoming clear that, as the campaign developed, the balance would shift more and more to a preponderance of American forces, while in Second Army, the shortage of battle casualty replacements would lead ultimately to disbandment or amalgamation of some divisions.

On 23 May, Dempsey held a final coordinating conference for his senior commanders. Concentrating on the latest intelligence of 711th and 716th German Divisions, he then went through his 'Balance Sheet', and revealed the latest airborne plan, under which only one division was allocated to Second Army. Latest intelligence from air photography showed that the areas designated for the gliders of the airlanding brigade were covered by extensive obstacles, erected against this specific threat. They would therefore have to come in a later lift, after parachute troops had cleared the landing zones. The 1st Airborne Division would be held in reserve and operations kept fluid.

After a final conference on 1 June, Dempsey attended Montgomery's dinner for the four Allied army commanders at 21st Army Group Headquarters, close to Dempsey's own, at Southwick Park, above Portsmouth. Patton, commanding the Third US Army, detailed to follow behind Bradley, was not impressed by Dempsey, who he took to be a 'yes man'. Given Patton's inability to find anything very favourable to say about any British commander – or many American ones – this judgement need not be given too much weight. Montgomery's assessment was that Dempsey, although he lacked the Guardsman's ruthlessness and drive of Leese (now commanding Eighth Army in Italy), was cleverer, and he possessed a legendary eye for terrain, ran a high-calibre headquarters and was, behind his quiet manner, completely imperturbable. During the evening Patton laid some wagers with Montgomery and Dempsey retaliated by betting Bradley £5 that the war would be over by 1 November. Bradley collected.

There was a very narrow window of possible dates on which the right conditions of moon and tide would be suitable for D-Day. The fifth of June was the first choice and it was therefore for 4 June that Dempsey arranged the service at Portsdown that was to precede the invasion. After agonizing deliberations occasioned by the deteriorating weather, a delay of twenty-four hours was announced, and on the evening of 5 June the soldiers of the 6th Airborne Division, commanded by Major General Richard Gale, filed into their aircraft for the first operations of the greatest amphibious assault in history. At twenty minutes past midnight the air transport command of the RAF began to cast loose the gliders and drop the paratroops. As a result of the very accurate work of the Pathfinders, the majority of the gliders came down on or close to target. The party charged with capturing the two bridges that span the River Orne and the Caen Canal at Benouville landed exactly as planned, rushed their objectives and captured them both intact. The men of the 9th Parachute Battalion were less fortunate. They were badly scattered and only 150 were available to fight their way through the wire and minefields surrounding the battery of great guns at Merville, which dominated the beaches on which so many men were about to come ashore. Its silencing was to prove a major factor in the success of Dempsey's plans. Further south, three bridges over the River Dives were blown to impede German movement into the area east of the Orne, where a small bridgehead was formed.

As dawn came up it revealed the huge invasion fleet which, under the direction of Admiral Ramsay, performed in the highest traditions of the Royal Navy. Battleships, cruisers, destroyers and monitors added their accurate fire to the huge weight of bombs already delivered by the RAF. Involving hundreds of heavy and medium bombers, they had delivered some 3,000 tons of ordnance over the 16-mile-wide assault area between 0315 and 0500, and were followed by ground-attack aircraft firing rockets and cannon. The naval gunfire, some pre-targeted, some closely directed by forward observers with the assaulting troops, continued for two hours as the force approached through channels cleared by the Navy's minesweepers. On top of this was the direct fire from the LCTs and field artillery firing from their decks. Many of the soldiers of the first waves were green faced from seasickness, having been afloat in a rough sea for twenty-four hours more than planned. They climbed down into their Landing Craft Infantry, while the tank crews mounted their vehicles and prepared their inflation kits.

It was the plan that the DD tanks would launch and swim in 4 miles from shore, to arrive five minutes before the first wave of infantry hit the beach. As they came into position, it became obvious that the sea conditions were such that this was impracticable and the majority delayed until their LCTs were as close inshore as those of the infantry they were supporting. This was undoubtedly the right decision.

On the right of Second Army, the veteran 50th (Northumbrian) Division assaulted on a two-brigade front between the fortified villages of le Hamel and la Rivière. Landing at 0725, one brigade encountered intense mortar and machine-gun fire, and did not take le Hamel until the evening. From the far end of GOLD beach, the other brigade finished the day 5 miles inland. The Division had fought in North Africa, and then in Sicily and Italy under Dempsey, which may explain why it was the only one of the Allied divisions to reach its D-Day objectives.

On JUNO, the 3rd Canadian Division assaulted astride Courseulles-sur-Mer at 0800 hrs and cleared the beach exits only after a costly process of infiltration and assault. Their final line at the end of D-Day was still 4 miles short of Caen. This was despite the fact that, at Dempey's request, all German troop movements in the vicinity of Caen were subjected to almost continuous air attack.

The 3rd Division, landing on SWORD at the same time as the Canadians 7 miles to their west, were centred on Colleville-Plage. Dempsey's plan was that they should land on a single brigade front, so that they would have depth, rather than the two brigades employed on the other beaches. His appreciation was:

> I did not want them to get involved on too broad a frontage, because that would have consumed two thirds of their strength … I was worried about the Germans on their left and on their front … I wanted to be able to push 3 British [Division] as far south towards Caen as I could and still keep sufficient troops in reserve to be quite sure of holding this flank … I needed to have plenty of troops in reserve to defend the line of the Orne if that were attacked. *I never expected 3 Div to get Caen on the first day, and I always said that if we didn't get it the first day it would take a month to get it afterwards.* The important task on this

sector was not deep penetration but strength on the flank, for it was against this flank that we felt sure the Germans would make their major effort.[4]

The 3rd Division's troops were quickly off the beaches, but as they moved south they met heavy opposition from strongpoints and by the evening of D-Day, although they were favourably positioned on the high ground leading toward the city, they were still 4 miles from this key objective.

The Germans' reaction was mixed and the greatest threat to Second Army came from 21st Panzer Division, which, on the initiative of its commander, sent a battle group against the airborne troops holding the Orne bridges. They had begun the attack when at 1000 hrs he was ordered to switch his attention to the 3rd Division advancing west of the river. By that evening a company sized group had penetrated as far as the coast, between the British and Canadian divisions. Fortunately the arrival of the second lift of the 6th Airborne Division, in the shape of 6 Airlanding Brigade, persuaded them to press no further. Asked later about the German tactics, Dempsey said that the Germans should have kept their armour further forward and committed them to immediate counter-attacks. 'His chance was to hit us in the very early days.' This was based on his own experience when planning the defence of the UK and on his fears that, in Normandy, his beachhead could have been rolled up from the flank if the Germans had had the Panzer forces in the right place to do so. He conceded that, with limited resources, Rommel faced a major dilemma in allocating priority areas for the stationing of armour, again emphasizing the value of the deception plan.

Thus by the end of D-Day, a beachhead had been formed, but it would take several days of heavy fighting before it could be declared safely established, and even longer before offensive operations to develop the strategy, set out by Montgomery from his first briefings, could be mounted. But for now, the exhausted troops could congratulate themselves that they had got ashore successfully.

It had been a close-run affair. At one stage, as the American landings at OMAHA appeared to be foundering, Bradley formed the impression that their forces had suffered an irreversible catastrophe. Dempsey was asked, in the utmost secrecy, if their effort could be switched to one of his beaches. During the run-up to D-Day, commanders at all levels were presented with theoretical scenarios to test their reactions and the flexibility of their plans. Dempsey had carefully thought through every nightmare contingency and he was quite sure that the difficulties involved in imposing a diverted formation of shipping, troops, tanks, vehicles and combat supplies to an already congested beach was a non-starter; he replied as such. It would be impossible, the area would simply be too crowded. As a result of inspired leadership on the beach and the bravery of the American soldiers, OMAHA was eventually secured. But it is interesting to examine the decisive factors in the success of D-Day and why the landings in Second Army's sector were so much more successful than in the American.

Of overriding strategic importance was the deception plan, which persuaded the Germans that the landings were but a prelude to, and probably a decoy for, a major assault in the Pas de Calais. The maintenance of this bluff for several weeks, giving the Allies breathing space in which to consolidate their hold on the Continent, was the fruit of the extraordinary, prolonged integration of the efforts of MI5's double-cross system, the inspired efforts of Dudley Clark's deception department, and Bletchley Park's interception and decoding of the German High Command's supposedly secret cipher traffic.

The Allies had enjoyed almost total mastery of the skies, and this had an adverse effect on every aspect of the German defence, from operational planning to logistics.

The weather had helped achieve surprise. The German forces, which had been at a state of 'immediate alert' during the fine weather of the preceding weeks, had been stood down when the seas began to run high. Rommel, commanding their forces in Normandy, went on leave. When the Germans did react, their counter-attacks were ill-planned and lacked coherence during the vital first few days.

Dempsey's Second Army, utilizing their experience of previous amphibious assaults, profited from four decisions which their American counterparts took differently. First, their naval gunfire support was planned for a full two hours during the run-in to the beaches, while the Americans' was for forty minutes only. One of the critical factors that turned the tide of battle at OMAHA was the fortuitous arrival of two Royal Naval fire support ships, able to identify and neutralize strongpoints dominating the shoreline. Second, the last-minute decision by Second Army armoured units to launch their DD tanks from close in avoided the fate which overtook their counterparts on OMAHA, where they were launched 6,000 yards out, and twenty-seven of the thirty-two sank before they reached the beach. Third, the Americans decided, with the exception of the ill-fated DD tanks, not to employ the 'funnies' of Hobart's 79th Division, and so lacked the protected firepower which could have eased the way off the beach. Both Montgomery and Eisenhower paid tribute to the value of these unconventional machines and to the effect on German morale of seeing armoured vehicles landing with the infantry. Finally, British experience and training emphasized the advantage of landing between enemy strongpoints in order to attack them from the side or rear. At OMAHA a tactical decision was taken to assault the main enemy fortifications head-on.

In discussion with Horrocks later, Dempsey emphasized the importance of tough individual training, careful planning and inspired leadership. He cited two examples. The first was the capture of Port-en-Bessin by 47 Royal Marine Commando, who were to land on GOLD Beach, then move across country to take this town on the junction with the Americans. Their landing was eventful, and several hours passed before about half of the main body was assembled and moved off overland. After a number of fierce brushes with the enemy, they arrived at the point where they expected to contact the Americans, who were to supply artillery fire support. This was not forthcoming and, after frustrating problems with their radios, they managed to contact the Navy and organize naval gunfire and air support. This was eventually provided and the marines launched their attack on the town, clearing it house by house, and then holding off the German counter-attacks. It then became apparent that, if they were to hold on to their objective, they would have to take the two hills that dominated it. The personal initiative of a young officer helped them achieve this and 47 Commando then held the town for two days until relieved.

Dempsey's second example was the work of the entire 6th Airborne Division and the inspiring leadership of their commander, Richard Gale, whom he considered one of the greatest airborne commanders to emerge during the war. A great trainer, Gale ensured that every man in his formation was briefed personally and knew exactly what to do on landing, even if things went wrong. Typical of this approach was the briefing given by Alastair Pearson, commanding a battalion of 'green' soldiers, whose task was to destroy three bridges and then reinforce the small bridgehead to be established at le Mesnil: 'Gentlemen, in spite of your excellent training and orders, do not be daunted if chaos reigns. It undoubtedly will.'

Despite the difficulties caused by many of the men being scattered over a wide area, the Division took all their objectives and Dempsey said that he was sure that this operation would be studied for many years to come. At one stage, a small body of paratroopers, whose objective was one of the Orne bridges, was completely lost. Suddenly, out of the sea-mist which covered the area, loomed the solid figure of their Divisional Commander. 'Follow me,' cried Gale, and as he passed through them he was heard to shout the famous lines from Henry V: 'And gentlemen in England now abed shall think themselves accursed they were not here'

Dempsey had deliberately employed a mixture of seasoned and raw troops in his initial landings. This was undoubtedly a factor in their success, but as D-Day drew to its close, there was an understandable feeling among those who had come ashore unwounded that they had delivered what had been asked for, and an almost miraculous result had been achieved. Their feeling of elation was replaced by the sobering realization that the countryside in which they were now being engaged by the enemy gave many advantages to the latter. Dempsey noted that this had a very pronounced effect on the veterans of the desert, particularly tank commanders, who suffered many casualties as a result of exposing themselves above their turrets in the way they had been used to doing in more open country. It became a feature of the campaign, as it developed, that the more seasoned units began to slow down and lacked the élan of fresh troops. Once this was realized, matters were put in hand to revitalise them, and they then regained their old flair.

Discussing the partial fulfilment of the plans for D-Day, Dempsey rejected the view that he had been too ambitious in allocating his objectives. He argued that:

> In a landing D Day is the attacker's day. Everything is in his favour, detailed plans: rehearsals: tactical surprise (time, place, weight); morale. This is the day when you capture ground. On D+1 everything is confused, units not sorted out, HQs out of touch, ships sunk, etc. It will take you days to capture what you fail to take on D. Troops must only be stopped on D Day by the enemy or by exhaustion.[5]

Seventy-five thousand men of Second Army had landed, in line with what had been forecast, and 4,200 casualties sustained, less than feared; but only 60 per cent of planned deliveries of vehicles and stores had come ashore. On the whole, however, he could be satisfied with the performance of Second Army and the position they were in. Much hard fighting would be required over the next few weeks and months; the immediate priority was to consolidate the bridgehead and then shape the battlefield in accordance with the Allied master plan. This he now set out to do.

CHAPTER 10

'Form Line'

Dempsey came ashore on the evening of D-Day, and had time to meet Crocker, commanding I Corps, before spending the night at Hilary. On D+1 he set up his tactical headquarters (Tac HQ) at Banville, a tiny village just inland from the seaside resort of Courseulles-sur-Mer. Tac HQ was where he lived and kept a small staff of his Military Assistant, two or three ADCs and liaison officers. It provided a small, mobile, self-contained headquarters with sufficient communications to enable him to fight his battle in the field. It consisted of a few caravans, radios, a Defence Platoon, some administrators and Dempsey's personal vehicles. It could be packed up and moved quickly, and enabled Dempsey to be at the critical point – be it corps, divisional or brigade headquarters – in any situation. From it he could roam freely around the battlefield. Sometimes he used a staff car, sometimes an Auster light aircraft, which he called his 'whizzer'. Horrocks was to recall an incident during the campaign in Europe when Dempsey arrived at his command post, calm and collected as ever. He gave his orders with his habitual clarity, then confirmed them in writing, using his left hand as usual. It was only after his departure that Horrocks learned that his Auster had turned over completely on landing, yet Dempsey never mentioned it. On another occasion, he flew, as he often did, with Harry Broadhurst, at the controls of a captured German Storch light aircraft. Unfortunately, the enemy markings had not been removed and they were met with a stream of anti-aircraft fire from their own side. Thereafter Dempsey was more circumspect in his choice of aircraft.

Some way to the rear of Tac, Main HQ conducted the current battle and planned future ones. Whenever possible, Headquarters 38 Group RAF was sited alongside, and the two staffs worked in the utmost harmony throughout the campaign. Main HQ was designed as a field headquarters, able to operate without buildings or permanent signal installations. The hub was a central combined operations room, in which the Operations, Intelligence, Air (Reconnaissance) and Air (Support) cells were collocated with the HQ of the liaison regiment and A Squadron of 'Phantom', the unit which deployed small patrols to all parts of the battlefield to report progress direct to Army Headquarters. This unit was tasked directly by the Chief of Staff, Maurice Chilton, who presided over Main HQ. Chilton was a gunner, slightly younger than Dempsey, dark and cadaverous, formidable and incisive, yet with a gentle side like Dempsey. They had spent two years together at Staff College and been companions on the Foreign Tour to East Prussia. They knew each other well and the six months preparation for the invasion had cemented a close relationship based on total trust and loyalty. He would meet Dempsey every day, usually at Tac HQ, and would then direct the hour by hour operations of the Army, based on the orders he had received, and his total understanding of Dempsey's methods and philosophy of command. Although Montgomery expressed reservations about his suitability for work at Army level, Chilton prospered, and ended his career as a four-star general. He would be replaced before the end of the year by 'Pete' Pyman, on promotion from Chief of Staff XXX Corps. Main HQ Second Army moved to France on D+6, and set up at Creully, alongside Montgomery's 21st Army Group Headquarters, where it was joined for a short period by Tac HQ.

Situated usually within 10 miles of Main, Rear Headquarters ran the logistics of the operation, and contained the heads of services and their staffs, under the direction of the Brigadier Administration. The extremely able Quartermaster General, Hardy-Roberts, later to become Master of the Royal Household, was based at Main HQ. The total strength of Second Army Headquarters was 189 officers and 970 men.

Dempsey's place in the hierarchy of command within the 21st Army Group has been the subject of much examination and speculation, arising largely because Montgomery tended to refer to all operations, particularly when they were successful, as if they were conceived, directed and overseen personally by him. While Eisenhower and Montgomery were responsible for the strategic direction of the campaign, Dempsey, as one of two, eventually rising to four, army commanders was responsible for that slightly nebulous area between strategy and tactics known as the operational level. Thus Horrocks was quite fair when he observed that Dempsey was not much involved in the higher strategy of the Normandy campaign. Horrocks summed up accurately why Dempsey has tended to receive less credit than he deserved for his contribution to victory:

> He has remained a somewhat shadowy figure and a General almost completely unknown to the general public. This was due primarily to the fact that he loathed any kind of publicity. It was also partly owing to the size of Second Army, which never therefore captured the imagination of the public as the smaller Eighth Army had.

Horrocks then goes on to say:

> I knew him to be one of the ablest soldiers in the British Army. He was
> very shrewd, he never flapped, and consequently Second Army HQ
> was highly efficient and devoted to their commander. I doubt whether
> anyone else could have worked so harmoniously with Montgomery
> as his immediate boss. The two were complementary – Montgomery
> the extrovert who loved the headlines; Dempsey the introvert who
> shunned publicity but got on with the job efficiently and without
> any fuss. Montgomery was not at his best with Allies; Dempsey went
> out of his way to iron out any friction so often caused by the other's
> tactlessness.[1]

Much can be made of Montgomery's involvement in the operations and affairs
of corps and divisions – even brigades and individual units – conventionally
considered not to be the preserve of an army group commander. Such views
tend to be coloured by the modern notion of 'mission command' and the
maxim that commanders should 'think two down' but 'command one
down'. This philosophy is based on the principle that a commander makes
his appreciation before an operation by considering its implications down
to the next but one level – in the case of an army group commander down to
corps level; but he gives out his orders only to his immediate lower formation
commanders – army level. These orders are given in very broad terms,
largely confined to his intentions and any essential coordinating instructions,
leaving it up to the commanders receiving the orders to make their own
plans and pass them on. In Normandy, and certainly in Montgomery's
case, and even more certainly with Dempsey, this was not the pattern. A
cursory reading of any work on Montgomery makes it clear that he did
indeed command 'two' and even 'three down' if he thought it appropriate.
The reason is not hard to find. Second Army was all that Britain had. If it
suffered a major reverse, Britain's influence on the war, and by extension
the commander associated in the public's mind with it – not Dempsey but
Montgomery – would be diminished. Montgomery considered it his duty
to mentor Dempsey, as he had other junior commanders throughout his
career. Freddy de Guingand, his loyal Chief of Staff, admitted that it was,
to an extent, true that Montgomery did not allow subordinates sufficient
initiative, but that on the whole his command methods worked excellently.
His commanders knew him well and accepted that this tendency to over-
control was balanced by the infinite pains he took to nurse them into their
command and give them the benefit of experience. However, he adjusted his
style to suit the individual. 'For instance, his treatment of Dempsey (Second
Army) or Crerar (First Canadian Army) differed, as with Americans.[2]

Discussing the question after the war, Dempsey emphasized that though Montgomery would always take all the praise and would not give public credit to others, he would also take the blame. He would not rat on you. He said that Montgomery's superiors found him 'impossible', yet his inferiors (with very few exceptions) found him a unique leader, an outstanding commander and a splendid man to work for. In Normandy and later, his relations with Montgomery were of the easiest. They were in constant touch. Dempsey issued the plans, but generally discussed them with Montgomery first. 'I would have been silly not to consult our finest military brain.'[3] Montgomery never sacked any of Dempsey's officers other than on Dempsey's recommendation, nor did he, with one exception, give him any written orders throughout the Normandy campaign.

On this subject, Dempsey emphasized two important points. First, Montgomery may have given orders – and particularly advice – to Dempsey that dealt with lower formations, but he did not bypass Dempsey and deal direct with them. To this should be added two caveats: first, 'unless Dempsey had been consulted and agreed the approach', as was the case with a particular problem that O'Connor brought up; the second 'with one or two significant exceptions', as narrated by Horrocks. In Bradley's opinion, Dempsey, while thoroughly competent to run his army, did not object to Montgomery's habit of occasionally usurping his authority, and that in his long association with him he knew how to tolerate it 'without jealousy or anger'.[4]

Second, the system that Montgomery instituted of liaison officers (LOs) who toured the battlefield, reporting direct to him each evening, was unpopular with some formation commanders, who thought of them as spies who could affect their future. Dempsey was relaxed about them and regarded them as a useful source of information for himself, as well as Montgomery. Indeed he adopted the idea and had two or three of his own LOs, who were quite invaluable. What has tended to escape attention is how Dempsey interpreted his role as commander and here it is interesting to observe the very careful phrasing he used in his Commander's Diary, his own day-to-day account of his activities throughout the campaign. While for the most part he gave orders only to corps commanders, he was careful usually to restrict his accounts of his dealings with lower formation commanders to the fact that he had visited them. At times, though, the protocol was breached, and it is clear that he did, when he considered it operationally imperative, give orders direct to formation commanders below corps level. The commanders had mostly been working together for years, they were big personalities, keen to win the war with the minimum of casualties and not likely to stand on their dignity. It worked and that is as much as need be said.

Before joining his Tac HQ on D+1, Dempsey went on board HMS *Faulkner* to meet Montgomery and Admiral Vian. After a briefing on the progress of the Americans and some coordinating points on the projected link-up between them and I Corps, Dempsey briefed them in turn and secured Vian's agreement to speed up the unloading of stores, which was impeded by the rough seas. He then visited the Main Headquarters of XXX Corps at Bulolo, and then its Tac HQ at Meuvaines, collocated with Headquarters 50th Division. They had made good progress and were on the line Thongues, east of Bayeux, to Putot-en-Bessin. After visiting the headquarters of 8th Armoured and 231 Infantry Brigades, he met up with his own Tac HQ, before returning to I Corps at Corseulles. The 3rd Canadian Division were on the line Putot to Franqueville, but the situation of the 3rd (British) Division, north of Caen, and the 6th Airborne Division was still obscure. Having been told later that evening that Bayeux had been taken, Dempsey could rest for the night secure in the knowledge that the situation on Second Army front, although far from ideal, was satisfactory.

Thus was set a pattern of command that was to be sustained, almost without respite, for a year. A study of Dempsey's War Diary reveals a master of warfare plying his trade, day in, day out, often in great danger, constantly visiting headquarters and units, weighing up the situation, 'smelling the battlefield', encouraging, advising, thinking and planning ahead to the next operation, while seeing through the ongoing battle. It is easy, with hindsight, to forget that the invasion was a truly gigantic enterprise which could have failed; the consequences of such a failure would have been unimaginably catastrophic. Until his headquarters was taken out of the line to plan the Rhine Crossing nine months later, Dempsey had no rest. Corps and divisions could be taken out of battle and rested, but he and his headquarters could not and the strain – physical, emotional and psychological – on a younger man would have been enormous. For a man in his late forties it could have been overwhelming. It speaks volumes for his character that, throughout this immensely taxing time, he remained his imperturbable, good-humoured, confident and reassuring self.

One of the ways he could relax was to maintain the correspondence with Patrick which had been such a feature of his time in Sicily and Italy. He found time to write shortly after D-Day:

I am sorry I have not written to you before. One never seems to get time in the early days of an invasion. I came over on the afternoon of 'D-Day' (June 6th) in a destroyer – Impulsive – and despite the extremely rough sea managed to get ashore without getting my feet wet.

I can't quite make out what impression the newspapers and BBC are giving to people in England. But you can take it from me that things are going very well. There were a great many hazards to be overcome; and there is no doubt it has been – so far – a pretty remarkable achievement. Nice country this Normandy – and the Camembert (is that how you spell it) cheeses are fine![5]

On D+2, 8 June, Dempsey began the process of 'tidying up' the battlefield. There was still a good deal of what he termed 'dog fighting' going on on the front of I Corps' assault divisions and some coordination was needed. He ordered Crocker to clear up the pockets of enemy, such as at Douvres, which had been bypassed; to get his armour under control and concentrated; and to use only sufficient forces in the east to bolster the 6th Airborne Division, who were quite happy. He also set in hand the operations that were eventually to lead to the fall of Caen, telling I Corps to be prepared to begin offensive operations in two or three days' time, with a view to capturing it from the east. He then saw Commander 3rd Canadian Division, and impressed on him the importance of getting his armour and artillery under proper control – definitely not 'mission command'! By the evening, the link-up between Second Army and the Americans had been successfully achieved. Finally he met Bucknall, commanding XXX Corps, to discuss his offensive south. His 8th Armoured Brigade had already started to move towards Tilly and Dempsey advised him not to commit 7th Armoured Division until 10 June.

The next day he saw Montgomery and impressed on him the importance of the Americans driving hard to the south in the direction of Caumont, so as to avoid exposing Dempsey's flank as the 7th Armoured Division of XXX Corps advanced on Tilly and Villers Bocage – Operation PERCH, which was due to start the following day. It made sense to him to concentrate on this operation, rather than the taking of Caen. With Crocker he again looked at the possibility of using the 51st Division east of the Orne to isolate Caen on 11 June. At this stage he was hoping that 1st Airborne Division would be dropped to the south of Caen to complete its encirclement and capture, and that afternoon he discussed this possibility with Browning. Plans had been tentatively prepared for a number of different objectives on the British front, so that such an operation could be laid on at short notice. Having satisfied himself by a visit to their headquarters at Ranville that the 6th Airborne Division was quite capable of holding on to its bridgehead east of the Orne without reinforcement, the next morning he discussed this plan with Bucknall, and that afternoon Dempsey, Browning, Crocker and Bucknall met to coordinate the operation. At this stage it was Dempsey's intention to advance south with XXX Corps to the west of Caen and I Corps to the east. On 13 June, the 1st Airborne would be dropped on the front of whichever was making the better progress; if XXX Corps was going well, Caen might be threatened from the west.

Bucknall's thrust south, PERCH, started slowly, experiencing great difficulty moving armour through the thick *bocage* country. Dempsey left him to get on with it on 9 June, but the next day he was with him early to hear that 8th Armoured Brigade was on the high ground north-east of Tilly, and the 7th Armoured Division was advancing west of them to Villers Bocage. Dempsey then moved on to Port-en-Bessin to meet Montgomery and Bradley, who could promise no immediate assistance, but would send one division south to Caumont on 12 or 13 June. For the moment 7th Armoured Division would be unsupported and their thrust was now producing a strong reaction from an alarmed enemy. Hitler ordered Rommel to put everything into stopping what he saw as the Allies breakout – exactly the reaction the Allies hoped for, but it was effectively to spell the end of PERCH.

On 11 June, enemy wireless intercepts showed that the Germans were concentrating for the anticipated armoured counter-attack from Caen. Dempsey met Crocker and told him to concentrate his armour on the high feature around Colomby-sur-Thaon, north-west of Caen, controlling all the ground between there and the sea, so as to stifle any attempt to cut his army in two. Dempsey told him that 'This bit of ground was the heart of the British Empire, and that he wasn't to move his armour from it except on orders from me.'[6] He reiterated this order the next day and by redeploying his 2 Canadian Armoured Brigade, and the skilful employment of artillery and air support, Crocker was able to break up the attack as it came in piecemeal. Part of the firepower still came from the Royal Navy, since Dempsey had already requested Admiral Vian to provide continuous support to I Corps in the Caen area, not just from smaller ships but from battleships and monitors.

However, Dempsey' plans to take Caen were struck a sharp blow the next day when it became apparent that there was no chance of a quick operation with 1st Airborne Division. The Divisional Commander, Major General Urquhart, wanted the drop to be in daylight, but the RAF considered this to be impractical, and a night drop was vetoed on the grounds that the aircraft would be at too much risk from all the ships in the Channel. The simple fact was that the RAF would not play and surprisingly, on this occasion, the resistance came from Leigh-Mallory, prompting Montgomery to characterize him as a 'gutless bugger'. He was to redeem himself later in the eyes of the Army, but for now Leigh-Mallory, although he was prepared to provide some air support, was not prepared to risk transport aircraft in such a risky undertaking. This was the first of a long series of projected, but aborted, operations by 1st Airborne Division which were to affect the planning for Arnhem some three months later. To Dempsey it was now clear that Caen could only be taken by a set-piece assault, for which he did not have the men or the ammunition. He would have to think again.

Meanwhile, on the morning of 12 June, Dempsey had visited Bobby Erskine, commanding the 7th Armoured Division, the 'Desert Rats', to see how PERCH was progressing. Irritated by the lack of progress of his Staff College contemporary, he gave him his orders, told him to get moving and said he would tell Erskine's Corps Commander, Bucknall, what he was doing. He then went on to meet Bucknall, who told him he was in touch with the Americans on his right. That afternoon, Dempsey was involved in a visit by Churchill and Brooke, who came to his Tac HQ, collocated for a few days with his Main HQ and Headquarters 21st Army Group. Having watched a raid by German bombers on the harbour at Courseelles, his visitors left, Churchill remarking on the apparent contentment of the French livestock they passed.

By the next day, while 6th Airborne and 51st Highland Divisions were engaged in heavy fighting on the eastern flank, intelligence warned that 2nd Panzer Division was moving to reinforce Panzer Lehr in the Villers Bocage area. It was imperative that Erskine speed up if he was not to be caught. By moving through the American area around Caumont, his armour could move faster. By 13 June, the operations of XXX Corps had progressed as far as Villers Bocage, which was entered by 7th Armoured Division that morning. It was hoped to capitalize on this by a thrust to Evrecy, but this failed, and they then withdrew to the high ground north-east of Villers Bocage. There the operation came to a close. Dempsey was not pleased.

> If he had carried out my orders he would never have been kicked out of V [Villers Bocage], but by this time 7AD [7th Armoured Division] was living on its reputation and the whole handling of the battle was a disgrace. Their decision to withdraw was made without consulting me, it was done by the Corps Commander and Erskine.[7]

On 14 June an extraordinary chain of events was set in chain by Coningham and Tedder, who claimed that there was a 'crisis' in Normandy. Prompted in part by the 'failure' of Second Army to capture the airfields which the (arbitrary and meaningless) phase lines of Montgomery's April briefing had led some to claim should have been completed, and fanned by Coningham's jealousy and dislike of Montgomery, a deputation visited 21st Army Group and Second Army. Any notion of crisis was soon dispelled – indeed the reaction of the Germans to the Villers Bocage operation showed that the master plan was working well – and Dempsey took the opportunity afforded by Tedder's presence to press his case for air support for the Caen operation on 14 and 15 June. His attempts foundered and for now he had to give up.

On 15 June, he met Bucknall at his headquarters near Nonant to discuss XXX Corps' projected operation using 7th Armoured and 49th Infantry Divisions, with his eyes on Thury Harcourt. He also met O'Connor to discuss a possible operation for VIII Corps east of Caen. This idea was to persist for several days.

On 16 June, Dempsey was visited at his headquarters by the King. Fortunately he had sufficient notice to prepare for this and had sent Captain Birkett Smith, PA to his Quartermaster General, back to England to buy a lobster and an umbrella at Bentley's in London. The lobster kept Birkitt Smith awake at night with its scratching, but it was safely delivered. The umbrella was unfortunately left at his overnight hotel – the reason for this oversight perhaps lying in the fact that he celebrated his wedding anniversary there – and he was somewhat apprehensive when he presented himself to Dempsey in France. Fortunately the weather for the visit broke fair and Dempsey let him off with the words 'I don't mind as long as it was not the Regent Palace!'[8]

By 18 June, the Second Army front ran from Caumont through Villers Bocage and Tilly, north of Caen, round the bridgehead east of the Orne, and down to the sea at Ouistreham. The Germans had four Panzer divisions opposite Second Army and the strategy of attracting them to that front, rather than to the Americans, was clearly working. Montgomery now issued an operational directive which aimed to harmonize the consolidation of their area with the expansion of the American sector. He set out Second Army's tasks as follows:

- To capture Caen and provide a strong eastern flank for the Army Group.
- The operations against Caen will be developed by means of a pincer movement from both flanks. The object will be to establish VIII Corps, strong in armour, to the south-east of Caen in the area Bourguebus-Vimont-Bretteville.
- From Vimont northwards the flank of the army will be established on the general line Troarn – thence along the River Dives to the sea at Cabourg.
- The right flank of the Army, forming the western half of the pincer movement against Caen, will swing south-eastwards through Aunay and Evrecy towards the bridges over the River Orne between Thury Harcourt and Amayé-sur-Orne.[9]

Montgomery followed up with a letter to Dempsey suggesting how he should regroup for the offensive. In the manner of an instructor at Staff College advising a student, he suggested he group the 15th, 49th and 11th Armoured Divisions into VIII Corps, 50th and 7th Armoured into XXX Corps and, as it became available, 43rd Division to make up a fourth division in

VIII Corps. The great thing was to make VIII Corps as strong as possible. In fact, although Dempsey accepted the spirit of this advice, he did not allot divisions as Montgomery had suggested. He made his own plan.

The intention was to start operations on 18 June and capture Caen by 24 June. However, nature now intervened in the shape of the worst storm in the English Channel for forty years. It lasted until 22 June and brought all ship-to-shore operations to a halt. The British Mulberry Harbour, across which the majority of Second Army's supplies were unloaded, was badly damaged and by the time the gale's fury was spent, their build-up was three divisions behind schedule by an average of one week. Dempsey's operation, which was given the code name EPSOM, had to be postponed.

But this delay gave him time to reconsider the feasibility of pushing O'Connor's newly arrived corps through the Airborne bridgehead east of the Orne. It was too small to assemble the forces, there were not sufficient bridges and the area was too exposed to enemy fire. Instead he proposed to Montgomery that he put VIII Corps in between I and XXX Corps, directed at Thury Harcourt far to the south.

On 22 June, Montgomery addressed the commanders of all corps and divisions in Second Army. He reiterated his intention to pull the enemy's reserves on to Second Army so that 1st US Army could carry out its task the easier. He privately expressed his confidence both in Bradley, commanding First American Army, and Dempsey, describing them as anxious to learn and doing so. Montgomery, however, was perhaps more tongue-in-cheek when he described Dempsey as unversed in Army/Air Cooperation, and in need of education in that area. In truth, it was Montgomery who, fuelled by the mutual dislike between himself and his opposite number, refused to deal with Coningham and instead either went direct to Leigh-Mallory (one level up) or Broadhurst (one down). In contrast, Dempsey worked conventionally and fruitfully with his opposite number, Broadhurst.

After two postponements, Operation EPSOM, involving 60,000 men and 600 tanks, began on 25 June. From the left of the British sector, 51st Highland Division, 3rd British and 3rd Canadian Divisions of I Corps were to maintain pressure on Caen from the north, while on the right the 49th Division of XXX Corps, with tank support, was to attack with the high ground around Rauray as its first objective. The main blow was to be delivered by VIII Corps, between the two, using 7th and 11th Armoured and 15th and 43rd Infantry divisions, backed up by two further armoured brigades. They were to cross the Odon and seize the high ground at Esquay in Phase 1, and then to cross the Orne and secure the area of Bretteville-sur-Laize in Phase 2.

The plan was ambitious, and although 51st Highland Division's preliminary attack north of Caen distracted German interest there, progress to the Odon was slow. The 49th Division went in to capture the high ground at Fontenay and Rauray which dominated the slopes of the Odon valley, rolling gently down to the river. The Odon itself was crossed by a number of narrow stone bridges, most of which the Germans had destroyed. The river banks were wired and mined, and the numerous stone buildings on its south side gave plenty of cover to the defenders. At 0730 next day, the 15th Division advanced to the Odon behind an artillery barrage of First World War proportions. They battled slowly through the formidable defences as far as Cheux that day and, on 27 June went through Mondrainville, surprising the Germans holding the bridge at Tourneauville, which became the main crossing point for VIII Corps. Dempsey met Bucknall at Saint Croix and told him to keep 8th Armoured Brigade in the Rauray area and maintain contact with the flank of VIII Corps. The Lowland Scots of the 15th Division struggled on to Baron and handed over to the 11th Armoured Division. A patrol of the 4th Wiltshires reached the perimeter of Carpiquet aerodrome but the area was still dominated by Hill 112, and although this was reached on 28 June, it was not held. Dempsey's view was that there was no point in holding 112, unless Hill 113 and Evrecy were also held. He did not feel he could afford the troops at that stage to make sure of getting there, because he was convinced that the vital spot to hold was the Rauray gap, an area he had looked at in detail and where he was convinced the Germans would strike. He was to be proved exactly right.

The Germans tried to counter-attack that night, but the infantry of 11th Armoured held on and the next day another crossing was made south of Mouen. A second attempt was made on Hill 112 and by 30 June they had a bridgehead over the Odon, 2½ miles wide, but only one mile deep. The 11th Armoured Division had lost 100 tanks and suffered 1,000 casualties, while VIII Corps in all had suffered over 4,000, the majority from the 15th Division. The farthest point was a long way short of the objectives Dempsey had set, and three brigadiers were sacked for not pushing their men hard enough. At the tactical level it was only a limited success, which, in the words of the official history, gave VIII Corps a firm bridgehead over the Odon, from which further operations to the south and south-east could be developed. However it had achieved a major gain at the operational level, which was about to be revealed.

Warned by ULTRA intercepts of the strong German reaction that his attack had prompted, Dempsey had to redeploy to meet a new threat. The Germans were convinced that EPSOM was the breakout that they had been expecting, and initially Rommel and von Rundstedt were in favour of abandoning Caen. They were overruled by Hitler and three new Panzer divisions were rushed in as reinforcements. By 30 June, Second Army had no less than eight panzer divisions, with 725 tanks, on its front, compared to 140 facing the Americans. They were achieving the strategy that Bradley had described as 'the sacrificial task' of attracting the German armour to their front, so the Americans could mount the breakout on theirs. Against such opposition, Second Army was obliged to concentrate on holding the ground won and to await the reinforcements delayed by the great storm. Dempsey now regrouped, pulling back the two armoured divisions and replacing them by infantry, ready for the next phase. Dempsey noted in his war diary that 'Second Army's task remains the same; to attract to itself (and to defeat) all the German armour, and when opportunity offers, to take Caen.'[10] Thus he opened himself to decades of criticism, especially from American historians, who failed to appreciate the Allied strategy. As Nigel Hamilton, the definitive biographer of Montgomery put it, Dempsey's modesty and his loyal post-war silence in the interest of Anglo-American unity are testimonials to the strength of character and self-abnegation of a great Allied general.

The press were now calling for Caen to fall. The Americans had taken Cherbourg, while the British seemed completely stuck. Dempsey was totally relaxed about this. In his view, the clamour would help convince the Germans to mass their strength on his front, which would provide the hinge for the American breakout south and then east towards the Seine. He had received his baptism of press coverage at the end of June, when the secrecy surrounding his appointment was lifted and the press had lauded him as one of 'the discoveries of this war', saying that at the age of forty-seven his appointment had bypassed many senior generals. Noting his extraordinary rise from lieutenant colonel at the outbreak of war, he was hailed as a tactician on a par with Montgomery. This publicity was not at all to Dempsey's liking, but he had been awarded his first knighthood and was now fair game for the press. One paper said: 'He has been called "Lucky" Dempsey. But in his case the luck has a background of study and experience, through knowledge, keen perception and memory and hard work. At 47 this bachelor soldier … looks at least five years younger than his age.'

However he used the opportunity afforded by the press interest to make a statement on the situation of Second Army:

> I am completely confident about the situation at the moment. We are ready for the enemy and prepared to meet him. Within the last 24 hours it has been established that German troops from Russia are fighting on the Normandy front. We are well disposed and properly balanced. We have got to kill the Hun somewhere. This is just as satisfactory a place as anywhere else. His communications are in a very dicky state. He may fight here or fall back and fight where his

communications are shorter and better … The rate of build up has been very high, but it does take time to build up a striking force, and we sat you may think very still for a fortnight, and the weather blew up delaying it … We are fully prepared. I have had experience of Hun reaction like this before. It is a good thing.[11]

At the end of June, Second Army's front ran in an arc from the north-east of Caen, then to the north and round to the west of the city. On 4 and 5 July the Canadians put in another attack on the west side of Caen, WINDSOR, but this failed. Dempsey was unfazed. All he had to do was hang on and in a few days the Americans would swing into action.

After a few days of Bradley's offensive, however, it became apparent that it was not going as well or as fast as hoped. Montgomery called Dempsey to his Tac HQ, where he told him that Bradley was barely off his start line and that he would need another two or three weeks to organize enough strength to break out. Dempsey would have to continue his 'holding battle'. Shortly after, Bradley joined them and confirmed Montgomery's estimate. Dempsey now appreciated that his main job was to stop the Germans relieving their armour with the infantry divisions which were just beginning to arrive from other parts of France, and to make them believe at Rundstedt's headquarters, and in Berlin, that Caen was regarded by the Allies as the key to the whole situation. They must convince the Germans that they intended to make the great breakout from Caen.

> I realised I would have to make the greatest possible show of force around Caen so as to keep Hitler's attention concentrated upon it. One way to do this would have been to continue the kind of attack we put in on the Odon. But these infantry battles were very costly and I had already been warned by the War Office that my resources were limited, and that I must keep a close eye on the casualties.[12]

At 0930 on 7 July, Dempsey briefed his five corps commanders that Second Army tasks were: to draw to itself and to contain the maximum number of German Divisions; to hold their present front intact; and, when opportunity offered, to capture Caen.

The defences of Caen by now were well prepared, with a system of interlocked anti-tank ditches, minefields and weapon pits in a belt 2 to 3 miles deep. Artillery and anti-tank guns were dug in, fields of fire cleared and buildings turned into strongpoints. In addition to three Panzer divisions, infantry and *nebelwerfer* units completed an extremely strong garrison.

Dempsey's solution was to make not only a major attack but also a major 'demonstration' by the Air Force. Mindful of his earlier unsuccessful attempts to enlist RAF resources beyond those available from Broadhurst's 83 Group, he realized that he would have to make a very convincing case, to 'sell the target', as it was known. This essentially involved exaggerating their case, which he did, with unfortunate consequences. The plan for Operation CHARNWOOD was for three divisions of I Corps, 3rd, 59th and 2nd Canadian, to attack in line. The attack was to be massively supported by Bomber Command, by the 16-inch guns of the battleship HMS *Rodney*, a monitor and two cruisers, and some of Hobart's 79th Division's 'funnies'.

At 2150 hrs on 7 July, 450 heavy bombers began to strike the northern outskirts of Caen and over the next hour dropped 5 tons each. At 0420 the next morning the infantry began their advance. The bombing raid was undoubtedly good for the morale of the attacking soldiers – although it prompted the playwright William Douglas Home to resign his commission in protest – but it had mixed results on the Germans.

The bomb line was set at 6,000 metres, which meant that although many defenders were left stunned and unable to resist, others had time to recover before the assaulting infantry were upon them; and the damage from the bombs was such as to impede the advance. Most Germans reacted violently and effectively, fighting fiercely for every street and every building. The next morning Dempsey was with Crocker to assess progress. The attack was going well and he was able to order 34th Armoured Brigade to pass into I Corps reserve. That evening he warned O'Connor's VIII Corps to be ready to take over the Caen sector at short notice. By the evening of 9 July, 9 Canadian Infantry Brigade was in the city centre and the whole of the city west of the Orne was in Second Army hands, at a cost to I Corps of some 5,500 infantry casualties. Although part remained in German hands, Dempsey had achieved his purpose of holding the German's attention, while at the same time giving him elbow room to manoeuvre west of the Orne.

Whatever the rights and wrongs of the bombing of Caen, there was no doubt where the sympathies of the inhabitants lay. They awarded Dempsey – 'Liberateur Glorieux de Cette Cité' – a large and imposing 'Diplome de Citoyen d'Honneur de la Ville de Caen'. Not much rancour there.

By now, Second Army had been fighting for a month and signs of strain were becoming apparent. Veteran divisions, which had been relied on to form the cutting edge of Dempsey's Army, had been found wanting. Commanders, even old hands versed in the hardships of war, had been slow and lacking in drive. The famous 51st Highland Division was, in the opinion of Dempsey and Crocker, not battle worthy, not fighting with determination and failing in every operation it was given. Even the 7th

Armoured Division, the famous veterans of North Africa, had lost their old *élan*. There were signs that they were too cautious, not inclined to take risks or be adventurous. In their case, the reason was all too human. After many years overseas – for some as many as six – they had returned to friends and loved ones in Britain to prepare for the invasion. The contrast between their previous hard, dangerous existence and the comforts of home life was exacerbated by wives and sweethearts imploring them not to take risks. They would have had to be inhuman not to feel that it was now someone else's turn. Michael Carver (later Lord Carver and Chief of the Defence Staff) commanded a veteran formation that had fought in North Africa, Sicily and Italy. He commented:

> One of the contributory causes was, I think, the emphasis placed before the campaign on the expected fierceness of the battle on the beaches. There was a tendency to build up a climate of feeling that, once ashore, it would all be fairly easy to get people to take exceptional risks, whether they were old sweats or keen young chaps, eager to win their spurs. Progressively both became disillusioned, either because opportunities created by bold action were not exploited – like Villers Bocage – or because boldness did not create the opportunities, but only led to certain casualties, particularly in the thick bocage. One was so often being told that the coming battle was the one that was going to break through and that no losses must deter one. Then the whole thing would come to a grinding halt, and instead of being told one had failed, *one was told that one had served one's purpose by containing the enemy.*[13]

Carver's remarks strike at the heart of Second Army's dilemma. Their task *was* to contain the enemy, but explaining that to soldiers and expecting them to fight hard for that purpose was not easy. The German soldiers were fighting to protect their Fatherland. The Americans were about to achieve glory by breaking out. When Bradley spoke about the 'thankless task' of the British, he meant just that. There was little glory for Dempsey's Second Army in their task on the eastern side of the bridgehead, and consequently little incentive to take the extra risk that might have produced brilliance. Commanders such as Bucknall and Erskine in XXX Corps, and Bullen-Smith, Dempsey's old brigade major from the 'phoney war' period, now commanding 51st Highland Division, had to pay the price.

Formations that had never been in action before were also found wanting, along with their commanders. In early July, Crocker, commanding I Corps, wrote to Dempsey to express his lack of confidence in Major General Keller, commanding 3rd Canadian Division. This was not the first time Keller had been reported on adversely. Prior to the invasion the Chief of Staff of the First Canadian Army had written to his Minister of Defence to warn him that Keller was pompous, inconsiderate, anything but brilliant and much over-rated, unable to command a brigade, let alone a division. Crocker was in a delicate position. As a British general it was difficult for him to recommend Keller's removal, as he might have done for a British general, but Crocker was aware that a Canadian Army was soon to be established, in which his corps would be grouped. He therefore tactfully drew attention to the problem by praising the Canadians' efforts on D-Day, but he then described their behaviour thereafter as nervous and their attitude as despondent. The steadying hand of the commander that was required was absent and although things had improved, their recent attack on Carpiquet once again demonstrated lack of control and leadership from the top. Crocker judged Keller unfit temperamentally and physically for command of a division. Dempsey agreed with the assessment and forwarded Crocker's letter to Montgomery with the comment that Keller had become undecided and apprehensive, and that had his division been a British one he would have recommended Keller's removal. By the time Montgomery had considered the matter, Keller's division had moved to join the newly formed II Canadian Corps, temporarily under Dempsey's command. The corps was commanded by Dempsey's old friend Simonds, in whom Dempsey had the utmost confidence; he later commented that Simonds was probably the finest Corps Commander in the whole Allied force. Montgomery therefore called for a report from Simonds as a fellow Canadian and a fresh commander. Two weeks later Dempsey forwarded Simonds's view that Keller's removal at that stage was likely to impact adversely on the morale of his division. Keller was therefore allowed to remain in command, but he, too, was living on borrowed time.

A worrying factor for Dempsey was the percentage of battle exhaustion cases, which were running at about one in five of all casualties. The fighting in the Normandy *bocage* was intense and extremely wearing on the nerves for those at the sharp end. The sunken lanes, high thick hedgerows and small fields gave excellent cover to the skilful German defenders. To the infantry platoon and section commander, life consisted of a series of heart-stopping dashes from cover to cover, never seeing more than a few yards ahead, dreading the mine placed at the only possible entrance to a field, or the machine gun in thick cover. For the tank commander, used to standing with his head out of the turret commanding a view of some hundreds of yards, the choices were either to continue this practice and risk being shot at close range by a concealed sniper, or close down and risk being 'brewed up' by a *panzerfaust*. Added to this, the tank crews were losing confidence in their ability to match the German armour. One crew out of four in each troop was equipped with the Sherman Firefly, with an excellent gun which could take on almost anything the Germans used. But the other tanks in the troop were not and the Sherman was acquiring a reputation for being easily combustible. The sight of comrades being burned alive in their tanks was enough to unnerve the hardiest of warriors. Dempsey called for reports on the effectiveness of British tanks. He concluded that at 30 yards the Sherman 75mm could not penetrate German armour, and that the Tiger was virtually immune to both the Sherman and the Cromwell. Although Tigers and Panthers only accounted for a part of the enemy inventory, it was generally accepted that British and Canadian armour was fighting under a considerable handicap.

As rest centres were established, as the opportunity was taken for whole divisions to be taken out of the line, reinforced and rested, and junior leaders replaced, the Army regained its old confidence. But the first thirty days had seen fighting of an intensity equal to that of the First War. From now on the husbanding of resources, and the strictest attention to unit morale, was more than ever necessary. This was to become evident in one of the most contentious operations of the campaign – GOODWOOD.

CHAPTER 11

'Charge'

Montgomery was convinced that strong and persistent action in the Caen sector would achieve the object of drawing the enemy reserves on to the Allies' eastern flank. The RAF, led vociferously by Tedder, demanded that strategy be guided by the need to capture airfields. This Montgomery was not prepared to do. He was satisfied that the close air support of Broadhurst's 38 Group, and the bombers that he could call on from Leigh-Mallory, were already giving Dempsey what he needed. His object was always to take ground that enabled him to dominate the area to the south-east of Caen. This would provide the hinge for the breakout, while at the same time drawing on to Second Army the bulk of the German armour. By doing so at the cost of giving the RAF the priority Tedder demanded, he was stoking resentment which was to cause him and Dempsey much difficulty.

During the period 10 to 18 July, while VIII Corps went into reserve, Second Army delivered a series of thrusts with the primary objective of making progress towards Thury-Harcourt, 10 miles to the south of their front line. These were sharp, stoutly resisted, infantry operations. The 50th, 49th and 59th Divisions of XXX Corps only progressed 3 miles at Tilly and the three divisions of XII Corps fared little better. The Canadian II Corps, with 1st and 2nd Canadian Divisions under command, took over the Caen sector, and the 51st Highland Division, part of I Corps, attacked the factory complex at Colombelles. They did not do well. On 11 July, they began the attack early in the morning and almost immediately ran into trouble. After a confused battle during the night, ten out of eleven tanks supporting the forward companies were quickly destroyed and the Highlanders withdrew with heavy casualties. Their own historian noted that they had failed to adapt to the conditions in Normandy in the way that their fellow North Africa veterans, the 50th Division, had.

Second Army's position was not helped by Eisenhower's failure to understand their role. In mid-July he was complaining to the Combined Chiefs of Staff of their 'inability' to break out in the east towards the Seine.

There was, of course, never any intention of breaking out on the eastern flank, as all the directives had made clear. Now Tedder joined Morgan at Eisenhower's headquarters, and Coningham commanding the Tactical Air Force, in claiming that Second Army had failed. It was Montgomery who was in their sights; but the fallout from their intriguing fell on Dempsey. The situation became so dire that the estimable Secretary of State for War, James Grigg, came over to see Montgomery and deliver to him a letter warning of Coningham's machinations – an almost unprecedented occurrence which begs the question as to why Coningham was allowed to remain in post.

The press, both in Britain and America, continued to be restive. The deception plan, Fortitude North, was kept active for as long as possible to convince the Germans that a huge American army, under Patton, was threatening the Pas de Calais. As a result, the press were kept under very tight control. Not unnaturally, a month after the invasion, they were demanding decisive action.

With the American breakout delayed, an operation was called for which could satisfy four mutually conflicting objectives. It had to continue the aim of convincing Hitler that the breakout was going to come from Second Army. It had to be presented to the press in such a way as to convince them that the British were acting as equal partners in the alliance, while at the same time masking their true intentions. It had to be presented to the soldiers in such a way that they would fight hard. Finally, it had to be 'sold' to SHAEF, the politicians and the RAF as a major blow that deserved their support. It was never going to be possible to achieve all four.

In addition to these concerns, Dempsey had some more practical matters to consider in planning his next operation. In a fascinating letter to Liddell Hart after the war,[1] he set out his reasons why he attacked on 18 July, and why at Caen. After emphasizing that Montgomery's master plan never changed, he went on to describe the meeting with him and Bradley at which it became apparent that the American breakout had failed. Montgomery encouraged Bradley to keep trying. Then he turned to Dempsey and said, 'Go on hitting; drawing the German strength, especially the armour, onto yourself – so as to ease the way for Brad.' After this conference Dempsey suggested in private that he could – and should – make the breakout. *But Montgomery vetoed the idea and it was never raised again between them.*

The primary consideration of the operation, which was to be called GOODWOOD, was the necessity to hit hard; attract the enemy's armour to the eastern flank; and wear down his strength there. But another consideration was the need to expand the bridgehead, which was becoming overcrowded as reinforcements and supplies poured in. To gain more room it was necessary to complete the occupation of Caen and the Bourgebus ridge to its south-east. This would have the subsidiary benefit of capturing airfields for the RAF. He also needed to expand the shallow bridgehead over the Orne on the left flank and to put Second Army in the best possible position to advance to the Seine, once the American breakout came into line to the south and permitted them to do so.

Dempsey then spelled out a series of factors which dictated his tactics. First was manpower. By 10 July, Second Army had suffered over 22,000 casualties, just under 4,000 of them killed, in the five weeks since D-Day. Most of these casualties were in the infantry and in early July Dempsey was visited by the Adjutant General, Bill Adam, who warned him that if infantry casualties continued at the same rate, it would be impossible to replace them. By contrast, his strength in tanks was increasing all the time. Replacement tanks were pouring in faster than the rate of tank casualties. An armour-heavy thrust would force the Germans to commit their armour in response. These two factors indicated that the operation should be based heavily on the use of armour.

A further consideration was that the nature of the ground dictated that the supporting artillery would not have enough room to be able to keep up with the armour. Also, a shortage of 25-pounder ammunition reduced the support they could give. Dempsey noted:

> It became necessary to depend on large-scale bomber support. To obtain this from the Air Staff and Bomber Command, who disliked being diverted to aid ground operations, Monty felt it was necessary to over-state the aims of the operation. In doing this he did not take Eisenhower into his confidence. But as an insurance against subsequent misconceptions he said to me 'Let's be quite clear about this' and wrote out a personal directive for me … it was the first time, and the last, that he gave such a written directive.[2]

Dempsey gave some thought to the possibility of German resistance crumbling, and decided to move his Tac HQ up with that of VIII Corps. His thought was that if the opportunity offered to seize all the Orne crossings from Caen to Argentan, it would be sensible to make sure he was able to do so. But he kept these thoughts to himself. He set about planning GOODWOOD, based on Montgomery's broad directive, but the plan was to be his.

He now had available the 7th, 11th and the Guards Armoured Divisions, the last just landed and ready for operations. He could also count on five independent armoured brigades and three tank brigades. By mounting a powerful armoured thrust into the Caen-Falaise plain, he could use this mass of armour to strike a hammer blow which would crush the German hold to the south of Caen. On 12 July, Dempsey saw Montgomery and obtained his approval for the plan. Montgomery's response was 'that should draw them in.'[3] At this stage, Montgomery had received a most unusual letter from O'Connor, which appeared to question the judgement of O'Connor's superior officer, Dempsey. It referred to the sequence in which preliminary operations should be carried out. These operations would begin on 15 July with diversionary attacks by Neil Ritchie's XII Corps from the Odon sector. Dempsey ordered that they should hold the ground from Evrecy to Esquay and develop a strong thrust south. They were to do all they could to lead the enemy to believe that Second Army's main thrust was coming in their area. At the same time XXX Corps was to secure the Noyes area and be prepared to exploit to the high ground north-east of Villers Bocage. Their operations were designed to draw enemy reserves into the thick country on their front. There is no record of Montgomery's response to O'Connor, but it is fair to assume he discussed this point with Dempsey during their consideration of the plan. Whether O'Connor was trying to upstage Dempsey or merely make a point in writing to cover himself for the future is not clear.

The main blow was to be delivered by O'Connor, whose VIII Corps Headquarters would take under command the three armoured divisions. They would be assembled in the bridgehead held by 6th Airborne Division, now reinforced by the 51st Highlanders east of the Orne. After a massive air bombardment this force of 750 tanks would smash through the German defences, outflank Caen from the east, and occupy the commanding heights of the Bourgebus ridge. They would be supported by attacks on their flanks by I and XII Corps, while Simonds would secure the southern half of Caen with II Canadian Corps. Dempsey now had a greater number of formations under his command than he was ever to have again.

The preliminary bombardment would be along the lines of CHARNWOOD. It was intended to allow the armour to penetrate the German positions and to neutralize their anti-tank defence in depth. But unlike CHARNWOOD, the bombing would precede the attack by only two hours. As well as RAF heavy bombers dropping 6,000 tons of bombs, American mediums were intended to join in with fragmentation and anti-personnel bombs. In the largest operation of its sort ever attempted, 700 guns and Naval craft would add their supporting fire. The heavy bombs were to be dropped on the flanks and the smaller, fragmentation and incendiary ones in the path of the attackers. It was hoped that heavy cratering, which would have impeded the attackers, would be avoided. A total of 4,500 aircraft of all types were employed.

However, Dempsey had a major problem with the ground over which he was to fight. The area where the armour was to assemble was dominated by the Colombelles steel works. This was in the hands of the Germans, who thus had unhindered observation of this mass of tanks as they prepared for an operation whose purpose was clear. Moreover, the area was limited and restricted the ability of formations to move through and deploy from it. Dempsey asked the Staff Duties branch to work out how long it would take to move three armoured divisions across the river Orne into this area. When he got the answer he realized that the traffic bottleneck would be so great that he could not get them all over in time. He therefore told VIII Corps not to worry about the supporting arms and services, but just to get the tanks and their supporting motorized infantry over. Even this limited plan was difficult.

Finally, the ground to the south-east, the direction of the attack, sloped gently up to the Bourgebus ridge and the villages of Bras, Soliers and Hubert Folie, from which the defender had perfect fields of fire, particularly for his deadly 88mm flak guns used in the anti-tank role. A further complicating factor was the presence of two railway embankments. Running almost at right angles to the direction of the advance, these two features at first appeared to offer cover to the attackers, but any armoured vehicle crossing them was dangerously exposed.

On 17 July, Dempsey visited O'Connor at Colombelles. He gave him the latest intelligence on the enemy, which appeared to be favourable, and then moved his own Tac HQ to Bény-sur-Mer. In fact, under Rommel's guidance, the Germans had created in the area to be assaulted the most powerful defensive system ever established in Normandy. In this sector alone they had three infantry and two armoured divisions, over 200 tanks and seventy-eight of the deadly 88mm guns. They were deployed in five belts, which included village strongpoints, woods and an armoured belt which included thirty-six Tigers. The final one included forty-five Panther tanks. Ranged against them were the 750 tanks of VIII Corps and the 350 in I and II Canadian Corps.

The bombing on 18 July appeared to go well, but dust obscured the target area and many of the bombs of the US Eighth Air Force fell widely scattered on the wrong places. Despite this the enormous weight of ordnance was sufficient to stun or even drive crazy those defenders left alive, and to destroy or damage much of their equipment. It was now that the German layout of defence in depth, and the quality of the German soldier, showed their strength.

At 0745 the tanks of the 11th Armoured Division began to roll forward, followed by the Guards Armoured and 7th Armoured. They had soon advanced 6 miles, and at VIII Corps and Second Army headquarters there was an air of quiet optimism. But as 11th Armoured reached Cagny, a battery of 88mm guns knocked out sixteen tanks. 'Pip' Roberts, the Divisional Commander, ordered Cagny to be masked, but as the Rifle Brigade and the 23rd Hussars moved into position they were cruelly exposed and more tanks were lost. The impetus faded. The forward units had outstripped the range of their supporting artillery, which was unable to move forward. The German anti-tank guns continued to take their toll and the supporting infantry struggled to keep up. The 11th Armoured Division stalled and Guards Armoured, following behind with the intention of swinging left and reaching Vimont, instead found itself stuck among the minefields and ant-tank guns of Cagny and Emienville. Although Cagny was taken that evening, Vimont remained beyond their grasp.

A mass of vehicles choked the approaches, thick smoke and dust obscured the battlefield and O'Connor seemed unable to grip the situation. By the middle of the first day it was obvious that Erskine, commanding 7th Armoured Division, did not have his heart in the operation and seemed unwilling to commit his tanks to battle. O'Connor also had a major row with 'Pip' Roberts, the 37-year-old commander of 11th Armoured Division, over the failure to bring up infantry to help out the armour. The advance was resumed on 19 July, and the 2nd Canadian Division and the British 3rd Division managed to secure the shoulders of the salient to the west and east respectively, but the operation was effectively over.

On 20 July, the weather broke and turned the battlefield into a quagmire. Dempsey moved his Tac HQ to Cairon and conferred with Crocker and O'Connor. Although Eisenhower stressed to Montgomery, 'I feel that Dempsey should keep up the strength of his attack,' Dempsey felt otherwise. He later recalled, 'Once it became evident that the armour was not going to break out, the operation became an infantry battle – and it was no part of the Goodwood plan to get drawn into a costly battle of that kind.'[4]

It was time to bring the operation to a close and tidy up the battlefield. Dempsey gave orders for the regrouping of the armour and infantry, and coordinated the handover of I and II Canadian Corps to the newly established First Canadian Army. O'Connor's VIII Corps would go into reserve. It was a difficult time. Everyone knew that the operation had not gone well and although, in the words of one of his staff, 'Wherever he went he inspired confidence and was a most welcome visitor to any harassed commander of a subordinate formation,'[5] it took a great effort for Dempsey to maintain his appearance of confidence.

The cost was heavy. Second Army had lost 400 tanks and over 6,000 casualties. Replacement tanks could be easily supplied, but the men, mostly infantry, could not be so easily replaced. One division had lost half its infantry and two Canadian battalions had lost 200 each. Eisenhower was not pleased and wondered aloud whether 1,000 tons of bombs for each mile gained was affordable. Recriminations followed quickly. First to go was Bullen-Smith, commanding 51st Highland Division. Dempsey was loath to sack his old comrade from 1940, but the unpalatable fact was, as Montgomery said to

Bullen-Smith, his men would no longer fight for him and his retention would have cost unnecessary lives. A further question mark was placed over 'Bobby' Erskine, who had commanded 7th Armoured Division since North Africa. They were seen to be slow and lacking in drive and O'Connor thought Erskine excessively cautious. Matters were not helped by a letter from Erskine criticizing the staff work of VIII Corps. O'Connor in turn came in for criticism. He was felt not to have exercised the tight grip which he had demonstrated in the desert

At the tactical level, GOODWOOD was a failure. The attacking armoured divisions were crowded into too narrow a front to avoid the congestion which prevented the proper tactical employment of the assets that the all-arms battle requires. The most important of these assets was infantry; indeed the whole concept of an armour-heavy battle in the *bocage* could only have been sustained if adequate infantry support could have been supplied. Dempsey made clear why he opted for the tactics he employed, but the impression remains of an untidy battle, in which VIII Corps was given a task with restraints so great that it was doomed before it began. His assessment was as follows:

> The attack we put in on July 18th was not a very good operation of war tactically, but strategically it was a great success, even though we did get a bloody nose. I didn't mind about that. I was prepared to lose a couple of hundred tanks, so long as I didn't lose men. We could afford the tanks because they had begun to pile up in the bridgehead. Our tank losses were severe but our casualties in men were very light. If I had tried to achieve the same result with a conventional infantry attack I hate to think what the casualties would have been.[6]

The official history of Second Army had this to say:

> To some extent the attack had been disappointing. The anti-tank cordon thrown around the area by the Germans had been quick and effective. 8 Corps had advanced 10,000 yards, and 2,000 PW had been taken. Sufficient elbow-room was gained for 1st Canadian Army to mount the operations which finally succeeded in driving the enemy out of the Caen-Falaise plain, which in turn materially affected the whole campaign.[7]

Brooke, gauging reaction in Britain and America, commented on 27 July:

> The strategy of the Normandy landings is quite straightforward. The British must hold and draw Germans on to themselves, while

Americans swing up to open the Brest Peninsula. But now comes the trouble. The press chip in and we hear that the British are doing nothing, and suffering no casualties, while the Americans are bearing all the brunt of this war.[8]

While Dempsey remained optimistic, his Chief of Staff, Maurice Chilton, was very upset by the press reaction. Dempsey told him, 'Don't worry – it will aid our purpose and act as the best possible cover plan.'[9] There was certainly no excuse for a message that Montgomery sent to Brooke that the operation had been a total success. To make matters worse, a disastrously optimistic press conference that Montgomery gave resulted in a *Times* headline 'SECOND ARMY BREAKS THROUGH'. It had not, it had never intended to, but now the pigeons came home to roost with a vengeance. Serious moves were made, spearheaded by Tedder, Morgan and Coningham, to have Montgomery removed. On 20 July, Churchill, roused to ire by the reports he was receiving, and Montgomery's personal fractiousness, visited in person.

Montgomery's position was perilous and he was as close to dismissal as he was ever to be. If he had gone, it is difficult to see how Dempsey could have survived. To maintain his own position, Montgomery could have thrown the blame on Dempsey. It was Dempsey's plan after all. But Montgomery did not. As Dempsey remarked, he did not rat. What he did was to face down his accusers and point out that the operation was in line with his long-term strategy. Indeed, at the operational and strategic levels GOODWOOD had been a qualified success. This was fortunately confirmed by ULTRA intercepts, which showed that, despite the obvious but unavailing attempts by Bradley to break out in the west, the main German strength remained doggedly arrayed against Dempsey's Second Army. Their appreciation was that the British offensive around Caen foreshadowed a breakout, and there could be no possibility of replacing Panzer formations by infantry in that sector. The accepted view has to be that if the Germans could have shifted even one single battered Panzer division towards Bradley at the end of July, it would have made his breakout far more difficult and costly – if not impossible.

Eisenhower's biographer, commenting on his subject's failure to appreciate the rationale behind the operation, wrote that what hardly anyone realized was that the British had fought the best formations in the German Army to exhaustion, kept them from even considering a counter-offensive and tied down fourteen divisions (six of them first-rate Panzer divisions) – 'no mean feat'.[10]

Fortunately for Montgomery and Dempsey, discussion of their battle was overshadowed by the momentous news of the attempt on Hitler's life and they both lived to fight another day. Churchill carried on to visit Dempsey, who showed him around Caen and then briefed him on his future operations.

In order to give even more help to the First American Army operation, Second Army was to carry out an operation at the beginning of August, either east or west of the Orne. *It would have no geographical objective* but would be a continuation of the policy which had held good for the whole time – that Second Army should deal with the main enemy force while First American Army swung forward with its right. Dempsey was to shift the direction of his main effort from the east to the west of his front. He gave orders for the regrouped VIII Corps to move from the area of Caen to Caumont and put in as strong an attack as possible on 30 July.

The plan for Operation BLUECOAT was set out by Dempsey at a conference for all corps commanders on 28 July. Noting that there were now eight German divisions between Troarn and Evrecy, he spelled out Second Army's tasks:

- To draw onto itself the maximum German strength – particularly armour – and weaken it.
- To hold the pivot secure, for on this the whole operation depends.
- To help First Army in every way possible to get Brittany
- To pivot, first north of Caen
  then on Caen
  then south of Caen.[11]

Next day he followed up with formal tasks. VIII Corps was to attack south from Caumont, where possible bypassing opposition, with its first objective le Bény-Bocage, while XXX Corps was to advance with its first objective the Bois du Homme. XII Corps was to swing its right forward until it rested on the high ground north-east of Villers Bocage. II Canadian Corps was to follow I Corps under command First Canadian Army, reducing Dempsey's command to three corps. A huge redeployment was now required to make all this work, within a very short time. Some formations had to drive 40 or 50 miles by roundabout routes through back areas from one side of the Orne to the other. Thanks to good staff work, good march discipline and complete air superiority, it was all achieved on time.

This time, lessons from GOODWOOD had been learned and divisions formed their own groupings of armour and infantry. On 30 July, after the area had been 'softened up' by Lancaster bombers of the RAF, VIII Corps headed off for Vire, and while 11th Armoured Division struck south to link up with the Americans, Guards Armoured and the 15th Divisions made good progress towards the hill country. They soon reached the top of the Caumont ridge, and the guardsmen and the Scots 'married up' to move forward. Gradually the enemy fire increased and the infantry halted. Here they consolidated for the moment. What happened to the Scots Guards battle group is described by Willie Whitelaw, later Deputy Prime Minister, then commanding a squadron of Churchill tanks: 'All at once I saw something so horrifying that my senses were completely dulled … In just five minutes I had lost three tanks and, most tragic of all, the lives of several members of my squadron, who were all my trusted friends and part of the happy family welded together by years of training.'[12] It was an example of the recuperative power of the Germans and the striking power of their anti-tank weapons.

In the centre, XXX Corps drove forward with 7th Armoured, 43rd and 50th Divisions. Initial movement was slow, but by the second day, as Montgomery urged Dempsey to 'throw all caution to the winds', the German front began to crumble in front of VIII Corps. An important early gain was the capture of the Bul bridge over the Souleuvre River by the Household Cavalry operating with 11th Armoured Division. Roberts saw the opportunity and took it, advancing so fast that he outstripped the Guards Armoured on one flank and the Americans on the other. He held on and waited for them to catch up. But he had opened the possibility that if Second Army could keep up the momentum, a whole pocket of troops facing Bradley's left flank could be rolled up.

But Dempsey, with his Tac HQ forward at Thiel, was unhappy with the progress of XXX Corps, so on the evening of the first day he rang Bucknall and warned him that he had better get on 'or else'. By the end of the first thirty-six hours, VIII Corps had advanced twelve miles, and Dempsey then met O'Connor and Bucknall at VIII Corps headquarters. He ordered that 11th Armoured was to secure le Bény-Bocage and then advance due south towards Vire, while Guards Armoured was to advance in the direction of Vassy. For XXX Corps, the eastern half of the Bois du Homme feature was to be captured as soon as possible and, without waiting for this, 7th Armoured was to 'be pressed through' on the axis Caumont-Aunay. Dempsey then met up with the Commander of the First American Army to coordinate the takeover of a segment of his front, to allow this to happen. It was now vital that 7th Armoured Division act with urgency and throw out a flanking shield if the opportunity were to be grasped. To Dempsey's disappointment, Erskine failed to rise to the challenge. Three German divisions were moving to counter the threat, 7th Armoured was too slow to move and Dempsey saw that it was too late. Erskine's desert instincts to worry about his flanks had been his undoing.

The next morning Dempsey rang Montgomery and told him he was tired of Bucknall. That evening, when XXX Corps progress was still unsatisfactory he told him he would have to go and wrote an official letter to Montgomery:

> I have already discussed with you the command of 30 Corps. The Corps Commander has failed during the last seventy-two hours to produce the results which the situation demanded. I must therefore recommend to you with regret that Lieutenant-General Bucknall be replaced in command of 30 Corps. In my opinion he is not fit to command a Corps in mobile operations.[13]

On the same day Montgomery endorsed Dempsey's recommendation to the Military Secretary and reported:

> Initially Bucknall did well in Normandy … but recently the problem has changed … it was clear that great energy and drive would be necessary, and great risks could be taken … It is in these latter days that General Bucknall has failed. He is very careful … he is nearly always 24 hours too late and the enemy profits thereby. General Dempsey and myself have tried to guide General Bucknall in the way he should go, and to quicken him up. But I am now convinced it is not possible.[14]

He then went on to make a very telling comment: 'Gen Bucknall was appointed to command a Corps at my request. I admit, frankly, that I made a mistake; and I must now remove him from command.'[15]

'Pete' Pyman, Bucknall's Chief of Staff, was in as good a position as any to judge whether this was fair. He wrote:

> It is always an unhappy event when a Corps Commander has to go. So it was with Jerry Bucknall. He had done a great deal for the Corps and he was a fine D-Day commander. But the open warfare was not nearly so much up his street. He kept getting out of position. He and those who were with him went with great dignity. In fact it was altogether a very dignified affair. Army Commander for his actions and Corps Commander for his reaction alike lost nothing in my young eyes. We got in Jerry's place *Jorrocks*, Lt General Sir Brian Horrocks, so the Corps lost nothing.[16]

Erskine also had to go; like Bucknall he was not responding to the need to press on. In Montgomery's judgement the Division needed a new general who could 'drive them headlong into, and through, gaps torn in the enemy defence – not worrying about flanks or anything'. Again Pyman approved:

'The dismissal of Bucknall and Erskine was fully justified – they made no effort to push hard, or carry out their orders.'[17] Pyman was probably being loyal to Dempsey – there is evidence that the sackings did cause resentment. Bucknall, whatever his demeanour at the time, was complaining within a few days of the difficulty of the task set XXX Corps by Dempsey, and maintained that he had protested in the planning stage and been overruled. His comments would have carried more weight if events on the battlefield had turned out differently.

Bucknall's departure and replacement by Horrocks was followed soon after by the capture of Mont Pincon in a remarkable operation. The commander of the lead group of tanks of 13/18th Hussars had found a small road, seemingly unguarded, leading to the summit. He led two troops upwards, pausing at one point as one tank came off the narrow track. By this time they were in thick fog, and British tanks and German infantry were within yards of each other on this vital piece of ground. The 13th/18th were followed by the 4th Wiltshires of 43rd (Wessex) Division. Although they had fought a savage battle the day before and had already marched 7 miles under shellfire, they pressed on up the track during the night. The next morning they repulsed a strong counter-attack and the most important piece of ground on the Second Army front was in British hands.

The realization now crept over the men of Second Army that they were on the brink of marvellous achievements. It was not before time. Second Army desperately needed a shot in the arm.

Horrocks wrote of that time:

> It soon became obvious to me that the seven weeks hard slogging in the thick Bocage country had taken their toll and the gloss had gone from the magnificently trained army which had landed in Normandy … This was obviously what had happened to the 43rd Wessex, one of the best-trained divisions which had ever left our shores.[18]

Another participant in these momentous events was Bill Deedes, later editor of the *Daily Telegraph*, then commanding a company of Riflemen in an armoured division. In a letter home he wrote:

> It seems slow where I am and rather expensive and tiring into the bargain …The CO [Commanding Officer] has gone and all the company commanders except me (have been) wounded or found other employment – now I remain the last chap in the battalion of 1939. One gets very tired, I find, even though we do not get all the blood and slaughter reserved for the infantry divisions. I find the endless slaughter and destruction wearing.[19]

A complete change in this mood was now achieved. The effect on morale of these gains, particularly the capture of Mont Pincon, was immense. The high ground that had brooded over the Second Army sector like an evil spirit was in British hands. Horrocks, newly appointed to XXX Corps, was able to sit on the summit with his Commander Royal Artillery and call on the support of 300 guns for any unit that needed it.

Now at last the Army sensed that their efforts were achieving solid gains, that the enemy was not invincible, that real movement was possible. Second Army was recovering its flair and within a week it had knocked out the 'key rivets' of Caumont and Mont Pincon, and secured the vital crossings over the upper Orne. Indeed, the possibility of a mighty blow was opening itself to the Allies – no less than the encirclement and destruction of the German Army.

Hitler now played into the Allies' hands. As the Americans began the huge wheeling turn which would bring their armies south and then east below the British and Canadians, he ordered a counter-attack at Mortain. Instead of falling back with all speed to a defensive line from which they could face the Allies on their own terms, the Germans now stuck their heads further into the lion's jaws. Five Panzer and two infantry divisions were held by the Americans, and the entire Allied Air Force was unleashed on them. First Canadian Army advanced south to take Falaise, with Ritchie's XII Corps on their right, and Dempsey moved his Tac HQ forward to le Bény-Bocage to keep pace. On 10 August, it became obvious that the Canadians under their new commander, Crerar, were in difficulties. Dempsey flew to Ritchie's headquarters and impressed on him the importance of the swift capture of Falaise, while the Canadians were to press on and close the mouth of the pocket. At one point it was even suggested to Dempsey by Bradley that he should send two divisions round through the American side of the pocket so as to complete the closure. This strange idea would not only have been wasteful in time and resources, it would have reduced Second Army's effective strength, already weakened, to dangerous levels. Already the 59th Division had had to be disbanded. It was not a starter.

Ritchie did take Falaise and, after noting that it was fully occupied on 17 August, Eisenhower acknowledged that the enemy resistance in this sector had exacted more Allied bloodshed for the ground yielded than in any other part of the campaign. Without the series of brutal, slugging battles, first for Caen, then for Falaise, the spectacular advances made elsewhere by the Allied Forces could never have come about. It was a welcome, if belated, acknowledgement of Second Army's 'sacrificial role' and the gallant, dogged way that it had been carried out.

Selwyn Lloyd's summary was:

Second Army has been opposed by very considerable numbers of enemy formations including the bulk of his armour. The country on our sector has been very close and difficult – and has greatly favoured defence – the constant attacks with limited objectives which Second Army has made have achieved a threefold purpose:

- They have kept the initiative firmly with us.
- They have forced the enemy to plug the holes as they have shown signs of appearing, and put his reserves into the line just as he was labouring to fill them up.
- They have inflicted heavy casualties on him.

We have broken through in a part of the front where progress has been made for some time; the enemy defences were well organised and there were minefields to be traversed which were deeper than any yet experienced on our front.[20]

By mid-August, Second Army's front ran west from Falaise to Conde, then south through Flers to Briouze. With the First Canadian Army on their left they formed the top and side of what became known as the Falaise pocket. The Americans formed the south side of an envelope 30 miles long. The intention now was to close it at the mouth, by the Canadians driving down from the north, and the Third American Army driving up from the south. Second Army, in Dempsey's words at his Cuilly headquarters, was to 'drive the birds into the stop lines'. This was the task of XII and XXX Corps, exerting pressure from the north and west and, as the Canadians and Americans strove to close the mouth of the pocket, Dempsey ordered them to clear the whole of the area Trun-Chambois-St Leonard-Argentan. This was done during the day and several thousand prisoners were taken. Here their operations came to a temporary halt as the contracting pocket denied them further room to manoeuvre.

The gap was not, however, closed as quickly as had been intended and, despite the sustained bombardment of both Air Forces and 300 guns into the pocket, one third of the German Army escaped to fight again.

The priority now was to move the whole Allied line forward to the Seine and Montgomery issued a directive to this effect. But a problem faced Second Army. Before they could move east, First Canadian Army had to get clear from their positions and begin their move up the coast. On the right of Second Army, the move forward of the First American Army took up road space that Dempsey needed. The solution was to share highways for three- or four-hour slots, a process that required good staff work and superb discipline. Dempsey flew up to Millebois to see General Hodges, commanding First American Army. He arranged that this sharing would start the next day for both XII and XXX Corps. Unfortunately, and very much out of character, at a press conference shortly after, Dempsey complained, or was reported as complaining, that he had been unnecessarily obstructed by American traffic across his front. Bradley was outraged and protested to Montgomery, who replied that Dempsey must have been misquoted. However, this did not stop him giving Dempsey an imperial rocket.

Dempsey decided to take VIII Corps into reserve and use their transport to increase the mobility of the rest of the Army. Although it may not have been to O'Connor's liking, his headquarters undoubtedly deserved a rest after their major role in so many of Second Army's operations.

The formation for the advance to the Seine placed XII Corps on the left, crossing at Louviers. They would come after XXX Corps, who were to cross at Vernon. By now, resistance had virtually ceased and both corps moved at such speed that at times they were ahead of Germans desperate to get back to safety. The heady elation of pursuit replaced the weary grind of the Normandy battle. Bill Deedes reflected this change of mood. Gone was the war-weariness of a few days before: 'It's thrilling here now to hear our tanks roaring east and the guns pouring up behind, and to see the RAF following up wave upon wave. I'm as peace-loving a chap as the next, but the Germans have bought this, and they deserve every stick of it.'[21]

The crossing of the Seine was carried out brilliantly. Preparations for this operation, which involved an opposed crossing of an obstacle 200 yards wide, had been made long before it began. At Vernon the assault was mounted from 120 miles west of the river by the 43rd (Wessex) Division under Major General Ivor Thomas. Known as 'von Thoma', Thomas was an imposing character who brooked no argument. He had trained his division hard and thoroughly in England before D-Day, and although Horrocks was probably right to observe that they had lost some of their edge during the hard fighting in the *bocage*, their capture of Mont Pincon had put new life into them. They were now back on peak form, as they speedily demonstrated.

For the operation the division was organized in three groups: the first 1,500 vehicles consisted of the assaulting infantry and engineers; the second 1,900 contained the artillery and the bridging train; the remaining 1,000 vehicles carried the remainder of the Division. Using their allotted two slots of four hours, they completed the approach march in thirty-six hours, with the two assault battalions mounted in DUKWs. Within two hours of arriving at the concentration area, assault boats and DUKWs were crossing under cover of a smokescreen and an intense artillery barrage.

At first light on 26 August, 4th Wiltshires were firm on the far bank and by that evening the Royal Engineers had constructed a 680-foot folding bridge. Despite German counter-attacks, within seventy-two hours of the first crossing a bridgehead over 4 miles deep had been established. The other main crossing, by XII Corps at Louviers, could not begin until 27/28 August; that too was successful and by the end of the month, earlier than the original pre-D-Day estimate, Second Army was east of the Seine. The battle for Normandy was over.

CHAPTER 12

'Pursue'

'One reaches the conclusion that these six short weeks saw one of the most successful advances of any British army – indeed of any army ever formed.'[1]

This summary of the period from the end of BLUECOAT to the arrival of Second Army at the border with Holland captures the spirit of those extraordinary times. Once over the Seine, the Allied plan of campaign, set out so comprehensively by Montgomery before D-Day, had run its course. It was now necessary to direct the huge mass of ground forces, with their supporting air armada, so as to defeat Germany in the shortest possible time. A Land Commander had to be appointed who could make and direct this plan. There were three possible candidates. One was Montgomery, who since D-Day had combined the posts of Commander 21st Army Group and Land Force Commander. He was the most experienced and arguably the most capable militarily, but tactless and politically maladroit; the American public simply would not have stood for it. Bradley was an excellent field commander, quiet and unassuming; and Eisenhower himself, woefully inexperienced at the tactical and operational levels of command, and with a poor grasp of strategy, was an outstanding personality, capable of greatness. Montgomery coveted the position, but was prepared to serve under Bradley if necessary. Possibly fearing that Bradley would not be able to control the headstrong Montgomery – an assessment that Dempsey shared – Eisenhower was ordered by his American superior, Chairman of the US joint Chiefs, General Marshall, to take on the mantle himself, in addition to his duties as Supreme Allied Commander.

The first decision Eisenhower had to make was whether to adopt a 'broad front' strategy, conforming to his natural inclination, as one of his observers described it, to 'urge everyone to attack at the same time, like a football coach roaring up and down the touchline', or to concentrate, as Montgomery urged, the maximum resources into one thrust at the heart of Germany. Eisenhower opted for the 'broad front', and the chase was on.

Second Army's immediate task was to advance north and establish itself in the area Arras-Amiens-St Pol. It would then capture crossings over the Somme in the shortest possible time. On 28 August, Dempsey was able to drive from his Tac HQ at Fontaine-Sous-Jouy to an observation point from which he could view the XII Corps bridgehead just established at Louviers. He visited the headquarters of 15th (Scottish) Division at Vieux Rouen and there congratulated the recently appointed commander, Major General Colin Barber, and his brigade commanders. Their action was one of many that were to result in the 15th Division being described by Carlo D'Este as the best in 21st Army Group.

To cross the Somme, XXX Corps, with 11th and Guards Armoured Divisions under command, were ordered by Dempsey to seize the crossings at Amiens, 70 miles distant, while the 43rd Division was stood down for a rest. By pressing on through the night 'Pip' Roberts's 11th Armoured Division, with help from the French Resistance, captured the bridges intact. They were led by the 2nd Household Cavalry Regiment, who advanced over 60 miles in forty-eight hours to arrive just before they were due to be blown. The advance now took on an air of exhilarating optimism. The country through which Second Army was speeding was open and rolling with wide fields, no hedges and good roads. It was very different from the close *bocage* which had proved so daunting in Normandy. The armour was able to revert to the formations and tactics they had employed so successfully in the desert. As they passed through villages, dusty and windswept, but exhilarated by their speed, the tank crews were greeted with enthusiastic welcomes. On the first day of the pursuit, XXX Corps travelled 21 miles, and in the last three days of August it covered 100 miles, through cheering Frenchmen, while church bells rang out. Members of the French Resistance appeared and played a useful part in providing information on local German forces, and guarding prisoners while the pursuit was resumed. Everywhere the French tricolour waved from windows and rooftops.

Isolated pockets of resistance held out and the Guards Armoured Division was held up by a determined German garrison at Pont-à-Marcq. The enemy had deployed anti-tank guns, mortars and machine guns in the houses and a factory on the outskirts. The Guards took over fifty casualties. But there could be no let-up for the advancing Army and commanders at all levels were seized with the need to press on. When necessary, as with Roberts's 11th Armoured Division, tank crews and their supporting infantry drove through the night. This was hard on the drivers, who kept going for thirty-six hours at a stretch, but the capture intact of the bridge at Amiens was followed in quick time by the remaining bridges over the Somme. Morale soared as the realization struck home that a major turn in the war's fortunes was possible.

On nearly every level of command intelligence officers were forecasting the imminent end of the war. The Combined Allied Intelligence Committee believed that the German situation had deteriorated to a point where it was beyond recovery. Eisenhower's headquarters was forecasting that the end of the war in Europe was in sight, almost within reach. By early September they judged the German Army to be no longer a cohesive force, disorganized and demoralized.

To take advantage of the situation, Dempsey was making plans for the employment of Browning's Airborne Corps, which would come under command Second Army on landing. His plans now were for XXX Corps to spearhead the advance, to be at Arras by 2 September and across the Belgian frontier on the morning of the third. Its axis was to be Tournai-Brussels and a plan was hatched – soon to be overtaken by events – for an airborne drop on Tournai in support. Meanwhile XII Corps was to strike for the area of Merville, to the west of Lille, and then to Ghent.

Events now moved with great speed. As the two corps raced north they motored so quickly that at times they were ahead of the retreating Germans. Resistance was feeble and the main difficulties came from mines, booby traps and blown bridges. Dempsey's Tac HQ moved five times from Fontaine to Perck in Belgium, a distance of 200 miles, in eleven days. Although movement was slowed at one stage to enable the drop at Tournai to take place, the operation was cancelled. Horrocks was to write:

> So late that night the airborne operation was fortunately cancelled and plans were made for the resumption of our advance into Belgium at first light. It was curious that during the whole of the advance we were constantly being 'threatened' by this sort of operation. *It soon became obvious that the vast, highly trained airborne army in the UK was bursting to go. Plan after plan was devised for their use, only to be discarded at the last moment.*[2]

The 11th Armoured Division reached Lens and in doing so overran launch sites for the V1 flying bombs which had become such a terrifying feature of life to the inhabitants of London and the Home Counties. The Second Army history noted: 'As a final plum from the fruitful tree of our advance, there fell into our hands the many flying bomb sites which had been set up just behind the French coast. From the viewpoint of the inhabitants of London, this was probably the most concrete result of the Allied pursuit.'[3]

In June, Herbert Morrison, Home Secretary, had warned the War Cabinet of the danger to civilian morale of these fearsome weapons. The location and destruction of both the V1 and, later, V2 weapons were to have a significant impact on Second Army operational planning.

Dempsey now issued a remarkable directive to Horrocks: 'XXX Corps is to capture a. Antwerp b. Brussels.' Admirably brief as it was, perhaps with hindsight it should have been worded a little more carefully. To take the second of these simple instructions first, Brussels was indeed liberated by the Guards Armoured Division in an astonishing operation. By driving hard through the day and night they arrived to occupy the city before the astonished Germans realized that they were anywhere in the vicinity. Brussels celebrated its liberation. Wherever the Guards halted, excited townsfolk swarmed over every tank, scout car or other vehicle, pressing bottles of wine on the crews. The noise was indescribable and as the lead elements headed for the Royal Palace, the Queen Mother of the Belgians was there to greet every soldier.

It was a brilliant operation and no less was the capture of Antwerp by the 11th Armoured Division. Heading straight for the docks, they seized them and their dockside equipment in full working order. Second Army had now advanced at an unparalleled speed for a week and Dempsey called a halt. He noted in his diary for 4 September:

> The very rapid advance of the past few days has placed a big strain on administration. Starting tomorrow, 1,000 tons a day are being flown in to Douai or Brussels for Second Army. Even with this it will not be possible to operate at full strength with three corps until we have in operation a proper port between Havre and Antwerp.[4]

On the same day, Dempsey was discussing with Browning and the staff of 21st Army Group a possible airborne operation against Nijmegen and Arnhem. Perhaps it was this that took his eye off the implications of his administrative problem. At this stage, Second Army, like all the Allies, was still being supplied almost entirely by what could be landed *over the beaches* in Normandy, hundreds of miles to their rear. With the capture of the docks at Antwerp, the problem appeared to have been solved. What everyone, from Eisenhower down, failed to appreciate was that holding the docks did not guarantee their use. Antwerp lies at the head of the Scheldt Estuary, both banks of which were held – and continued to be held for months – by the Germans. By failing to take this into account, the Allies made one of the greatest errors of the campaign.

On the day that Antwerp fell to Second Army, Admiral Sir Bertram Ramsay, Eisenhower's Naval Commander-in-Chief, sent him a signal at Supreme Headquarters Allied Expeditionary Force. He warned that if Antwerp and Rotterdam were to be opened quickly the enemy must be prevented from mining and blocking the Scheldt. If the enemy were to succeed in these operations, the time it would take to open the ports could not be estimated. Eisenhower, having become the Land Force Commander, had the responsibility of appreciating the strategic significance of this message. Unfortunately he was 400 miles from the front, with a badly twisted knee and poor communications. He failed to act. Some blame must also attach to Montgomery, also operating at the strategic/operational level. He admitted as much in his memoirs: 'I underestimated the difficulties of opening up the approaches to Antwerp so that we could make free use of that port. I reckoned that the Canadian Army could do it *while* we were going for the Ruhr. I was wrong.'[5]

Dempsey, commanding at the operational level, must also take some responsibility. Perhaps his order to Horrocks, so admirably terse in mission command terms, might have been better framed so as to include a rider 'and ensure that it is opened for our use', or something similar. Horrocks was quite open about his failure to appreciate that the Scheldt might be mined, and that 82,000 first-line troops and over 500 guns were being ferried across the estuary and would soon be threatening his left flank. He had the reasonable excuse that as a corps commander he was concerned with the tactical battle and nothing higher. The fact is, the headlong pursuit had engendered an air of overconfidence, an expectation that the war was almost won, and eyes were off the ball.

Not everyone was convinced that the Germans were finished. Stuart Hills, a junior officer in the Sherwood Rangers Yeomanry, was at Renaix in early September:

> General (later Sir Miles) Dempsey, Second Army Commander, called in to see us and declared that there was almost nothing to oppose us once we reached Germany. Some believed this kind of guff from on high, but not many. We had seen how the German Army had defended France and Belgium, and it seemed very unlikely that their resistance would suddenly disintegrate when they were defending their own homeland.[6]

Hills was right. Beyond Brussels, resistance was stiffening and his regiment was about to engage in some of the most bitter fighting it endured during the whole war. The German Army's headlong retreat had been slowed and then stopped by one man. Lieutenant General Chill of the German Army concluded that the only way to avert catastrophe was to set up a defensive line on the Albert Canal. Taking the remnants of his own division, he welded onto it a mixed bag of units and individuals from every part of the German armed forces. They were joined by parachute troops from General Student's

Air Army in preparing defensive positions and demolitions on the crossings. It was a remarkable demonstration of the power of recuperation of the enemy, directed by one man of energy and determination.

Second Army now had two tasks: to prevent the Germans breaking out of the 'bag' which had been tied by taking Antwerp; and to gain a bridgehead over the Rhine.

On 6 September, the Guards Armoured Division, leading XXX Corps, was ordered to capture two bridges over the Albert Canal. One bridge had been destroyed but the other, at Beeringen, was still usable by infantry and a small bridgehead was established. German resistance was now stiffening, and reinforcements were on their way down. The 50th Northumbrian Division was tasked to make another crossing and advance to Gheel, but they found themselves under heavy counter-attacks from German tanks and infantry. On 9 September, Dempsey noted:

> It is clear that the enemy is bringing up all the reinforcements he can lay hands on for the defence of the Albert Canal, and that he appreciates the importance of the area Arnhem-Nijmegen. It looks as though he is going to do all he can to hold it. This being the case, any question of a rapid advance to the North-East seems unlikely. Owing to our maintenance situation, we will not be in a position to fight a real battle for perhaps ten days or a fortnight. *Are we right to direct Second Army to Arnhem, or would it be better to hold a LEFT flank along the Albert Canal, and strike due East towards Cologne in conjunction with First Army?*[7]

Two days earlier, as his army was brought to a temporary halt to allow the badly stretched logistic chain to catch its breath, he had noted that operations were strictly limited by the administrative situation. Until a port capable of handling 5,000 tons a day was taken, until Dieppe was working, and until they could get a regular airlift of 1,000 tons a day, Second Army could not 'be developed' beyond Arnhem. The question now was whether Arnhem was the right place to strike at all.

The story of Arnhem – Operation MARKET GARDEN – is so well known that there will be no attempt in this book to retell it. Instead, it addresses the part played by Dempsey as Commander Second Army, responsible for the land operation, and the imperatives behind the use of the Airborne Corps. One thing should be made clear from the outset: the Arnhem operation was heroic. It was heroic in conception, heroic in execution and heroic in the actions of the individuals – British and American, soldiers and airmen – who engaged in that great undertaking.

Pressure was growing to employ the powerful Airborne Army. Commanded by an American, Lieutenant General Brereton, it consisted in one formation of all the Allied airborne assets, together with the air transport, RAF and USAAF, that could carry them into battle. The air assets, however, were not permanently tied to Brereton, and could be used elsewhere if so directed by Eisenhower. Indeed, his Chief of Staff, Bedell Smith, was already complaining of the effect on air resupply – necessitated by the tenuous lines of communication to which Dempsey alluded – of projected airborne operations. Each time a mission reached a certain stage, troop carrier planes had to be taken off lifting petrol to the front, grounded and made ready for parachutists.

The airborne elements included the American 82nd and 101st and the British 1st Airborne Divisions in the Airborne Corps, commanded by 'Boy' Browning. Brereton, who was only appointed in August, was an outstanding airman with no experience whatever of either land or airborne operations. He was, in Browning's view, confused, weak-willed and overcautious. They had a fundamental difference of view over the employment of airborne forces. Brereton insisted that the primary responsibility of any air operation was that the first troops on the ground must secure landing zones for resupply. Browning favoured the immediate capture of tactical objectives while the element of surprise was still in favour of the attacker. In this he had the full backing of Dempsey, who had planned and launched more airborne operations than either of them.

Browning, concerned that morale was suffering at the repeated cancellations, joined in the clamour for action. On 3 September, he signalled to Montgomery that since thirteen operations had been cancelled, four of them having reached immediate readiness, and without 1st Airborne or the 52nd Lowland Division having fought in France, he requested that his headquarters and both divisions be landed in Europe for operations immediately.

Looking back on the build-up to Arnhem, Horrocks believed that:

> The fly in the ointment was General Brereton's powerful Allied Airborne Army in the UK. By now it was bursting at the seams, having had no fewer than 16 operations cancelled at the last moment, owing to the rapidity of our advance … Back in Washington, General Marshall, the Chief of Staff of the US Army was urging Eisenhower to use this immensely powerful force in one operation to finish the war in 1944.[8]

Eisenhower had indeed been searching for both a target and a suitable opportunity to employ the force. He had been pressing Brereton and the various army commanders to develop bold and imaginative airborne plans calling for large-scale mass attacks deep behind the enemy's lines. A series of contingency plans had been drawn up, some in advance of D-Day, to employ airborne forces, most of them involving 1st Airborne Division. The first of these, Operation TUXEDO, was intended to drop a brigade anywhere required at four hours' notice. This was then upscaled to a divisional plan, and others followed in quick succession. Some of them even proceeded to the point where troops actually emplaned, but were aborted on the runway. Each plan involved a huge effort by air force and airborne staffs to prepare the detailed instructions demanded of any combined operation. The projected – but cancelled – operations immediately preceding Arnhem were for the capture of Boulogne and the V1 sites; support to the Seine crossings; landings ahead of the advance from the Seine; capturing Tournai; the Walcheren Islands; and Operation COMET, the first of the plans to capture a Rhine crossing, using two or three brigades only. There was indeed a huge head of steam, at all levels, to employ these superb soldiers, who were as frustrated at being denied action as their commanders were frustrated at being unable to use them. There was an intense desire to take the chance of any action that was offered.

Arnhem was not the only option. Having decided on 9 September that COMET must be postponed until the night of 11/12 September at the earliest, Dempsey now had the chance to rethink his plans. His preferred choice now was to cross the Maas at Venlo and the Rhine at Wesel, 40 miles further east towards the flanking Americans. Dempsey's reasoning was this:

> After Brusssels there were various plans for the use of the Airborne Forces, and by about the 8th or 9th I was convinced we ought to go for Venlo and Wesel. The reasons were that this only involved two major river crossings rather than three, and it also brought us down closer to the Americans. We had asked Bradley to extend 1st Army's boundary northwards, so as to help us if we went to Arnhem but he couldn't do this because his right wing was being continually dragged southwards by Patton. Consequently I felt that if Bradley couldn't come up to us we would have to go down to him.[9]

However, it was not to be. On 9 September, Montgomery received a signal from London concerning the landing of the first V2 rockets, with a request to 'report most urgently by what approximate date you can rope off' the area from which they were launched. When Dempsey flew up to see him the next day with his plan for Wesel, Montgomery met him at the door to his caravan with the telegram in his hand and said, 'Let us save England.' 'That decided the question. I don't think Monty had really made up his mind on Arnhem before he got the telegram.'[10] This begs consideration of two factors. The first relates to the importance of the V2 threat in making up Montgomery's mind. The second is the wisdom or otherwise of this decision.

On the first, it must be remembered that at this very moment Montgomery was consumed by one consideration – the adoption of a narrow thrust strategy, spearheaded by 21st Army Group, with overriding priority for logistic resources. This thrust would go north into Germany and then wheel right towards the Ruhr. Montgomery had been badgering Eisenhower, in the intense and unremitting fashion of which only he was capable, to be allowed to adopt this plan. He thought he had received Eisenhower's blessing and his agreement that 21st Army Group should 'have priority' for logistic support. But whether Eisenhower said this with his fingers crossed behind his back, in an attempt to rid himself of this turbulent field marshal, or whether it was an example of the 'common language dividing them', and 'priority' meaning 'absolute priority' in English English – but less than 'absolute priority' in American English – the fact was Montgomery was not to get it. On 10 September, though, he thought he was. This consideration may have persuaded him to stick with Arnhem, so as not to unsettle the overall plan.

The V2 menace was certainly a very real consideration. It was having an unsettling effect on civilian morale, particularly in a war-weary London. But it is hard to justify this – purely British – consideration as the basis on which to make a decision fraught with potential consequences for the whole Allied cause. If the war was indeed so close to its end, one course or the other would make little difference. Conversely, if German resistance was hardening, the better reason was to go for the more tactically viable plan. For in addition to the points brought out by Dempsey, the Maas at Wesel is considerably less of an obstacle than it is below Arnhem. And Dempsey, as the commander at the operational level, should have said so. If he had one great failing in the whole story that is Arnhem, it was that he did not stand up to Montgomery and argue the case against Arnhem as the objective. There are excuses. First, Montgomery's reasoning – questionable though it was – was couched at the strategic level, not strictly Dempsey's preserve. Second, Dempsey, like every other senior British commander, was in total awe of Montgomery. He had been proved right on so many occasions and he dominated any discussion, not by bluster but by cool, reasoned, military logic based on a lifetime of study and experience. So Dempsey, to his everlasting regret, acceded.

The decision taken that the objective should be Arnhem, Dempsey obtained from Montgomery his agreement that 'In view of increasing German strength on Second Army front in the Arnhem-Nijmegen area the employment of one airborne division in this area will not be sufficient. I got from C-in-C his agreement to the use of three airborne divisions.'[11] Dempsey immediately returned to his headquarters and began the planning with Browning, who had been in North-West Europe with a small planning staff for the last few days. They fixed the outline of the operation, to be known as MARKET GARDEN, which Browning estimated could be carried out on 16 September at the earliest. Browning left to fly back to Britain to plan his part, MARKET, and Dempsey then saw Horrocks, who had been summoned to his headquarters, and gave him the plan. Horrock's XXX Corps would be the major player in the ground role, GARDEN, with the cooperation of VIII Corps on its right, and XII Corps on its left. But now a major stumbling block on the planning of an airborne operation became apparent. Unlike the assaults into Sicily and Normandy, the troops to be committed to the operation, *and their headquarters*, were back in Britain, separated by hundreds of miles from the headquarters of the land battle. Once landed, the Airborne Corps would come under Dempsey's command, but until that point they were under Brereton.

Allied intelligence had, until very shortly before MARKET GARDEN, been bullish. A Joint Intelligence Committee Appreciation of 5 September suggested that German resistance might end by 1 December, or even earlier. By 10 September, this appreciation was beginning to change, but it is difficult, looking at the intelligence on German forces available to the Allies, to discern, with two possible exceptions, any sense that the forthcoming operation was likely to encounter insuperable opposition. The first exception is ULTRA, the intelligence produced by the deciphering of the German top-level codes, through the work of the Government Communications Centre at Bletchley Park. A worker at the centre wrote afterwards:

> This was the atmosphere in which the Arnhem operation was planned. It had a dulling effect on thought … which made it easy to dismiss the inconvenient and mutually supporting evidence of ULTRA and photographic reconnaissance instead of examining it with the care its provenance deserved. Even ULTRA's strong indication that two or more Panzer divisions were quartered on or near the MARKET GARDEN battlefield could not penetrate the wall 'cemented by confidence, complacency and an uncharacteristic refusal to weigh evidence' which some of its recipients had erected to protect their presuppositions.[12]

It cannot be denied that during the three or four weeks before the Arnhem operation ULTRA regularly produced intelligence about II SS Panzer Corps, consisting of 9th and 10th Panzer Divisions. This included the direction that any elements of these divisions not operating should rest and refit in the Venlo-Arnhem-s'Hertogenbosch area. However intelligence on these units dried up after 4 September, and the ULTRA evidence was neither complete nor entirely up to date on 17 September, the day the operation started. There was less ULTRA information about the German troops in the Nijmegen-Veghel-St Oedenrode-Son area. There was one major problem with ULTRA. It was so secret, so sensitive, that its distribution was extremely restricted. The lowest level to which it could be sent in 'raw' form was Second Army Headquarters, where a special handling team had exclusive control. Its content could not be passed, even to the Intelligence staff, unless it was camouflaged, and the intelligence obtained by some other means such as aerial reconnaissance. Certainly Second Army Intelligence Summaries in the period leading up to MARKET GARDEN show little awareness of any enemy location or activity which would materially affect the operation. On 15 September, two days before the launch, Summary No. 103 reported that on the eastern flank 116 Panzer Recce Regiment had 'provided its usual contribution to the day's battle' by revealing the location of 9th Panzer Division. ULTRA had reported 9th and 10th Panzer as being somewhere between Eindhoven and Arnhem as early as 6 September, but the area indicated in the summary nine days later was so large as to be of little tactical use, and it was certainly not on the outskirts of Arnhem. The next day's summary reported the presence of General Student, commanding the Parachute Army, in Tilburg, only 10 miles from XXX Corps' start line, but the summaries were only graded SECRET, not the highest classification, so it is unclear whether more precise intelligence was passed on directly to Dempsey himself. He certainly maintained after the war that his intelligence about German strength round Arnhem was faulty. Let Horrocks have the final word on what was known to the ground troops about to undertake GARDEN:

> I had no idea whatever that the 9th and 10th Panzer Divisions were refitting just north-east of Arnhem, nor had Dempsey as far as I know, yet both Montgomery and Browning knew that they were there, as they had been identified by air photographs ... and Montgomery eagerly grasped the chance of *an advance at last on a narrow front, which had originally been turned down by Eisenhower.*[13]

Back in Britain, Browning was receiving his own intelligence briefings on the enemy's dispositions in the Arnhem area. It is well known that Major Brian Urquhart (no relation to the Divisional Commander), the GSO2 Intelligence in the Airborne Corps headquarters, obtained aerial reconnaissance photographs which seemed to show a small number of modern tanks only 10 miles from Arnhem. The evidence was discounted and not passed to Dempsey or Horrocks. More importantly, it was not passed to the 1st Airborne Division. Browning pressed ahead with his planning, based on the discussions he had had with Dempsey on 10 September. There was one week before the off and a lot of planning to do.

The plan agreed between Dempsey and Browning for MARKET was for the American 101st Airborne Division to be dropped to secure the bridges north of Eindhoven; the American 82nd the five bridges over the Maas and the lower Rhine at Nijmegen; the British 1st Airborne at Arnhem; and a further brigade to be dropped at Elst to aid the advance from Nijmegen to Arnhem. The preferred option was for these drops to be made in the shortest possible time and at night. It was now that the fundamental divergences in philosophy between Brereton and Browning became apparent. Brereton insisted that the drops must be in daylight, be spread over three days and could not include the extra brigade at Elst. The American pilots did not have the navigational skills of the RAF, and he would not even consider a request from the RAF's 38 Group that a quick turnaround on the first day could enable one early drop and one late drop to be made. This would require that the approach flight at least be made in darkness – doubtless Brereton was mindful of the awful disaster fifteen months earlier when American pilots had dropped most of a British airlanding brigade in the sea off Sicily during a night operation. Restricting his room for manoeuvre was the fact that, despite Eisenower's promise – or what was understood to be a promise – to give 21st Army Group priority, aircraft were needed elsewhere.

More worrying, and fatal to the plan, the drops at Arnhem could not be made at the bridge, even by glider, as had been done with Pegasus bridge (in the dark!), or even on the Deelen airfield, close by. Reports of anti-aircraft defences – later found to be inaccurate – persuaded the airmen that the nearest drop to the bridge must be some 6 miles, and the furthest 8 miles, from the main objective, the road bridge. Dempsey considered that 'the distance of the DZs from the bridge was of course fatal'.[14] Of all the decisions that affected the outcome of the operation, this one, combined with a misappreciation of the enemy's capacity to react, was the most important. Another was Browning's order to Major General Gavin, the young and brilliant commander of the 82nd Airborne, to land on and secure the high ground overlooking the Nijmegen bridge, rather than land on the bridge itself. But Dempsey was unable to influence this part of the planning. The Airborne Corps did not come under his command until it had landed. Moreover, a further consideration now entered the equation. The option was open to place the three airborne divisions directly under either Dempsey's or Horrocks's command once landed. They were so spread that there was little coordination that the Airborne Corps could do that could not be done by a headquarters more intimately concerned with the other, inextricably connected part of the operation, GARDEN. In fact, as was later to be experienced, artillery support was more easily and intimately arranged directly between the air-dropped troops and XXX Corps than in any other way. Added to this was the possibility that the removal of the Corps Headquarters would free up thirty-eight gliders that were desperately needed for fighting troops. Dempsey could perhaps have insisted on this, but again physical distance was a barrier to communication and he did not do so. Browning and his headquarters were to land.

On 13 September, Dempsey flew to the headquarters of XXX Corps at Diest. There he discussed the forthcoming operation with Horrocks. Although the Airborne Corps would retain command of the 82nd and 1st Airborne Divisions, the 101st, on landing, would come directly under command of XXX Corps to secure the road between Eindhoven and Grave. He set the date for 17 September, at a time to be selected by Horrocks. He than flew to his Tac HQ at Perck and there confirmed with O'Connor and Ritchie the roles of VIII Corps, on the right with the 11th Armoured and 3rd Divisions, and XII Corps on the left with 7th Armoured, 15th and 53rd Divisions. To enable Ritchie to concentrate on this task, First Canadian Army would relieve him in Antwerp.

Changes to the plan continued to be made. When Dempsey discussed the plan with Browning three days before the operation, the intention was to put one brigade down at Elst on the first day, and to land the other two brigades north of the river. 'They had to change this because of shortage of aircraft, and the failure to secure Elst plus the attempt to hold the DZ and LZ were fatal to the plan.'[15]

On 16 September every commander in XXX Corps down to regimental and battalion level gathered in the cinema at Bourg Leopold to be briefed on GARDEN. Dempsey introduced the operation, stressing the vital importance of getting through to relieve the three airborne divisions before they could be overrun. He was followed by Horrocks, who described the plan to advance over an 'airborne carpet' along the one road available, to join up, eventually, with 1st Airborne at Arnhem. Some 20,000 vehicles would have to use this one road, which stood above the Dutch polder on either side. The country was very wooded and marshy, and Horrocks was in no doubt about the likely enemy reaction. Stressing that tough opposition could be expected, he said that the only possibility was to blast their way down the road. The Guards Armoured Division would lead initially, then the 43rd (Wessex) Division. Artillery support would be provided by 350 guns already in position and by rocket-firing Typhoons of Harry Broadhurst's always supportive 83 Group RAF. In case any of the bridges were blown, 9,000 sappers were organized in groups to replace each one. Traffic control would be a nightmare, and an elaborate system was set up to cope. But Horrocks, despite his conviction that they would have a very tough battle, was absolutely convinced that the operation would be successful.

The next day, as the vast airborne armada passed overhead, Horrocks gave the order, the guns opened up, and the Guards Armoured Division began their advance. The story of what followed is too well known to repeat here, but certain aspects deserve study. The first is the selection of the lead division and its performance at the time. Major General Adair, divisional commander, did not have an outstanding reputation, and was at times described as 'sticky'. Certainly the decision of Brigadier Gwatkin, commanding the lead formation, to harbour for the first night, rather than pressing on in darkness, has been questioned. They were also to be criticized for their alleged slowness to press on unsupported beyond Nijmegen. But Horrocks had selected the division because, in his words:,

> I was sure that if told to break out the Guards would certainly do so. The Guards tradition is such that when ordered to do something they will do it no matter what the cost. Guards Armoured had the better infantry and those splendid young officers who were prepared to give their lives without qualm or question.[16]

This high opinion was endorsed by Montgomery, who was heard to say that the Guards were the best troops he had under his command, because they would carry out their orders unquestioningly. Whatever the opinion of hindsight, it is worth recording the opinion of the American Major General Jim Gavin, in a personal letter after the war: 'I always thought the Guards were the best soldiers that I saw on either side during the war – not only because of their soldierly qualities, but because of their nonchalance and style; they seemed to enjoy what they were doing ... It was a remarkable division.'[17]

For all their quality, they could not prevent the enemy blowing the vital bridge at Nijmegen which delayed them by forty-eight hours. Nor, given his orders from Browning to take the Groesbeek heights as his priority, can Gavin be held totally responsible.

It is easy to say that there was insufficient drive, but Dempsey was certainly well forward with his Tac HQ. Having conferred with all three corps commanders at Bourg Leopold on 18 September, he moved to Son as soon as that was taken, and he arrived with the 82nd soon after they landed at Nijmegen. He came up to Gavin, shook him by the hand, and said, 'I am proud to meet the commander of the greatest division in the world today.' Leonard Rosen, a paratrooper of the 82nd, had an unusual encounter. During the fighting for the town, he was approached by Dempsey, who had come to observe the 504th Regiment's attack on the bridge. 'Our squad was practically wiped out,' said Rosen. 'We lost a lot of men there. He said to me "Who's in charge?" I said, "All dead." This did not stop the British general. "You're in charge," Dempsey shot back.' Although he was impressed that the general was near him in the thick of the action, Rosen took his sudden promotion with a grain of salt. 'He was a fine man,' he said of Dempsey.

On 21 September, Dempsey met Horrocks and Browning just south of Nijmegen, and urged Horrocks to keep up the pressure. Horrocks needed no urging. He was consumed by the need to get his corps spearhead forward to relieve Arnhem. The following day Dempsey was at Schaft, coordinating the assistance that O'Connor and Ritchie could give to the security of XXX Corps' route. On 23 September, he moved back to St Oedenrode to confer with all three corps commanders to ensure that everything possible was being done to keep open the axis of advance, and impressed on the commander of 227 Brigade the vital role his formation would have in protecting the bridge at Son.

For the first few days of the operation, little news came back from 1st Airborne. They had major communication problems, both externally and internally, so that initially all was assumed to be well with them. In fact, due to the capture of an entire set of orders for the operation from an American glider pilot, carried against all standing orders, the Germans arguably knew as much as the Allies. As it became obvious that the original timetable for their relief was not going to be adhered to, Browning raged at his impotence. But there was little that he could do to influence the outcome. Once the gallant men of the 2nd Parachute Battalion were forced from their tenuous hold on one end of the bridge at Arnhem, the entire *raison d'etre* of the operation was lost. As 43rd Wessex passed through Guards Armoured and prepared to cross 'the island' between Nijmegen and Arnhem, Dempsey at last became aware of the true situation. The heroic remnants of Urquhart's division were beleaguered at Osterbeek, west of the town, with a precarious foothold on the north bank of the river. General Thomas drove his men of the 43rd Wessex unsparingly, and on the night of 24 September, he determined to make a final push to cover the last 400 yards that separated them from the Paras. As Dempsey and Horrocks conferred by telephone, Lieutenant Colonel Tilly, commanding 4th Battalion the Dorsets, gave out his orders for the crossing. As he was about to lead his men off, he was told that the plan was no longer to expand the bridgehead, but to get the survivors out. Tilly was told that there was now no point in him leading the assault. In the expectation of certain death or capture, he did, and against all the odds survived.

Dempsey and Horrocks met that night at St Oedonrode. They agreed that unless 43rd Division were able to make a quick left hook further downriver, there was no point in maintaining the bridgehead. The next night they conferred further by radio, using a code. 'Little one' meant withdrawal, 'Big One' further crossings. Horrocks suggested that it would have to be 'The Little One'. Dempsey agreed and gave the order to wrap the operation up. The bridgehead must be withdrawn and all prospect of an early thrust into the heart of Germany was at an end.

Dempsey's critique was scathing. A huge admirer of Airborne Forces, he was less than complimentary about the planning of MARKET GARDEN, and some of those involved. It has been suggested that Montgomery's order that the ground attack should be 'rapid and violent, without regard to the flanks' was not complied with. Dempsey rejected any notion that XXX Corps lacked vigour in their push up the narrow axis dividing them from Arnhem. Horrocks might have faults, he said, but lack of drive was not one of them. He rated as the outstanding performance of the whole operation the way the 82nd Airborne Division fought at Nijemegen. 'It was easily the best division on the Western front.'[18] He thought 1st Airborne Division had little chance of success because their plan was so bad. It would have been better if they had never tried to bring in their third brigade and had instead concentrated on getting their original two brigades to the bridge. He later said that Arnhem failed for two reasons. One was the cancellation of the brigade drop at Elst, because of aircraft shortage. The other was Urquhart. Most unusually for the mild-mannered and charming Dempsey, on the subject of the commander of the 1st Airborne Division, he was, by his standards, vitriolic. In a letter to the official historian in 1962, he said: 'It would, I am sure, be the opinion of all those who know the facts that Urquhart was the most vocal, though not the most able, of the divisional commanders.'[19] He had earlier spelled it out in more detail:

> The primary reason was inept planning by 1 Airborne Division, loss of control by Divisional HQ, and the failure of their communications. They were never in the battle as a formation. Let me make it clear that the troops fought magnificently, and could not have done better individually … I had 1 Airborne Div under my command in Sicily and Arnhem, and 6 Airborne Div in Normandy and on the Rhine. The latter were far better at the top. There was no comparison between the two divs in that respect.[20]

An optimistic gloss was put on events in the Second Army Official History. As a rather low key aim it said that: 'Second Army was directed to place itself astride the Rivers Maas, Waal and Lower Rhine … and to dominate the country between the Rhine and the Ziyder Zee, thereby cutting off communications between Germany and the Low Countries.' It could therefore conclude optimistically that:

> At the time of Arnhem the enemy was well aware of the implications of the operation and that we were trying to finish the war in 1944. He fought with great determination to prevent a breakthrough. Nevertheless it was clear that the army task, to a very large extent, had been carried out. True, there was no bridgehead over the Rhine, and the more ambitious plans to sever Holland from Germany had been shelved. Apart from this curtailment, which had been conceded only after a fine stand by 1 AB Division, the Army had successfully advanced 60 miles into enemy territory, crossed the Rivers Maas and Waal in strength, withstood counter-attacks, and finally expanded the shaft of the spear with a secure lodgement in Southern Holland. This deep penetration was to serve as the springboard from which further attacks could be launched.[21]

The bitter fact was, though, that the daring attempt to pursue a 'narrow thrust' strategy had failed. The heroism of the soldiers of the Airborne Corps and of XXX Corps had not been sufficient to carry through an ambitious – some would say an overambitious – plan. There were some examples of poor planning; some of poor leadership and poor communication; of incomplete intelligence and intelligence ignored; and any number of examples of bad luck. If things had worked out a little better, these would have been overlooked. Although it may be claimed that Arnhem was a success at the operational level, but not at the strategic level, the verdict of history is that it was a glorious failure.

Dempsey did not attempt to deny responsibility: 'The plan was mine. It was not perfect – few plans are – and in several ways a calculated risk was taken. We secured a good bridgehead at Nijmegen, and we failed to get the final objective, which was a good bridgehead at Arnhem.'[22]

It was to be the last loud roar of the British lion in this campaign.

CHAPTER 13

'Halt'

It is with the greatest pleasure we are now able to record that Lt General Sir Miles Dempsey commands our Second Army. His meteoric rise from Lt Colonel to Lt General and from Battalion Commander to Army Commander in the space of a little over four years must surely constitute a record difficult to beat. On behalf of all members of the Regiment we extend to General Dempsey our very sincere congratulations in his responsible position, and to say how proud we feel and that our thoughts and good wishes will always go with him.[1]

The Regiment's congratulations and good wishes, though belated, were genuine, and were renewed shortly afterwards when Dempsey was advanced from KBE to KCB. He recorded the occasion, when the King dubbed him with a borrowed sword, with his usual understatement in the one word: 'Investiture'. It was held in an open field, with the sound of gunfire in the background, and inevitably invoked comparison with the knighting of Dempsey's ancestor 345 years earlier.

The period after Arnhem had been as busy as ever. On Urquhart's return from the battle, Dempsey debriefed him alone. Since his report was written up at the time, it is worth recording verbatim:

Owing to the shortage of transport aircraft, the landing of the Division had to be spread over three days, and owing to the suspected flak the dropping and landing zone was eight miles west of Arnhem. This meant that, of the force which landed on 17 September (1 Para Bde and AL Bde less one battalion), the Para Bde had to remain eight miles from Arnhem to guard the dropping zone for the subsequent arrivals. As was almost inevitable, the enemy came in between the two Bdes, each of which became isolated.[2]

They might both have been cheered to know that General Student, their opposing commander, had considered MARKET GARDEN to have been a great success, which brought the Second Army into possession of vital bridges and valuable territory. It had been a complete surprise, which, in his opinion, created a good platform for the offensive which contributed to the end of the war. But, whatever the thoughts of the enemy, the opportunity for a 'narrow thrust' – if it ever existed – was over. Despite Montgomery's efforts over the next few weeks to kick its embers into life, the policy was dead. Dead also was any pretence that Britain was any other than a very junior partner in an alliance that was dominated by the Americans. The British contribution had shrunk, following the disbandment of the 50th and 59th Divisions, to just three armoured and eleven infantry divisions compared to the American contribution of sixty.

The Allied front line now ran in an arc that followed the direction of the Rhine as it curved south to the Ruhr through Wesel and Homburg. To the west of the great river, the Germans occupied the territory up to, and in some places over, the Meuse, with the exception of the small salient at Nijmegen. The Allies now had to clear this belt, about 15 miles wide at the northern end, and 30 at the southern, between Venlo and Roermond. To enable Second Army to concentrate, it was proposed that the First American Army take over a major portion of the area west of the Meuse. On 26 September, Montgomery, Dempsey and Hodges, Commander First American Army, agreed that an American force would be assigned a corridor, 16 miles by 40, protruding into the British zone. Bradley, Hodges' superior, gave three reasons for not placing these forces under command of Second Army (and therefore under Montgomery's 21st Army Group). One of them was the American dislike of British rations, but it is hard to escape the notion that Bradley was unwilling to trust Montgomery, for whom he now entertained a hearty dislike, with command of American troops.

The Canadians were allotted the task of clearing the Scheldt Estuary, while Second Army was to clear the remaining pockets of German resistance south and west of the Rhine between the Canadians and Americans. It was time to put XXX Corps on the defensive, and for VIII and XII Corps to take on the burden of offensive operations. On 3 October, Dempsey saw Horrocks at his headquarters near Nijmegen. He impressed on him that in view of the persistent counter-attacks which the enemy were making north of Nijmegen, it was most important that the reliefs there should be properly handled. After a similar discussion with Browning, about to withdraw to England, he then moved on to discuss the VIII Corps situation with O'Connor. He was concerned with their right flank, also the flank of Second Army, which the American 7th Armoured Division was protecting.

Autumn was now closing in with a vengeance. Every day seemed to bring rain, and the polder, assisted by German engineers who opened the sluice gates, reverted to flood plain. The wet, the mud and the cold sapped morale. The almost sacred duty which British regimental tradition held should be accorded to providing at least one hot meal every day to every soldier, however far forward or however exposed, was never more important. Dempsey was acutely conscious of the conditions his men faced and made extra efforts to ensure that each division was rested, replenished and retrained. Over the next few weeks he visited as many formations as time allowed, usually talking to all lieutenant colonels and above. On 10 October, it was the 15th Scottish Division, a week later 7th Armoured at Nistelrode, where he gave a morale-boosting address. The 51st Highland Division followed, then all ranks of his own Rear Headquarters, then Guards Armoured, but it was not until 3 November that he could report, after a visit, that the 43rd Wessex Division was well rested and completely ready for offensive operations. The provision and quality of infantry reinforcements continued to be a major cause for concern until the end of the war.

In these conditions, attacks had to be small in scale, have limited objectives which could definitely be achieved, and have overwhelming firepower in support. On 28 September, the operation to clear the Peel Marshes began with the move of the American 7th Armoured Division, commanded by Major General Lindsay Silvester, through Second Army's area. Due to an underestimate of German strength, their attack through Overloon stalled. British artillery joined with the Americans to produce enough firepower to blast their way a little further forward, but by 5 October, 7th Armoured was halted. Dempsey came forward to discuss the situation with O'Connor, and at midday O'Connor and Silvester met him at his Tac HQ. It was clear to Dempsey that, with its present plan, the Division was unlikely to make any further progress. He was also concerned that, with the Division deployed as it was, they were not effectively protecting his right flank. 'Until sufficient American troops are made available, and are positioned correctly, a number of Second Army units will have to be used to fill the gaps – and these will be required on 10 October to take part in the attack.'[3]

Still concerned, the next day he flew to see Hodges. He repeated that it was quite clear that the American 7th Armoured was not going to make any progress, and agreed that they should side-step to the south-east and join up with the Belgian Brigade. Meanwhile Second Army would take over the Overloon area. But now Dempsey was becoming concerned that his whole command was becoming unbalanced. Enemy attacks on XXX Corps had been continuing, and he needed three divisions to defend the bridgehead there whilst an attack was launched in a south-easterly direction between the Rhine and Meuse. To clear the area west of the Meuse as far south of Roermond he needed at least two and probably three divisions. His conclusion was:

I have not enough divisions in the Army to carry out at one and the same time:

(a) A successful defence of the Nijmegen bridgehead.
(b) The elimination of the enemy on my right flank west of the R. Meuse; and
(c) An attack south-east between the Rhine and the Meuse.[4]

On 8 October the boundaries were adjusted again, to hand the Peel Marshes back to the British, at the same time placing American 7th Armoured under command of VIII Corps.

O'Connor's plan was to use the 3rd Division to take Overloon and push on to Venraij, while Silvester's division made a feint eastwards from Deurne. Despite the difficult terrain of marshes and woods, and dogged German opposition, supported by artillery and *nebelwerfers*, the 3rd Division's attack was successful. On 12 October, Overloon was taken, and on 17 October they were in Venraij. Operations in the southern sector were now halted temporarily while priority was given to the clearance of the Scheldt Estuary. Dempsey gave orders that XII Corps was to prepare to take over a slice of Canadian territory on Second Army's west flank; XXX Corps would take over the whole of XII Corps area; and VIII Corps should hand over the 15th Division to XII Corps, accepting that this would limit VIII Corps's operations.

This gave the Germans time to regroup and prepare a counter-offensive, which was launched on 27 October. The weight of the attack fell on Sylvester's men and Bradley now had to endure the mortifying spectacle of an American formation being baled out by the British. O'Connor sent his own armour to relieve the bridgehead at Deurne, and the arrival of British infantry and the employment of their artillery blocked the German advance from Meijel. The 53rd Division was also brought in to reinforce the sector and the German effort ground to a halt.

Bradley had had enough and Silvester was sacked. He believed that he owed his relief to a personality clash with Bradley and misunderstandings. Dempsey and O'Connor were horrified, the latter offering to resign. Perhaps they were not aware how quickly and easily, compared to the practice in the British Army, American commanders at all levels were summarily dismissed. One unit had eight commanding officers in one month. Prompted by a letter from O'Connor, which spoke of Silvester's 'whole-hearted cooperation, and his own dogged fighting qualities', Dempsey wrote to Montgomery:

There is no doubt that up to the time he was relieved in command of 7 US Armd Div, General Silvester co-operated wholeheartedly with Comd 8 Corps; I consider that this fact should be made known. The Division showed a fine fighting spirit in the battle at MEIJEL, where at the start it was heavily outnumbered. I have already expressed to the new Commander my appreciation of the Division's work.[5]

Montgomery, who may have been complicit in Silvester's removal, was unimpressed. Changes now took place at the top of Second Army. Dick O'Connor left for India, where he was to be GOC-in-C of Western Command, a promotion. The move was initiated by Brooke, but it was not opposed by either Montgomery or Dempsey. O'Connor was replaced by Evelyn 'Bubbles' Barker, another infantryman, two years older than Dempsey. Barker had commanded a brigade with distinction in 1940, but had seen no active service between then and D-Day. His command of the 49th Division, particularly during EPSOM, had impressed both the Army and Army Group commanders, and he was leading VIII Corps as Operation NUTCRACKER came to its successful conclusion.

At the end of October, Montgomery, Dempsey, Bradley and Simpson, commanding Ninth American Army, met. In view of the widening gap between Second and Ninth Armies, and the need to drive the enemy back behind the Meuse, the First Canadian Army would now take over the sector held by XXX Corps. The 7th US Armoured Division would revert to American command, and XXX Corps would take over the sector between Geilenkirchen and Maeseyck from the Americans. Dempsey would then order XII Corps on the right, and VIII Corps on the left, to clear the whole of the Venlo area west of the Meuse. Dempsey left the conference and headed straight for Ritchie's and O'Connor's headquarters where he briefed them on their roles in the forthcoming operation.

The move of Horrocks's XXX Corps to its new sector placed it alongside the Ninth American Army, now charged with taking Geilenkirchen. This town lay on the River Wurm, and from it radiated six roads which Ninth Army needed for their deployment. The Americans agreed that XXX Corps should run the battle to take it, with the American 84th Division under operational control. The British had three advantages: they had built up greater stocks of artillery ammunition; they had call on the 79th Division's 'funnies'; and they had experience, which the 84th, newly arrived in theatre, lacked. The 43rd (Wessex) Division, now rested and up to strength, was tough, well trained and experienced. The enemy was from the 15th Panzer and 10th SS Divisions, and the weather was appalling. As a young tank officer in the operation, Stuart Hills, said with masterly understatement, referring to the Americans, 'It was certainly not the best of circumstances in which to be taking an untried unit into battle.'[6]

On 18 November, the attack began, with the Americans of the 84th on the right, supported by the Sherwood Rangers Yeomanry and XXX Corps artillery, and the 43rd on the left. They fought their way into the outskirts of the town, but as the freezing rain came down in torrents they were counter-attacked. It was now that the Americans' inexperience began to tell. Despite the gallantry of their soldiers, their untried staffs were found lacking. In the 43rd Division the men received a hot meal and a fresh pair of socks every day; the American soldiers did not. To the reader sitting in comfort, this may sound rather irrelevant. To a soldier in a muddy field, cold and wet through, tired, lonely, hungry and frightened, and about to be called on to advance against the best infantry in Europe, it was the world. Horrocks tactfully suggested how the 84th could improve and, with the readiness to learn and adapt that was the hallmark of the American Army, they did. The battle consisted of a six-day slogging match against the carefully prepared concrete positions of the Siegfried Line. The weather remained awful and the ground was a sea of liquid brown mud. Progress was painfully slow and Geilenkirchen was not taken until 23 November. Dempsey and Horrocks were effusive in their congratulations to those involved. The Sherwood Rangers Yeomanry was described as one of the most experienced regiments in the western European theatre. The only trouble with such accolades, reflected Hills, is that you get to fight too often.

NUTCRACKER was the VIII Corps operation to knock the Germans out of the western part of the Maas (Meuse) region, near Venlo. To help overcome the awful conditions, VIII Corps used everything that Hobart's 79th Division could offer in the way of specialized equipment. In addition to the flail and bridgelayer tanks, and the Crocodile flame-throwers, O'Connor had introduced the Kangaroo. Similar in concept to a vehicle pioneered by the Canadian, Simonds, the Kangaroo was a tank with the turret removed, which carried infantry. Originally distrustful, Dempsey was now a convinced enthusiast of these strange beasts, and in the 'perfect battle of Blerick' they proved their worth.

Blerick was on the west side of the Maas opposite the larger town of Venlo. It was surrounded by a wide, deep, anti-tank ditch and extensive minefields. Its capture was entrusted to the 15th Scottish Division. In early December the flail tanks beat cleared lanes up to the anti-tank ditch, which was crossed by the bridgelayers. As the infantry in their Kangaroos crossed, the flails were already clearing further lanes beyond. Again, they stopped to allow the infantry forward, and in a few hours the town had been taken along with 250 prisoners for the loss of fifty British casualties.

At the end of the year, Maurice Chilton moved to Headquarters 21st Army Group and was replaced as Dempsey's Chief of Staff by Brigadier Harold Pyman from XXX Corps. 'Pete' Pyman was a Royal Tank Regiment officer who had excelled as Commanding Officer of 3 RTR in North Africa. Aged just thirty-six, he was an outstanding officer at both staff and regimental duty. He described his first meeting thus:

> It was about this time that I met our Army Commander. With his usual courtesy he rose from his seat as I entered the room. His name was Dempsey, who subsequently became one of my best friends, as I was one of his greatest admirers. I will not attempt to give a full description of his personality. Let me just say that I grade him as the perfect British officer, without peer. Self-assured yet modest, he had all the essential qualities of a great commander and a great soldier without any distracting qualities.[7]

He made an excellent team with Colonel Selwyn Lloyd, a civilian turned soldier, later to follow a distinguished career in politics. He had attended the first wartime Staff College course, and was now Colonel GS to Pyman and Dempsey.

Early the next year Dempsey wrote to O'Connor, now in India:

> We finished off the Venlo operation satisfactorily just as you left. We prepared and mounted the Sittard operation (clearing the Hun salient up to R Roer), but directly the snow set in we cancelled it for the time being and started re-grouping for the Reichswald operation – the drive South-Eastwards between the two rivers.
>
> As you know, Cdn Army were to carry out this attack as there was only one road by which it could be mounted – the bridge at Grave.
>
> Just as I was handing over the necessary divisions to Cdn Army the Hun's suicidal Christmas offensive started, and I had to block the gap quickly – roughly on the line Huy-Namur-Dinant-Givet. From that line we advanced Eastwards beyond Laroche-St Hubert, until the broken ends of First and Third Armies had been joined together again.
>
> The Americans, as you realise, were strung out at more or less equal density along their whole front and had no strategic reserve.
>
> For the sake of good relations our part in the Ardennes battle had to be kept pretty quiet. The Hun suffered considerably in this month and a minor Falaise was brought about – limited in result by the bad flying weather and difficult movement on the roads. But there is no doubt that Panzer Army 6 had taken a heavy knock when it was urgently required and moved to bolster up the Eastern front.

I was very stretched during all this, with 8 Corps from Gennep to Maeseyck, 12 Corps from Maeyseck to Geilenkirchen, and 30 Corps (the other side of Ninth and First Armies) in the Ardennes.

Directly all this was over I did the Sittard operation with 12 Corps. This went very well. Neil handled the whole thing excellently and casualties were not heavy.[8]

The references to the German Ardennes offensive, known popularly as the Battle of the Bulge, sum up in a few short paragraphs an extremely intense period in which, in short order, Second Army had to: reform, taking back under command formations recently grouped elsewhere; redeploy to cover the massive gap torn between the two American armies; and become the backstop against which the offensive would finally be halted before Brussels. It was an enormous load for commanders and staffs at all levels who had been virtually stood down and, although very little by way of fighting came their way, Second Army rose magnificently to the challenge. Dempsey was sanguine about the chances of German success, believing that he had plenty of reserves with which to stop them. During a visit to the Guards Armoured Division he remarked that the problem in winter was to get enough Germans out into the open to fight and now they were doing it themselves.

By Christmas Eve, as the German offensive was running out of steam, he was with Horrocks at Hasselt. He ordered him to move on to the offensive, with 29th Armoured Brigade operating east of the Meuse. With the 6th Airborne Division on its way from the United Kingdom, he could regroup from the quickly scrambled formation he had been compelled to adopt, and he could prepare to welcome its commander, Richard Gale, for whom he had plans for the future. By 30 December, he was confirming with Horrocks the move of XXX Corps under Canadian command for the clearance of the Reichswald. The emergency was over, but the fallout was not. Montgomery's disastrous press conference, tactless and misrepresented by a chauvinist press, worsened relations with the Americans still further.

Dempsey's reference to 'the Sittard operation' related to Operation BLACKCOCK which began in mid-January, with the object of clearing the Roermond triangle. This was the area bounded on the west by the Maas, the east by the Wurm and Roer, and to the south by the Siegfried Line, along the course of the Saerfeiler Beek. For this, XII Corps was given the 43rd Wessex and 52nd Lowland Divisions, as well as 7th Armoured Division. They were to be the major players, coming in to the triangle from the south, while VIII Corps was to hold the line of the Maas on their left flank.

The attack was on a north-east axis, with the 7th Armoured on the left aiming for St Odilienberg, the 52nd in the centre aiming for Heinsberg and the 43rd Division on the right. After four days the 7th Armoured Division was at Seint Joost, halfway to their objective. After twenty-four hours of intense fighting, the village fell to the Durhams and the Rifle Brigade, and by the end of the month the triangle was in British hands. Dempsey now prepared and briefed the 3rd Division under Major General Galloway for an assault crossing of the Maas further north at Venlo. This was to be his final operation for six weeks. Second Army was now stripped down to just three British and two American divisions, and put into reserve. Dempsey and his staff were to prepare for the last major operation of the campaign, the crossing of the Rhine. It was an opportunity for Second Army Headquarters to stand down for the first time in nine months.

Horrocks, suffering from exhaustion, had been sent on leave in January, and now Dempsey himself took the opportunity to fly to Pocklington, outside York, and then visit Kilnwick Percy. As well as a day watching his horse in training nearby, he visited the headquarters of the Royal Engineers bridging establishment, which had been experimenting at Goole, on the Yorkshire Ouse, with the equipment required to cross major obstacles. The Ouse at that point was particularly suitable because it was tidal, and Dempsey wished to confirm that he would have the capability to deal with a deep and fast-flowing river. He was away for only a few days and on his return he caught up on some regimental business. Among the hundreds of units in his army were two wartime battalions of the Berkshires, the 30th and the 5th. The latter were Lines of Communication troops, who carried out the humdrum tasks that fell to the lot of a second-line unit. Dempsey's visit was received with rapture and remembered for years afterwards. He was able to raise their morale by announcing that they would be employed in his next operation – they were to be part of a bank control unit for the crossing of the Rhine. He hinted at this enormous undertaking in early March in a letter to O'Connor: 'I am handling the next operation, the scheme and scope of which will be obvious to you. It needs some care and preparation, which I have been engaged in for some little time. Everything is going very well in this way, and I hope it will go with a bang when the time comes.'[9]

The crossing was to be launched on a 25-mile front between Emmerich and Rheinberg. Dempsey's plan was for the main Second Army effort to be made by Ritchie's XII Corps, supported by airborne landings, between Rees and Wesel, and by XXX Corps between Emmerich and Rees. The Ninth American Army would also make a crossing as part of the same operation, but to accommodate Allied sensitivities they would not come under Dempsey's command. The river crossings were to be known as Operation PLUNDER and the airborne operation, to be carried out by the British 6th Airborne and the American 17th Airborne Divisions, was to be VARSITY.

The greatest water obstacle in Western Europe, the Rhine here was a third of a mile across, flowing at between 2 and 4 knots. Defending it were four parachute and three infantry divisions, supported by two Panzer divisions. They were low in strength and the quality of their soldiers varied, but Dempsey was not going to take any unnecessary risks. The ability of the German Army to fight tenaciously in defence in the most disadvantageous circumstances had been demonstrated time and again. The anti-aircraft defences were also considerable and much planning was required to subdue them to allow the airborne operation a chance of success. In favour of PLUNDER was the crossing at Remagen, made just beforehand, which drew some German reserves southwards.

Elaborate measures were in hand to protect the security of the crossing points, which included strict control of reconnaissance parties. A dense and continuous smoke screen 50 miles in length was laid and kept in place before the assault, and an air bombardment of 50,000 tons of bombs softened up the defences. Thirteen hundred guns were in support of Second Army. Lessons had been learned from MARKET GARDEN and the airborne assault would not go in until the far bank was in safe hands. They would be close enough to ensure that a link-up was effected on the first day.

Preparation for the bridging itself had been under way for months, and the necessary 22,000 tons of assault bridging had been brought forward. This included 25,000 wooden pontoons, 2,000 assault boats, 650 storm boats and 120 river tugs. As well as the assault boats, 'Buffaloes' of the 79th Division would be used to carry troops and equipment across the river, and across the marshy ground on both banks. Another innovation that came to full flowering at the Rhine was Canal Movement Light, a rather ponderous name designed to conceal the use of anti-aircraft searchlights, divorced from their original role, to provide artificial moonlight as an aid to night operations. Based on trials by XII Corps, they had been used on an ad hoc basis in the Normandy battles. Now a battery was established in each corps, and they came to be regarded as an essential tactical aid, enabling the commander to 'make the weather' to suit his operation. They were employed for administrative purposes, such as speeding dumping programmes, as much as for tactical use for night attacks.

On the evening of 23 March, the 51st Highland Division assaulted across the river at Rees under cover of a huge artillery fire plan. Just after 2100 the Black Watch were the first British troops across. They were followed early the next morning by the 15th Division in the centre and by 1 Commando Brigade at Wesel, behind a concentrated attack by Bomber Command which flattened most of the town. At 1000 the air drop began and, although there were, again, some navigational errors affecting the Americans, it was deemed successful. Dempsey noted in his War Diary that out of a total of 1,587 troop carrying aircraft, fifty-four were lost, as were sixteen of the 240 supply aircraft. Second Army had suffered over 3,000 casualties, 1,400 of them among the airborne units.

Dempsey watched the landings from the high ground at Xanten, and then he himself crossed between Xanten and Bislich. After discussions with his RAF and American colleagues he flew up to Goch to find that the 51st Division, having established their bridgeheads, were now facing bitter opposition from German parachute units. One of the casualties was their popular and highly respected commander, Major General Rennie, who had done so much to restore the Division's morale and reputation. He was killed by a mortar bomb as he visited his men.

That evening, as news came that Wesel was in British hands, Dempsey could record that a very successful start had been made to the operation, but it was to be another twenty-four hours before Rees was secure. This obviously affected the construction of the bridges, but by the evening of 24 March several ferry sites were in operation, and the first bridge was completed thirty-six hours later.

On 25 March, Dempsey was at the headquarters of XVIII Corps of the Ninth American Army to confirm the handover of 1 Commando Brigade, who now had Wesel under control, and visited the commander of the 15th Division near Xanten. He watched the rafting operations at Wardt and saw Ritchie to confirm that the 53rd Division, followed by 7th Armoured, would follow up the next day and capture Bocholt. He then saw Barker to confirm that VIII Corps would relieve the American XVIII Corps on his right.

At this stage it was considered safe for Churchill and Brooke to accompany Montgomery on a visit. On 25 March, they drove to Wesel, where Churchill rather ill-advisedly scrambled about on the ruins of the bridge. The next day they picked up Dempsey, motored on to pick up Ritchie at his headquarters and then to Xanten. There they drove over the newly completed Class 40 bridge and on to Bislich, before returning to experience a ride in a Buffalo. At one point Churchill disappeared to have a victorious pee in the Rhine and Brooke summed up the feelings of all of them: 'I find it almost impossible to believe that after these 6 years of endless heartbreaking struggles, that we are now at last on the threshold of the end.'[10]

VARSITY was not without its critics. They focussed on what they called the excessive caution which had dictated such a large and complicated operation, contrasting it unfavourably to the 'bounced' crossing at Remagen. They also pointed to the casualty list, notably among the airborne troops. It is therefore interesting to look from the 'other side of the hill' at what the Germans thought might happen. ULTRA intercepts gave 'abundant evidence that 21st Army Group's attack was expected at the time and place at which it eventually occurred … Warnings of possible air landings were so frequent that they ended up seeming like cries of 'Wolf Wolf'.[11] With hindsight, then, it was only sensible to take the precautions that Dempsey did. It was, as Ronald Lewin wrote, the last time that mountains of metal and many thousands of men would be thrown into a large enterprise on a limited front where British power was predominant. But there was another consideration. If Second Army were to make the most of the opportunities offered by their crossing, they needed to move the enormous stocks of supplies and equipment, particularly bridging, that would be required to support a rapid and sustained advance to put the maximum area of Germany under British occupation. For not only did Britain need to demonstrate to its American allies that it was still a player to be reckoned with in the post-war settlement, it had to consider the Russians. At this stage, the occupation of Berlin by the Allies was still a possibility and Second Army was ideally placed to reach it.

By the evening of 28 March the bridgehead was 35 miles wide and had a depth of 20 miles. By the end of the first week, 2,000 tanks and self-propelled guns had crossed, and Second Army was ready for operations to exploit the opportunities offered. Above Dempsey's level, however, there was confusion and inertia. Lacking any overall direction from SHAEF Headquarters, each army group was free to develop its own plans and, within Second Army, commanders were straining to push on. Inevitably each had a compelling reason why the Second Army reserve, the 11th Armoured Division, should be employed in his particular sector. Pyman said afterwards that one of the aspects of Dempsey's handling of his corps commanders which he most admired was his tight control of his reserves. Although transporters were ready to bring the 11th Armoured Division forward 'at one jump', he was in no hurry to allocate them. He would place them in whichever sector showed the best prospects of a breakthrough. At that stage it looked to be an equal bet between VIII and XII Corps, who led the advance initially; but as VIII Corps moved out on to the right flank of his army, Dempsey gave Barker the reserve to add to the 15th and 6th Airborne Divisions, fighting in an infantry role. They captured Osnabruck, Minden and Celle, before crossing the Elbe at Lauenburg in the vanguard of Second Army. The 6th Airborne got to Wismar a few hours before the Russians and had the honour of saving Denmark from a second occupation.

Ritchie's men had been first over, with substantially the whole of XII Corps across on 27 March. The 7th Armoured Division led their advance across the Westphalian Plain and by 4 April, it was on the line of the Dortmund-Ems Canal. The 52nd Division crossed and by 10 April lead elements were within a few miles of Bremen. Taking this large city was going to be a major operation and it was left to XXX Corps, advancing on their flank. Dempsey summed up the situation in a letter to brother Patrick: 'As usual – ever since June 6th last year – opposition has been much stiffer on the left than elsewhere. Fanatical hordes are fighting to keep us away from Bremen and Hamburg – and will I think continue to do so. Blowing every bridge and culvert and hanging on to the numerous river lines.'[12]

The assault began on 24 April, and after some heavy fighting the 52nd Division broke through the German defences into the city centre, while the 3rd Division, supported by 'Buffaloes' and flame-throwing tanks, penetrated the southern part of the city. Along with Guards Armoured and 43rd Wessex, they now swept on to clear the area between the Elbe and the Weser.

Bremen was unusually hard, but not an exception. Such resistance as there was in the main came from old men or very young boys armed with the occasional *panzerfaust*. But they could do damage. Of 1,000 tanks in Second Army, 125 were destroyed or badly damaged, and 500 more were temporarily incapacitated in the few weeks after the Rhine crossing. No one wanted to be the last British soldier to die and it took all Dempsey's powers of leadership to press his advantage home.

To 'Pete' Pyman, his devoted Chief of Staff, this period showed Dempsey at his best. When two SAS troopers, Albert Youngman and Gordon Davidson, escaped from German captivity after a deep penetration operation behind enemy lines, they were taken in front of Dempsey for debriefing. After asking about German movements he said he presumed they thought they had some repatriation leave due to them. Yes, they replied, but Dempsey was having none of it. Knowing that the end of the war, and all the leave they wanted was close at hand, he sent them back to the SAS to pass on their first-hand knowledge.

The River Aller was crossed by the 53rd Division in mid-April and by the end of the month XII Corps was investing Hamburg. On 2 May, the 11th Armoured Division reached Lübeck on the Baltic in VIII Corps's last operation of the war. Berlin, to Montgomery's dismay, was not on the agenda for Second Army and fell to the Russians.

Despite the fact that history was being written around him, Dempsey refused to allow himself to be ruffled out of his calm routine. When Himmler was arrested, Dempsey took the news from Pyman with total detachment. Later that evening, he was dining out Selwyn Lloyd, who was about to return to civilian life, when Pyman rang him at Tac HQ to say that the acting Head of State had committed suicide. 'What is the matter with you tonight, Chief of Staff ?' asked Dempsey. On being told, he simply replied, 'Good. Good night.'

It was during these last days of the war that Dempsey became aware of the existence of the concentration camps that his men were uncovering.

Reports came in of the suffering undergone and the brutality meted out on a massive scale that had stained the Germans' reputation; on 15 April, Belsen was liberated. Dempsey went in with Selwyn Lloyd to find 10,000 unburied corpses. In the next few days a further 17,000 inmates died and hearts were hardened as surrender negotiations got under way in early May. For Second Army, events took on an almost comic turn when a delegation of senior German officers turned up to arrange terms. On 3 May, they were seen by Dempsey at Tac HQ. After a short period of questioning it became apparent that General Admiral von Friedeberg was a representative of General Keitel, who wished to surrender to Montgomery. They were sent on their way and Dempsey then began to deal with Major General Wolz, commander of the Hamburg Garrison.

Dempsey sat with Pyman, facing Wolz and his staff officer, while his orders were passed on through an interpreter. He started with his conditions, each of which was accepted, with the exception of some minor points, such as the preservation of all records, codes and so on, with which Wolz could not promise immediate compliance. Dempsey ordered him to do his best to maintain law and order in the city, make sure that the radio station was undamaged and ensure that all aircraft were grounded. It was, in Pyman's opinion, a model of the way such negotiations should be conducted, and a few days later the same procedure was initiated with Blumentritt. The general principles of administration of millions of German, Danish and Dutch civilians, and hundreds of thousands of German soldiers, were coordinated at this first meeting, after which Pyman took over for subsequent ones.

Montgomery was quick to show his appreciation of Second Army's achievements under Dempsey, who replied to his congratulatory letter:

My dear Field Marshal,

Thank you very much indeed for your letter, which I appreciated more than I can say.

Though we had occasionally met before, it was only two and a half years ago that we started serving together. A comparatively short time – but every day has been historic.

I am quite sure I could not have kept up the pressure under anyone else. Loyalty goes both ways – up and down – and the certainty of your loyalty to me – that you were behind me – has made things easy, even in the more difficult times.

I only hope that I may continue to serve under you in the days that lie ahead.[13]

It was time for mutual congratulation and it is appropriate to reflect, as Dempsey ceased, for the last time, to command British soldiers on operations, how he ranks in the body of Second World War commanders. Inextricably woven into all he did was his relationship with Montgomery. The point has already been made that he was one of 'Monty's men'. In fact, he could be said to be, above all others, 'Monty's General'. Although he undoubtedly owed his extraordinary preferment in part to Brooke, the same could be said of almost any other British general of the period. The eighteen months in which Brooke shaped the future army saw virtually all of them stand or fall. But it was only a chosen few who were picked up by Montgomery. Service in the front line in the First World War, the hardening of ambition and the training of the intellect arising from his service in north-west Persia; the long years of grind preparing for and studying at the Staff College; peacetime service in a first-class county regiment; and the flowering of his military talent in the BEF of 1940 – these were the preparation. But there must have been something else that caused Montgomery to select him, above all others, mostly senior to him, to command Second Army.

The obvious answer would be that he considered Dempsey to be a 'yes man', as Patton described him. But this facile explanation does not bear scrutiny. An easily malleable character would not have been able to command the respect of his highly capable and ambitious corps commanders. Nor would he have been of use as a sounding board for Montgomery's ideas. What Montgomery saw in Dempsey was someone who shared his philosophy of leadership, his lofty ideals and unshakeable belief in the rightness of their cause, and the ability of the British citizen soldier to prevail; but he also recognized that he possessed certain personal qualities that were the opposite of his own. Where he was convinced that he was right, Dempsey possessed the patience and tact to persuade him that another course was really his own; he was content to allow glory to go to Montgomery, while seeking none himself; he was prepared to give total loyalty to him; and he was a superb battlefield commander whose judgement could be relied upon.

Dempsey's qualities were tested to the full, not least in Normandy, where Second Army took on and maintained the unglamorous and taxing role of attracting the German armour, while the Americans broke out; and in taking responsibility for the Arnhem operation and the Rhine crossing. But in return he received Montgomery's full confidence and backing. Where there was glory, Montgomery took it; but where there was blame, he also took it. They complimented each other perfectly.

When Ronald Lewin asked O'Connor for his opinion of Dempsey, he found it interesting that O'Connor had nothing illuminating to say, beyond the routine response that Dempsey was a decent chap, nice to serve under.

But when asked what he had contributed, beyond being a usual channel between Montgomery and his corps commanders, there was really no answer. The point has been made by others, and it is a fair one, that Dempsey played little part in the shaping of strategy; but that is as it should be. His was the operational area of command that fuses the strategic and tactical. From the Combined Chiefs of Staff, through Eisenhower and his Army Group commanders, strategy was formulated and disseminated. Dempsey's task was to put the nuts and bolts in place to achieve the strategic aim; to organize, disseminate and supervise the unfolding of the plan. He was not the artist, creating the design, but rather the artisan, polishing and perfecting the execution. He was Soult to Montgomery's Napoleon. It is open to speculation how he would have fared in an independent theatre of operations, if he had, like Allenby, been taken from command in a theatre where his actions were circumscribed by conditions, and his own genius allowed to flower as Allenby's did in Palestine. Pyman had no doubt on that score:

> So far I have said little about Dempsey as a soldier, but let me, now, just very briefly, say this. He was superb. He commanded the only British Army in North West Europe … He really understood the British soldier, and we all trusted him. His regimental and staff duties (which included one job as Chief of Staff of a Canadian corps) had given him a wide basis of experience to which he brought his own unique qualities. He trusted his subordinates to do their job and demanded (and got) trustworthiness in return. He was, by nature, almost merciful to a fault, but when his duty demanded it he could be utterly merciless. I am quite sure that Miles Dempsey could have run anything. His powers of leadership were boundless. It is not every soldier one can say that about.[14]

Let the last word rest with Selwyn Lloyd, a 'hostilities only' soldier who owed no allegiance to the British Army establishment. As a politician with a brilliant career at cabinet level, his view demands respect:

> He was a great commander and a remarkable man. That this was not more widely realized was solely due to his modesty. He disliked publicity. He shrank from anything that seemed like self-advertisement. He would not tolerate any notion of flamboyant anniversaries of his Army's achievements.
>
> He was an outstanding commander. I crossed the Channel with him on D-Day in the destroyer Impulsive. He was calm, fresh, fit and confident. He was ashore early on D plus one, and wherever he

went he inspired confidence, and was a most welcome visitor to any harassed commander of any subordinate formation. Time and again he realized the tactical opportunity and saw that it was exploited. But his experience in the First World War, particularly at Passchendaele, had made him determined to have no unnecessary casualties. He was very careful of the lives of his soldiers.

His military gifts were obvious to all who served with him. He was an immensely able, dedicated professional.[15]

Pyman's judgement was about to be fulfilled. For the next two years Dempsey would take on huge responsibilities in a world now at peace.

Chapter 14

'Stand Fast/Cease Firing'

Immediately the surrender document was signed, Dempsey issued an instruction that his troops were to stand fast on a line from Donitz to Bremen. No advance beyond this line was to take place without his personal orders. The immediate problem facing Second Army was conversion from a war-fighting organization to the administration of an occupied country, and the next day he issued the following directive:

1. That chaotic conditions, both military and civil, exist in the unoccupied portion of GERMANY is now known. The full extent of these conditions is still under examination.
2. Second Army will proceed to disarm the remnants of the German armed forces, to organise the return of Allied prisoners of war and displaced persons, to organise prisoner of war areas and to restore law and order within its zone.[1]

Directing each corps to maintain law and order within its area, he ordered that large prisoner-of-war zones be set up by three of them, each capable of holding 700,000 men. To deal with the German Army, a temporary system of control and administration was instituted. The counterpart of Headquarters Second Army was set up and commanded by Blumentritt.

On 12 May Dempsey issued a further directive:

1. Matters are now beginning to take shape in Second Army area. There is much to be done; a large measure of decentralization is necessary, and it is important that everyone should be quite clear as to the policy to be followed and the immediate tasks to be carried out.
2. In order to get the area controlled and organised as we wish, the following tasks have to be done:

(a) The concentration of German prisoners;
(b) The evacuation to the UNITED KINGDOM of British and American ex-prisoners of war.
(c) The handing over of Russian ex-prisoners of war to the Russian Army.
(d) The evacuation Westwards of displaced persons, other than Russians.
(e) The spreading of German refugee civilians over a wide area so that they can feed off the country; and
(f) The concentration of Russian civilians East of the British boundary.[2]

The simplicity of the orders conceals the state of near anarchy to which the Third Reich had descended. Millions were on the move: German soldiers trying to return home; German civilians fleeing the Russians; liberated prisoners and slave labourers living off the country; Allied soldiers going about their business. The roads were choked, law and order was almost non-existent. The policy of unconditional surrender had left no German central authority. Fear of reprisals had caused most of the officials that remained to go into hiding, so there was little administrative capacity at local level either. There was no food distribution, no services, little shelter. Devastation by bombing and ground fighting had shattered the infrastructure and the economy.

One of Dempsey's priorities was to adjust the mindset of his soldiers from a wartime to a peacetime mentality. He issued another order: 'Now that the fighting has ceased it must be realised by all ranks that wanton and unnecessary damage and stealing are not permissible and any case will be treated as a very serious offence.' The reminder was salutary, but returning to peacetime standards of discipline was a minor problem compared with some of the moral dilemmas that faced British soldiers on a daily basis. Dempsey was able to discuss some of these problems when he visited the First Battalion of his own regiment, who were now based at Wunsdorf. The Berkshires had had a distinguished record in the war, with many battle honours gained, most of them in the Far East. Dempsey was received rapturously by the Battalion, commanded by Lieutenant Colonel Hogg. He spent a happy day with them and came away refreshed in spirit.

The sort of problems that he could discuss on an informal basis were now commonplace for soldiers throughout the Allied zones. There was a strict policy of non-fraternization; but how did that apply when a German child was starving? Russians were to be repatriated to their zone, but how did that apply to a Ukrainian who had served in the German Army and was facing death if handed over? How were concentration camp guards to be handled? How were slave labourers to be prevented from taking revenge on their erstwhile masters? The potential pitfalls became apparent early on when Horrocks was attacked in the British press for staging a party for German children. These matters now became Dempsey's daily concern, but only for a few weeks.

Some months earlier Dempsey had been nominated to become Commander-in-Chief British Troops Austria, but this was now cancelled. On 4 July, he was called to an interview with Brooke, who told him he was for the Far East. Brooke was very disappointed at his attitude and recorded in his diary: 'He is suffering from a swollen head, and I took some pains to deflate it.'[3] This account of Dempsey's future appointment to take over command of the Fourteenth Army from Bill Slim makes uncomfortable reading. If there is one quality that everyone who knew Dempsey agrees on, it is his humility. The explanation possibly lies in Brooke's and Dempsey's tiredness at the conclusion of years of superhuman effort during which neither had spared himself; indeed Dempsey had remarked, only half in jest, to Pyman that they might take a year or two out to write the Second Army history. But there is another possible ingredient. The move of the popular Slim, still fighting the Japanese in Burma, had been initiated by Leese, who had moved to South-East Asia as Land Force Commander the previous year. He had unwisely tried to shunt Slim sideways to command another army. Slim had threatened resignation, but it was Leese who had to go and Slim who took over his job. Dempsey could well have seen his move in a similar light to Slim, and moreover one that he, as a bachelor, could be told off for at a moment's notice. He was mollified by a charming letter from Mountbatten, Supreme Allied Commander South East Asia, mentioning that Slim's promotion had left a vacancy for which he had been offered Dempsey:

> You can imagine that I jumped at it. Although I only met you for a brief while with Field Marshal Monty in Sicily, I know from Boy Browning and others what a wonderful job you have done throughout the war, and we shall all count ourselves extremely lucky that you are coming to run the 14th Army.[4]

Happily, Dempsey was only to be in command of Fourteenth Army – double hatted as GOC-in-C Malaya – for a matter of weeks before he was promoted to Slim's new post, while Slim moved on to the Imperial Defence College, and in good time to the post of CIGS. Happily also, because the incumbent had been damaged by the spat with Leese, Pyman was moved to be Chief of Staff Allied Forces South East Asia (ALFSEA) at almost the same time. The team were back together, but the command set-up was not entirely to

Dempsey's liking. Shortly after his arrival, while still at Fourteenth Army, he wrote to brother Patrick:

> There are too many large HQs here now, and the obvious solution is to fold up 14 Army. I would do it today – because I know it's the right answer. But I am afraid it will take longer than that! Meanwhile I have got absolutely nothing to do – and am merely wasting my time and the Govt's money.[5]

and to his old friend Dick O'Connor in India:

> My dear Dick
>
> I have not written to you before – because I had hopes of seeing you. But I do not see much chance of that now – at any rate in the near future.
>
> I realise only too well how true your letters to me were. What an extraordinary business this is. I will not comment on the plan for capturing Malaya – beyond saying that it is a good job the Jap chucked it when he did! I have never seen such a fantastic set-up, as was planned.
>
> Now we have all these large HQs, tumbling over each other, and an apparent desire not to demolish any of them. I have had no troops at all in the Army since I took over, and when I am inserted into the scheme – in Singapore – it will look like this:

<pre>
                        Supremo
                           |
                   Army Group (Alfsea)
                           |
                        14 Army
                           |
          _____
          | |
     34 Corps Malaya   15 Corps Singapore
       (Two divs)   (One div)
</pre>

> I have never felt quite so useless – or more like a spanner in the works – in my life! I hear that you are leaving E. Comd and going north-west. How does that appeal to you?
>
> At Cam Nicholson's invitation I went to see 2 Div yesterday. A fine division – almost unique these days in that they have, thanks

to low casualties, so many men of long service. I impressed upon the B.M. 5 Inf Bde the necessity of maintaining the standard of his predecessors!

Good luck, Dick, I am longing to see you again.

Yours ever, 'Bimbo'.[6]

'Bimbo' was a nickname that Dempsey used sparingly, and then only to those he considered lifelong friends, or equals. Its provenance has never been explained, but since it seems to lie in some mildly embarrassingly incident in Dempsey's past, perhaps this is not surprising. The mention of the Brigade Major of 5 Infantry Brigade was of course a light-hearted reference to the fact that both O'Connor and Dempsey had filled that post during their careers. The invasion plan was an altogether different story.

The plan to recapture Malaya – Operation ZIPPER – involved a number of assault landings on the coast. Although the full operation was rendered unnecessary following Japan's surrender, the landings went ahead. It was thought that a demonstration of what had been planned would be a salutary lesson to the defeated generals. They were lined up on one of the target beaches and the invasion fleet was unloosed – only to founder abruptly a quarter of a mile from shore on a sand bar that had not been properly reconnoitred. The Japanese watched the performance with inscrutable expressions. This was not the only flaw in the plan. Dempsey, who rightly considered himself something of an expert in combined operations, was scathing: 'You will understand something of what I mean when I tell you that – at the end of a month, without opposition, and with virtually no ammunition – there were two days supplies ashore.'[7]

The command organisation under Mountbatten continued to irritate Dempsey, who wrote: 'The organization of command in S.E. Asia I can best explain by quoting a remark which Dickie M. made to S of S for War and myself: "I always like to have my three advisers round me" (Power, Park and Slim). But he's a grand chap!'[8]

Dempsey had arrived in the Far East as the war against Japan ended, following the atom bomb attacks on Hiroshima and Nagasaki. Many of the problems confronting him were similar to those in Europe at the conclusion of hostilities. There was one great difference. The peoples of South-East Asia, with the exception of Siam, were in theory subjects of the British, French and Dutch empires. As the war ended, the Command's boundaries were extended and now stretched from Burma through Siam, French Indo-China, Malaya and Borneo to the whole of the Dutch East Indies. In all of these countries, nationalist movements, quiescent or actively anti-Japanese during the war, now began to work for independence from their colonial masters. Their activities ranged from armed insurrection in the Dutch area to *dacoity* in Burma.

Within the command were 122,700 British and Dutch prisoners of war and internees to be rescued, and 733,000 Japanese soldiers. The economy was debilitated by war and Dempsey wrote to O'Connor from his new headquarters in Singapore:

> I spend most of my time on semi-civil matters; trying to get rice into the country is the problem which overshadows everything else. The Colonial Office administrators are nice people, and pretty good: but they are accustomed to taking their time. There are all sots of interesting – lesser – problems; collecting and evacuating our P.O.W.; running Singapore (800,000 souls) without a police force; getting Rubber going again – and, more slowly, Tin: I brought 5 Para Bde into Singapore directly I took over, and they are quite first class – as one would expect.
>
> We have a wonderful opportunity in Malaya, and I pray that the right men are appointed as Governors. Harold Mac M. I met for the first time when he landed a few days go; what a splendid person: we rather naturally talked of you! He is out here fixing up things with the Sultans.
>
> What of the future? I would love a talk with you as we had in Aldershot in 1934. I think the time really is coming now![9]

The reference to the 1934 talk reveals that already, so soon after the end of the war, Dempsey was thinking of retirement. For the moment, he soldiered on. An article in a local paper gives a very good idea of how he was viewed in his capacity of General Officer Commanding Malaya, one of many hats he wore:

> The average citizen is still not yet conscious of the fact that GOC Malaya is virtually the Military Governor of Malaya, with all the powers of a Military Governor – and that is no small compliment to Lieut General Sir Miles Dempsey. So far from there having been any attempt to rule the population of Malaya in a spirit of army discipline, the man-in-the-street still does not know that the ground-plan of the present temporary government shows General Dempsey at the head with two staffs under him: the staff of the Fourteenth Army, and the British Military Administration. To bring out further the main outline of the picture, it should also be stated that this dual machine of power and organisation under the GOC's hand has been directed recently

at four main objectives: firstly the disarming and concentration of the Japanese forces; secondly, the repatriation of Allied prisoners-of-war and internees; thirdly the relief and rehabilitation of the civil population; and finally preparation for the restoration of civil administration at the earliest possible moment.

We have seen for ourselves the progress that has been made along these four parallel lines. Malaya will soon be cleansed of the alien taint more completely and quickly than we had believed possible, and we trust that the hundred thousand Japanese troops and civilians who are to make a temporary home of their own on an island in the Rhio Archipelago will be given the object-lesson they so badly need in civilised standards of treatment of prisoners.[10]

Dempsey's anger at the behaviour of the Japanese was fully expressed when he met their commander in September. Referring to the prisoners he said:

I shall ship the whole bally lot of them to a group of Dutch islands south of Singapore. They will be dumped on the beaches and left there. I am allowing them 10 oz of rice daily, which should reduce their waists a little. As most of the islands are uninhabited the Japs will be able to start a brave new world for themselves, but they will not be able to harm anyone outside.'[11]

The end of the war resulted in a demand to run down the forces as quickly as possible and return the large proportion of conscripts to civilian life. For Dempsey this involved a juggling act, as he retained enough armed strength to deal with the numerous trouble spots within his command, while reducing where possible. He had his eyes particularly on the headquarters and their staffs, of which he thought there were too many. By October, his strongly stated opinions had convinced Mountbatten, who agreed to cut his own staff by 90 per cent, and insisted that subordinate commanders do likewise. In November, the famous Fourteenth Army was disbanded and Dempsey became Commander-in-Chief Allied Forces South East Asia.

The situation in the colonies was not settled so easily. The most pressing military problem was in the area colonized by the Dutch, now known as Indonesia, where in August, Soekarno had proclaimed a republic. His followers had armed themselves with weapons surrendered by the Japanese and one of Dempsey's first decisions was to send the 23rd (Indian) Division to reoccupy Java, along with a small Dutch military mission. They were followed by further reinforcements, but in the interim Japanese soldiers were used to fill the vacuum and help keep the peace. This was highly embarrassing for the Allies and in October, Japanese troops used against insurgents in Semarang and Ambarawa performed so well that General Christison, Commander Allied Forces Netherlands East Indies, asked that some of them be granted special commendations for gallantry. By the time the request reached Dempsey, Christison had been replaced by Monty Stopford, Dempsey's fellow brigade commander in the dark days of the BEF. Dempsey had no difficulty in declining the request.

At the same time as the Japanese were involved, British Indian forces were engaged in a major confrontation at Surabaya. Brigadier Mallaby, commanding a brigade in Major General Hawthorn's division, was killed by nationalist insurgents while negotiating a ceasefire. The Division, reinforced by the 5th (Indian) Division, was now involved in serious house-to-house fighting as it cleared Surabaya and lost several hundred killed. It was the bloodiest engagement of the insurrection and concentrated minds in London. Operations continued to rumble on into December, but further reinforcement was difficult due to the shortage of shipping, and further embarrassment was added to the controversy over the employment of Japanese troops when a number of civilians were alleged to have been massacred by Indian troops at Bekassi. The affair was highlighted in the British press and a belated finding that the casualties had been suffered in the course of operations, and not as a reprisal, came too late for the Chiefs of Staff to make suitable representations.

Mountbatten agreed with the Atlee government that using British troops to assist the Dutch to regain their empire was not a suitable or feasible proposition. The granting of independence, which Britain now supported, was but a matter of time.

By January 1946, Dempsey was wondering about his future and wrote to Patrick:

> Heaven alone knows what my plans are! I am warned – keep this to yourself – by Brookie that I will probably leave here in April or May 'for another appointment' ... Directly we can get this damned Java business settled things will be fairly straightforward out here – and I might be able to start leave in April: anyway I want to see The National. We have reached full deployment now – having put troops into Borneo and Celebes to collect Japs – and I have got W.O. and India to agree to my withdrawal plan, which has started at full bat, and is limited only by shipping. I was in Borneo and Labuan this week; they are exactly my idea of where Robinson Crusoe lived!
>
> But apart from all this I don't know that I want 'another appointment' ... For not too long a period this is a very attractive place – with a

good, though lazy, climate. I have got by far the best house I shall ever live in … So for the months of December, January and February it is not a bad place to live. When March comes – that is another matter altogether.[12]

The restrictions on shipping continued to be a headache for the next six months, limiting the rate at which troops, the majority from India, could be repatriated, either for redeployment to their home stations, or for demobilization. A paper prepared for Dempsey in early 1946 outlined the plan. From a strength of 600,000, the garrison of ALFSEA was to run down over the year to 200,000 – but only if shipping were not to be reduced further. But the Chiefs of Staff were considering a cut and the long-term deployment plan depended on how the situation in each of the countries involved turned out.

The Andamans and Nocobars, a group of islands off the south coast of India, were reoccupied by a brigade and the Japanese garrison evacuated without trouble. Within two months, trouble within the local police force resulted in the return of British troops to restore order. Within Malaya, Singapore, North Borneo and Brunei, the situation was largely peaceful. During the Japanese occupation, the Malayan People's Anti-Japanese Army, composed largely of Chinese communists, and assisted by the British Force 136, had resisted on a small scale. They agreed that, once Japan was defeated, they would disarm. Their leader, Chin Peng, was decorated by the British and it was hoped that, once Malaya was freed from the Japanese, they could be reintegrated into civil society. In fact, many of the weapons supplied by the British were never handed back and as soon as the war was over, the MPAJA rushed to establish a presence throughout the peninsula. In many towns and villages the hammer and sickle flew for weeks before proper administration was restored. The 'secret units' then went under cover and might have remained there, doing no harm, if political development had kept pace.

Dempsey's military administration was well received:

We could not ask for a more genuinely sympathetic, considerate and liberal attitude towards the civil population by the military government. Five years go we would not have believed that the establishment of a theoretically autocratic military government could have been compatible with the restoration of true freedom in Malaya. But in practice it has been so. No civil government in Malaya has ever had so much power as General Sir Miles Dempsey, and none has ever used it less. We have all found a good deal to criticise and complain about in relation to the British Military Administration viewed as the practical day-to-day equivalent of the Straits Government and the Singapore Municipality, but we have every reason to be thankful that they came in with their cut-and-dried scheme of civic reorganisation, and considering that half their personnel are still waiting to be transported from India, they have got the essential services going and tackled a multifarious array of social and economic problems with very considerable success in the short space of six weeks.[13]

But Chin Peng was not satisfied. For now, although the British were treated as liberators and the situation throughout the British area was peaceful, a series of unwise decisions in Whitehall sowed the seeds for the conflict that was to break out later and last twelve years. Dempsey had been prescient, indeed, in his hint to O'Connor concerning the quality of the restored civil administration.

French Indo-china – the area now composed of Vietnam, Laos and Cambodia – was, by contrast, in turmoil. The French administration there had declared for Pétain's Vichy government in 1940 and the Japanese were, therefore, officially garrison rather than occupying forces. On Japan's surrender, the Chinese forces under Chiang Kai Shek occupied the northern half of Vietnam, while the Allies were responsible for the south. The introduction of de Gaulle's forces was delayed due to the shortage of shipping. The local French authorities, fearing the breakdown of order and the potential of the nationalists for ending their rule entrusted to the Japanese the task of maintaining law and order, pending the arrival of British Indian troops from Burma. But on 17 September, the Annamite Independence Party declared the independence of the Republic of Vietnam. With the majority of the countryside already in the hands of the Viet Minh, the groundwork for the eventual end of French rule was laid.

Meanwhile, the repatriation of three quarters of a million Japanese soldiers was proceeding very slowly. Known in the spirit of the times as Operation NIPOFF, it was initially hoped that this could be achieved using Japanese shipping captured after their capitulation. Mature reflection revealed that this would take up to five years and, although there was no urgency to return them, many predicted that their discipline would deteriorate if they remained too long. Some 100,000 were to be retained as labour and 3,000 to face war crimes tribunals. Dempsey applied to the Chiefs of Staff for help. An initial lift of seventy-five Liberty boats would carry half by the middle of 1946, a second lift of a quarter of a million would follow and the Chiefs were invited to provide a final lift by early 1947 for the remainder.

Dempsey had huge distances to cover to supervise his command. Although for local visits around Singapore he had the use of a fast launch crewed by the Royal Army Service Corps, the usual method was air and

Pyman reckoned that they averaged about 10,000 miles every week. The farthest of his eight subordinate headquarters was in Burma and it was here that Dempsey felt that his efforts had been least rewarded. Describing it as his 'disappointing child', he said in his farewell address that he did not think that the good start to rehabilitation made by the military had been retained by the civil. The problem of *dacoity* – lawless bands of armed men who preyed on villagers – had resurfaced after the surrender of the Japanese. They had kept the dacoits under control by simple, if savage, methods. In one area, a gang was captured with its leader. He was strung up to dangle with a meat hook through his jaw; for the two days that it took him to die, the remainder of his gang were forced to watch him struggle. Such methods were thought inappropriate by the returning administration.

Mountbatten was fulsome in his compliments to Dempsey on his departure:

> In two and a half years I have had twenty Commanders-in-Chief; five Fleet; five Land Forces; five Air Force; and five Commanding Generals U.S. Forces. None of them could have risen to the great heights of a Commander-in-Chief in war without tremendous competitive selection.
>
> If I could only keep one out of the twenty to continue in partnership with me, I have absolutely no hesitation in saying that that one would be you.[14]

CHAPTER 15

'Last Post'

Less than a year after arriving in the Far East, Dempsey was on the move again. His destination was Cairo and his new title was Commander-in-Chief Middle East Land Forces. He took over from General Sir Bernard Paget, a most competent officer, who as C-in-C Home Forces had spent a large part of the war training the soldiers who were to invade Europe. There was no Supremo, as there had been in the Far East, and so he answered directly to Whitehall on the many responsibilities he had inherited. Shortly before Dempsey took over, Montgomery visited the region. Although he was not yet CIGS he wasted no time in setting out his priorities and giving instructions. Dempsey, arriving in theatre just as Montgomery became the professional head of the Army, was pretty clear what he had to do. Soon after arrival, he wrote to Pyman, temporarily sporting bowler hat and umbrella at the War Office:

> My object out here is to eliminate unnecessary commitments; get the Army properly organised on its peace-time basis; and prepare for the next war. A fascinating job, and one must be quite clear about one's L of C. You know my views on this. If they are accepted, there is nothing to prevent us going ahead – putting all our money into communications.[1]

The reference to Lines of Communication (L of C) concerned Dempsey's – and Pyman's – emerging philosophy on the state of the world and the British Army's strategy in future conflict. It was a preoccupation that was to dominate his thinking for the next year. It is hard to imagine, sixty years after the event, how Britain then stood in the world. Although she may have regained her Empire 'on the coat tails of the Americans', it was still an empire on which the sun never set, and with it came responsibilities for a large part of the world's population. Headquarters Middle East commanded troops in Egypt, Aqaba, Libya, Sudan, Eritrea, East Africa, Aden, Malta, Cyprus, Greece and Palestine. A 1,500 strong military mission was also in place in

Greece and smaller missions were in Turkey, Saudi Arabia, Abyssinia, Iraq and with the Arab Legion in Transjordan.

Dempsey's own appreciation of the situation in the different parts of his command is illuminating:

Now for some remarks on the Middle East.

(a) GREECE. You know as much about this as I do. I have had no opportunity of going there yet; I do so, in fact, next week. It is a commitment which I very much want to see brought to an end – and I keep 31 Dec 46 as the target date.

(b) Miscellaneous – CYPRUS, DODECANESE, TRIPOLITANIA, CYRENAICA & SUDAN. I have a small garrison in each and few, if any, difficulties at present. Nor, in fact is there a dark cloud on the horizon.

(c) IRAQ. A brigade at BASRA. Another Brigade on the way from INDIA. As usual INDIA is being very helpful and meeting us in every way. There are possibilities of trouble here in the oilfields: I liken it to SUMATRA.

(d) PALESTINE. We await a political decision. Meanwhile, both dogs are enjoying an uneasy sleep.

HQ PALESTINE (Barker) at JERUSALEM.
HQ 1 Div (Gale) at HAIFA.
HQ 6 Airborne Div (Cassels) at BEIT DARAS.

A good team – disposed at present to look after the Jews. So, if the Arabs have to be looked after too (or in place of the Jews) we shall have to do a certain amount of repositioning.

(e) EGYPT. The sooner we get out of the cities and down to the Canal the better and I hope to have GHQ there by the end of the year. What happens after that will depend upon the TREATY, which has not yet been signed. I have had to spend a good deal of my time lately with Stansgate and the Ambassador on this subject, and one has to be very clear what one is after.

Meanwhile there are the everyday Police problems; a few in GREECE and IRAQ; rather more in EGYPT: and quite a lot in PALESTINE. It may be that the last named will become a *major* Police problem! But one must not let oneself be drawn off the subject by these distractions. It is just the same as South East Asia, though it differs in degree.[2]

The treaty negotiations over the future status of the British base in Egypt had been under way for some time, and had reached a temporary standstill. In peace it was necessary to have the use of the Suez Canal and such other facilities as were needed for imperial communications to Australia and the Far East. It was also important to maintain the base installations for use in war. The Whitehall view was that if the forces then in Egypt could be rapidly slimmed down and moved out of the delta cities, the Egyptian King and his politicians would recognize Britain's good intent, and negotiations could resume on a more favourable basis.

In his inaugural address to his own headquarters, Dempsey set the tone very clearly. The whole organization had to be slimmed down drastically and moved from Cairo to Fayed on the Great Bitter Lake. After making clear that commanders of operations would always have enough men and materials, he said that he intended to lead the way in finding economies to get everything onto a peacetime basis. The move had to be completed quickly and efficiently:

> Viewed in a purely local and narrow-minded way reduction in strength can be depressing. If you resist it to the bitter end, and finally have numbers of your troops removed against your will, you will get a feeling of defeat creeping in.
>
> You and I are going to look at this in quite a different way. We realise that every unnecessary soldier we keep out here means a man kept off production at home; a man who should be growing food, or building houses, or engaged in one or other of the urgent jobs at home.[3]

Comparing the task with his previous one in the Far East, he briefly described the contrast between the operational tasks and the large-scale reduction of forces that had been accomplished: 'We are not going to sit here resisting reduction, grudgingly and unwillingly giving up soldiers when the demand becomes insistent. On the contrary we are going to lead the way in reduction.'[4]

The execution of the rundown plan was the responsibility of Lieutenant General Allfrey, Commander British Troops Egypt. As the plan progressed, Dempsey expressed his appreciation for the way he had handled this difficult task. After briefly mentioning the full and difficult year he had endured, with thousands of troops in transit, the move from the delta to the canal and the situation of great delicacy with the Egyptian government, which had placed great demands on his command, he summed up: 'He can seldom have accomplished more than he has done in 1946.'

By the end of 1946 the situation in Greece was more or less under control, and the large British military mission, backed by a few battalions of infantry, was able to plan a withdrawal as the commitment was handed over to the Americans.

The Palestine issue was not so easily settled. During the war, immigration of Jewish settlers had continued at low level, aimed at changing the imbalance between them and the native Arab population, who hugely outnumbered them. As the war ended, a clamour arose, backed by the United States, to increase the level of immigration, largely from Jews displaced or disadvantaged by the war in Europe. Britain, under a United Nations mandate, had the thankless task of maintaining law and order. This responsibility rested in the first place on the High Commissioner and the Palestine Police Force. General Sir Alan Cunningham had had a controversial career during the war, having been sacked as Eighth Army commander in North Africa. He came to Palestine in 1945, but was still regarded with a rather jaundiced eye by his military contemporaries. Although he could always be relied upon to do his duty, he was thought by Montgomery to be weak and vacillating, as was the policy of the Labour government now charged with solving an intractable problem. The Balfour Declaration of 1917 had stated that the British government viewed with favour the establishment of a national home for Jews in Palestine, but not to the detriment of the local Arab population. Here lay the paradox: the two policies were incompatible, and as Britain strove to maintain some sort of balance between the two, the general situation deteriorated.

As Dempsey succeeded Paget, the Army under Barker was responding to a series of outrages committed by the Jewish underground forces. Leaders of the Jewish Agency and their underground army, the Haganah, were detained. Montgomery signalled to Dempsey:

> At a Cabinet meeting on 1 July it was clearly stated that the Government policy is to suppress and root out all illegal armed organizations in Palestine whether Jew, Arab or any other. Your present operations should proceed at a high tempo. Arrest the leaders and collect in the arms and generally stamp on the HAGANAH and its associated organizations. Please give my congratulations to Barker and his troops on the skilful way in which the whole business was planned and carried out and say I have every confidence they will finish the business in the shortest possible time.
>
> I would welcome by return some information as to the extent to which captured documents incriminate the Jewish Agency and/or other highly placed Jews.[5]

In Jerusalem, the King David Hotel was blown up, killing and injuring British soldiers. The Irgun and the Stern Gang, extremist groups proscribed even by the Jewish Agency, were targeted and a few days later Montgomery signalled again:

> HMG have decided that illegal immigration into PALESTINE is to be stopped. An order is to be sent to the High Commissioner that he is to stop it ... I consider that you will have to see that CUNNINGHAM does not begin to wobble or try to sit on the fence. Once we begin the business it must be got on with firmly and with great energy and there must be NO repeat NO question of looking over our shoulder. I rely on you to let me know privately the moment the PALESTINE Government shows any sign of not wanting to face up to its responsibilities or to shirk the issue. Once we begin we must go through with it whatever the Jews may do. Take the initiative and use plenty of troops and always be one move ahead of the Jews.[6]

The Palestine Police were woefully undermanned and overstretched, and the British Army was now fully engaged in counter-insurgency. Families were sent home, soldiers were armed everywhere they went and emergency regulations put in place. Towards the end of October, the Colonial Office, Cunningham's masters in Whitehall, decided that if the imprisoned terrorist leaders were released and arms searches were to be suspended, an atmosphere more conducive to sensible dialogue would be created. It was even hoped that the Jewish Agency would denounce terrorism and back the High Commissioner's efforts to restore law and order. On 11 November, Montgomery signalled personally to Dempsey:

> It looks as if the Haganah have decided to go into battle in Palestine against the Stern gang and other extremists. Our own attitude will require most careful consideration. I am definitely opposed to cooperation with the Haganah in order to maintain law and order as it is an illegal organisation. From the military angle we are at war with all illegal organisations and we must not be led away from this clear cut issue.
>
> This aspect of the problem must be clearly understood by all military commanders in Palestine and by the Police. From past experience impress on Barker not to put anything in writing.
>
> Let me know if there is any tendency to depart from this simple issue on the part of the civil power.[7]

As more and more restrictions were placed upon the Army, British soldiers and members of the Palestine Police continued to be targeted and killed. By the middle of November, Dempsey and Barker were becoming exasperated by what they saw as weakness in the face of terrorism. Their soldiers were being killed and wounded, at the rate of two a day, while the extremists responsible seemed to be immune from preventive action. Dempsey wrote to Montgomery:

> The situation in Palestine is steadily getting worse. There are murders and acts of sabotage every day and not a terrorist is caught. During the last forty five days seven British soldiers have been killed and fifty two wounded. During the same period six British officers of the Palestine Police have been killed and eight wounded. All trains have stopped running at night, and there are no passenger trains at all between Lydda and Jerusalem.
>
> The main reason why we catch no terrorist is that the people of this country take no action, either directly or in the giving of evidence. Somehow we must make them do so. We recently adopted a policy of appeasement without any QUID PRO QUO. We laid off the searches for arms and we released the internees without a guarantee that terrorism would be fought.
>
> It seems to me that we can get these people to combat terrorism in one of two ways:
>
> (a) By bringing a little pressure to bear, that is to say by negotiation between HMG and Jewish leaders.
> (b) By bringing physical pressure to bear that is by resuming searches for explosives and weapons and so on. And the murder and wounding of seventy three Britons in the last six weeks surely gives us the right to do so.
>
> We soldiers had the initiative in Palestine in July and August and things were satisfactory. Then we stopped and handed over to Civil Govt. We are getting mighty near now to the time when the soldier takes over again.
>
> I am slipping up to Palestine again one day next week chiefly so that I will have the latest picture when you are here. If I have any further points I will signal you again. Meanwhile I wanted you to have my views before you leave London and hope that they may help.[8]

A personal reply came from Montgomery on 20 November:

> I made a statement today in the Defence Committee on Palestine. I said the Army was on the defensive and was being held back from searching for arms and explosives and was not even allowed to search

the locality of each outrage directly it occurred. I said we had lost the initiative and the situation is growing steadily worse. I asked that the Army should be allowed to take the initiative against the terrorists.

Colonial Secretary said he knew of no orders to restrain the Army as outlined in Para one above. We must have law and order in Palestine and the High Commissioner was responsible for securing it. He said he knew of no change of policy in this respect and of no order that the Army was not to be used to put down terrorism.

Prime Minister gave it as his opinion that searches should certainly take place in the locality of any outrage. He asked by whose order was the Army held back from taking offensive action against terrorists. He said he knew of no such orders.

In view of Paras two and three above please send me by return the information I require to substantiate my statement that the Army is being held back. Who has given such an order. Who has ordered that searches are not to take place in the locality of an outrage. Who has ordered that the Army is not to act offensively against terrorism.

I am to see the Prime Minister again on Friday before I leave U.K. Please send above information urgently and by return.[9]

In discussion with Attlee, armed with information from Dempsey, Montgomery suggested that if Britain was not prepared to maintain law and order in Palestine, it would be better to withdraw. He then left for a tour of the area, and on 29 November met Cunningham and Dempsey to discuss the situation. Cunningham, who was not of course answerable to Montgomery – although he my well have been in awe of him – agreed that the Army was unable to assist the Police Force meaningfully because of the restrictions placed upon it. The conversation then became stalled in the way that is common to many insurgencies. The solution has to be a political one; the role of the Army is to hold the ring while that political solution is found; use of force has to be carefully controlled as one of the factors in achieving a political solution; where politicians are unable to deliver a political solution, violence increases and the Army are blamed for not suppressing it. There was no political solution in Palestine that would satisfy either both sides, or natural justice; Britain was under huge pressure from the United States to allow unhindered immigration of Jews. This would alter 'the facts on the ground' by changing the balance of the population in favour of a Zionist state.

Montgomery, frustrated at what he saw as lack of will on the part of the government, and armed by Dempsey with first-hand knowledge of how restricted the Army was, prepared for a showdown with the Colonial Office. Surprisingly, perhaps, Montgomery's views prevailed and a new directive was prepared for the High Commissioner more in line with his ideas. But by mid-January, Montgomery was on the warpath again. The particular case in point was that of leniency to terrorists sentenced for militant activity, without the sentence being carried out. Describing this as a weak and thoroughly bad policy which could only make things difficult, he made his views clear to Attlee. Signalling again personally to Dempsey he said he had the Prime Minister's agreement that leniency towards terrorists was not only an unsound policy, but would put Britain on 'a bad wicket with the Arabs'. He demanded that sentences be carried out unless there were some technical irregularity to prevent them. The problem arose with his last paragraph, in which he urged Dempsey to take the matter up with the High Commissioner. This put Dempsey in a most difficult position. The matter was purely political and was for the Colonial Office, as Cunningham's masters, to take up, not Dempsey. The way that soldiers were to react in the event of a shooting or explosion was a fair matter for negotiation with the civil power, which Cunningham, although a soldier, represented. Commutation of sentences was not.

Montgomery now went even further. At the end of January, a British judge and an ex-officer were kidnapped. The High Commissioner threatened that if they were not set free within forty-eight hours, military administration would be set up in certain areas. On 30 January, Montgomery signalled personally to Dempsey:

> I am absolutely horrified at what is being allowed to go on in Palestine, and have given my views to the Colonial Secretary in no uncertain voice. It is quite monstrous to negotiate with illegal organizations and to say that unless they do this then we will do that. To give them 48 hours notice of what we will do is merely giving them added time to prepare to meet the blow …
>
> I am all in favour of 'a firm policy' but have never seen one yet in Palestine since I have been CIGS. We have been led into the present situation by a policy of weakness and of weak will power and by futile and ineffective methods which have been in force for many months and we have only ourselves to blame for what is now going on. The new directive to the High Commissioner is of itself useless. The result will depend on how that directive is interpreted and implemented. What we want is a stronger will power to stamp on this lawlessness and a firm determination that we will NOT repeat NOT tolerate insults to the British rule from a lot of gangsters.[10]

He then burned his boats completely. Bad enough that he had, by inference, described the Prime Minister and his government as weak willed, and their methods as futile and ineffective, but he then added: 'You can show it to anyone you like in Palestine.' This was outrageous and next day he was forced to backtrack: 'My telegram … was a bit over the odds and you will consider it as cancelled. The High Commissioner has had a perfectly clear directive from H.M.G. and I would be glad if you would give all your help and support to the High Commissioner towards carrying it out effectively.'[11]

Montgomery was quite happy to have stirred things up, but for Dempsey it was an example of the sort of manoeuvring and dealing that was an integral part of life for a senior officer in peacetime. He was already considering his future and this episode helped him make up his mind. The previous autumn, Oliver Leese, now GOC-in-C Eastern Command, had written to Dempsey to tell him of his decision to retire. Dempsey replied that he was surprised and sorry. Montgomery was determined that Dempsey should replace himself as CIGS, but by early November, Dempsey had made up his mind to go and told Montgomery that he would have to look elsewhere.

He wrote to Patrick:

Thank you very much for your remarks about myself. They are a great help – but are you not being rather optimistic when you say that I will be able to take my choice of several … well-paid jobs. I have every intention of leaving in June 47. I told Monty it was my firm decision: he agreed. I have discussed it no further with him since I was in London – but we both (I do anyway) regard it as settled. I am in fact longing to get out now. There are a good many things about Army policy I don't much care about – and I hate the social life and atmosphere of Cairo more than I can say. It is not my line! – as I am sure you will understand.

In order to keep you in touch with developments, this is what Hamilton of D. wrote to me on Oct 21st: 'I have told Home Office you will be available to take on the Chairmanship of RBCB at the end of June. It is the Home secretary's appointment. I hope most sincerely that he gives it to you. I think you would find the work interesting, and I do not think it would be unduly onerous.'

I am sure – from what he and the Duke of Norfolk told me – that it would not take up more of my time than I wished to give it.[12]

He was pressed on all sides to reconsider. Typical of the reaction was a letter from Mountbatten:

I saw Monty and Boy recently, and was staggered and shocked beyond measure to hear that you are contemplating leaving the Army.

> I hope you will allow an unbiased person to tell you that your departure would be nothing short of a National disaster, as I honestly consider you are in a class by yourself, on whom the future of the Army must, to a very large extent, depend.[13]

Dempsey was giving up the chance to become the professional head of the British Army. After command of one's own regiment, this post must be the ultimate ambition of any professional officer. To reject it must have been an enormously difficult decision and his reasons bear close examination. He replied to Mountbatten:

> You took an interest in the fact that I am retiring. May I tell you why? My reason for going is – with me – very strong. It is a very bad thing for the Army that officers at the top should continue to sit there moving from job to job. We saw it after the last war.
> I have been in succession – since January 1944:
>
> Comd. Second Army
> Comd. Fourteenth Army
> C-in-C S.E. Asia
> C-in-C Middle East
>
> I regard command of an Army in war as being at the top. Do you really want me to go on sitting there for another 3 years or so. And do you really think it would be good for the Army? I am quite certain it would not. Further, I am not going to fight the next war. Let those who are, come rising up, and have the say in shaping the Army correctly for it. Those who have been at the top in this last war think of the present (and the past). That, too, I feel very strongly.
> There are other points of lesser military importance, but of considerable influence with me: my dislike of certain aspects of present military policy; the heavy reaction (inevitable perhaps) which follows high command in war – it is stronger in my case than you imagine; and finally the impossibility of becoming in peace-time an unmarried Commander-in Chief (this is a very personal reason!).
> There it is; and my decision is right.[14]

Mountbatten reluctantly accepted Dempsey's arguments, but his reply gives an indication – even allowing for a little hyperbole – of the regard in which Dempsey was held:

Anyone who knows you well could not doubt for one moment that you were acting from the highest motives, and the whole of your argument holds water completely until we come to the last stage, which you in your inveterate modesty, have seen fit to omit.

It boils down to this, who is to succeed Monty as the next CIGS? The whole Army, I go further, all the fighting services, and all intelligent people in the country looked upon you as not only the logical successor, but as the only candidate of the right calibre immediately available. For all these reasons, I cannot but regret your decision most deeply although I of course absolutely respect your reasons.[15]

Dempsey wrote to Leese:

Yes – I am leaving in July. I don't feel I can go on sitting at the top, playing musical chairs, any longer. I remember too well how you and I felt after the last war. The post-war army is going to be a tender plant – and we must see that the chaps who really matter (Lew Lyne, Jimmy Cassels, Hughie Stockwell, Pete Pyman etc.) get a proper run. And I find the reaction is very great. I think that is inevitable after what we did. If you told me now to take a violent interest in training the new Army for the next war – I would have to say 'I'm sorry: it just can't be done!'

So I leave in July, and I know I am right. I am Colonel of my Regiment, which will give me a little Army work, and I have accepted the Home Secy's invitation to be chairman RBCB. This too (I am told) is very much a part-time job, but – as I am interested in breeding and racing – I hope to enjoy it.[16]

Dempsey showed his customary flair for picking winners – a trait of which he was very proud – in naming four of the Army's brightest and best. Although Lyne retired early, the other three (Cassels a future CGS, Stockwell a future Deputy SACEUR, and Pyman, who could have been CGS) were the future leaders of the peacetime army.

In another letter to Patrick he spelled out his thoughts on retirement:

My commitments look like being;

Colonel R.Berks
Chairman RBCB
Governor Shrewsbury (between ourselves for the present)
"Anything else"

I want to keep a cow or two, a pig or two, a hen or two. I want green grass (like anything!). I want to be not too far from the southern racecourses, nor from London: nor, I think, from the Epsom gallops.[17]

Life was not all work. One of Dempsey's pleasures was that Africa was on his doorstep, and he could return to South Africa and Roberts Heights for more relaxing diversion from problems such as Palestine. Nearby, Freddy de Guingand had retired to Rhodesia and over Christmas the two of them enjoyed reminiscing. From there he visited Eritrea, where members of the Stern Gang were incarcerated under the watchful eye of the Military Police at Keren. Dempsey was received by Brigadier Tapp, the Garrison Commander, inspected a guard of honour from the Eritrean Police and the Sudan Defence Force, and enjoyed a glass of the local Melotti beer in the NCOs' mess.

He had a particular reason to take an interest in what was then the recently named Corps of Royal Military Police, now granted the royal prefix, as he had been invited to become their Colonel Commandant, a post he assumed in March. It was an association which Dempsey and the Corps were to enjoy for many years.

In February 1947, the British Government appealed to the United Nations for help in the intractable problem of Palestine. While their fact-finding committee pursued its deliberations for the next six months, the country became increasingly lawless and the hopelessness of the situation there informed Dempsey's thinking, first on his future, second on the direction of British strategy in the Middle East. Having declined the offer to become CIGS and stated his definite intention to leave the army, for now he formulated his views on strategy.

In March 1947, he and Pyman crystallized their thoughts on the Middle East in a world in which Russia was the likely enemy. Identifying the British Empire's vital interests in the region as oil in Iran, Iraq and Saudi Arabia, and airports in North Africa, they rejected Suez Canal access, among other possible candidates, as being in this category. The lines of communication which must be safeguarded were through Capetown, Nairobi and Cairo by land, and Capetown, Aden and Suez by sea. Dempsey's concentration on Africa, as the strategic lynchpin, was becoming apparent.

If our MIDDLE EAST base has to leave EGYPT for a time then … the Base Troops must change to BT EAST AFRICA and we must prepare an advanced base in CYRENAICA, TRIPOLITANIA or ERITREA … We must … get agreement to keep an advanced military base in Iraq …The main axis must run from SOUTH to NORTH.[18]

In June 1947, as he was preparing to leave his last post in uniform, Dempsey finalized his thoughts on the future of British forces in the region. Rather in the manner of a 'haul down report', he presented his views in June 1947. It should be remembered that these views were shaped by the assumptions then current: first, as the Cold War era began, that Russia was the likely enemy in the event of war, and that war could be nuclear; second, long before the 'wind of change' began to blow through Africa, that Kenya would remain a British possession; and third, that South Africa, in that pre-apartheid era, would be a reliable and uncontroversial ally.

He began by saying that Britain was without a firm policy to which energies could be directed. This endangered her position with the Arab world, with which ties should be strengthened. Noting that the 'old' or Mediterranean strategy was now out of date, he recommended that sources of supply must be spread through America and the Dominions, and a new and safe line of communication in the Middle East must be found. What was required was a 'new', or African, strategy. Focusing on that continent, to which his thoughts had become increasingly drawn, he went on:

> It is fortunate for our interests in the Middle East that there exists a great industrial potential in Southern Africa, and that, with development, adequate and safe lines of communication can be brought into existence through the Continent of Africa, from west to east, and from south to north. It is in Africa that our source of supply must be built up, our bases established and our communications developed. It is in Africa that the bulk of our Middle East forces must be housed and trained. It is from Africa that our influence in the Arab countries must be directed; and it is from Africa that our reserves will move and supreme authority will function if the next war comes.[19]

He then focused on how, if Africa were to become the centre of gravity and bases were relinquished in the Arab world, British influence was to be retained where our vital oils assets lay. The answer was to establish strong and well-staffed military missions, and to ensure that the supply of British arms and military equipment was guaranteed. A strong and fit reserve, able to move quickly by air, must be available. Quoting as an example the reinforcement of the Sudan by air in October 1946, he emphasized that the reserve must be based in a stable location. The most difficult section of his appreciation was the attempt to forecast how a future war would be fought. His guess was that it would be a battle of medium- to long-range weapons delivered by aircraft or missile. This, again, pointed to bases as far forward as North Africa, or as far to the rear as the Sudan. This in turn pointed to Kenya, whose climate, communications and training facilities made it the ideal location for a major base, with forward bases or equipment stockpiles in the Middle East.

To establish Kenya as a major strategic centre, two things were necessary: communications throughout the African continent must be developed wherever they might be required; and Africa must be brought firmly into the British orbit by building up the population of British immigrants in the south of the continent. In a final flight of the imagination, Dempsey envisaged an 'African Army' replacing the Indian Army as a major tool of Imperial strategy.

> These Africans are fighting men and what has been achieved in India in the past can be repeated in Africa. The record of the African soldier in Burma is encouraging … with foresight and energy these men can be trained to take their place in Empire defence and are eager and ready to do so.[20]

He was suggesting that Britain turn from a Mediterranean to an African strategy; that the Persian Gulf and the Red Sea be the 'new lines of approach to the Middle East; British forces be withdrawn from the Middle east and replaced by military missions and equipment stockpiles; and forward airfields established on the line Iraq-Saudi Arabia-Transjordan-Cyrenaica'; the corollary must be that Kenya would be 'the base from which our effort must spring'.

Dempsey summed up the argument:

> Agreement with these views will enable us to take up once again the reins of leadership in the Middle East and shape our course along our own lines. It will enable us straightway to remove our Middle East base from Egypt to East Africa: and allow us to proclaim to the world the treaties of friendship we have made with certain Arab states, and our intention of moving our fighting troops from those countries such as Palestine and Egypt where no benefit can accrue but where our strength and prestige are suffering so much.[21]

His paper summed up all Dempsey's experience in thirty-three years in uniform, in which he had served King and country in two world wars, and held high command in two theatres of great responsibility. It reflected his deep conviction that Britain was a force for good in the world, and that the British Empire, despite the loss of India, would continue to flourish. It was of course dominated by the Cold War, then gathering force, and the notion that another world war was inevitable. In many ways he was ahead of his time and many of his proposals were later to be adopted. The Canal Zone continued to be a running sore until the Suez debacle; British bases in the Middle East continued to be the focus of discontent until the last of them was withdrawn from Aden in 1967; and a British base in Kenya flourished as the location of our theatre reserve with little or no friction for many years. Training missions were major tools of military/diplomatic influence and continue to be so today. Finally, the forward stockpiling of equipment was an idea ahead of its time, later to be widely adopted by American forces with their POMCUS depots.

The paper, by its nature, reflected one man's views. It would have been interesting to see the reaction of Dempsey's Royal Navy and Royal Air Force colleagues. What is fascinating is the light that the handling of the document sheds on his relationship with Montgomery. Writing to Pyman on the subject he forecast:

> Of course it is going to go 'Africa'! But the CIGS is not going to accept your scheme or my scheme – or anyone else's scheme. That is not his way. It is going to be his scheme. I do not feed it into Monty any more; he has got it all. And if I let it lie, it will come out all the easier as his plan.[22]

As Dempsey's departure and retirement drew closer, his thoughts turned more and more to the future, and his part in it. In his address to the last course to be held at the Haifa Staff College, he said:

> The time is coming now when those of us who held high command in the war will be quitting the stage and handing over to others. There is nothing more certain to produce inertia and a lack of intelligent planning for the future than that those at the top should overstay their time and so prevent a normal upward flow. In my view such a flow is essential. But it is our duty – before we quit – to pass on to those who follow the more important lessons of our experiences.[23]

He enlarged on the theme in his address at his farewell dinner in GHQ on 6 June 1947. After paying a warm tribute to the Royal Navy, and in particular to his old cricketing friend from Staff College, and comrade in arms in the war, Admiral Tom Troubridge, he continued:

> I had intended to try and explain to you how completely qualified for the madhouse I have become after 3 years; but the Chief of Staff has done it for me ... And now fate in the shape of my own conscience has said 'Time' – for there must be no clinging on to office after the spark has died.[24]

This most humble and self-deprecating of men then went on to make an unusual boast:

> But one branch of the military art in which I claim to have no equal is in the skill of picking men. I have never boasted before ... A commander depends so largely on his subordinate commanders and staff; if he achieves success he must be a good selector ... I claim wisdom in selection, you have brought me the prize of achievement. . It has been a difficult time...but it has served to show me what a fine team you are. It would be an understatement to say that I am grateful.[25]

As Dempsey was travelling home, a very special piece of regimental news was received. In late 1946 he had assumed the Colonelcy of the Royal Berkshire Regiment. Let his predecessor, General Collins, now take up the story:

> In the absence of General Sir Miles Dempsey, who is not due to reach England until June 11th, it seems to be up to me to tell the story ... When the news arrived that the King was going to honour the Regiment by assuming himself on May 12th the Colonelcy-in-Chief, it came without warning and so was a delightful surprise. The official letter was only received by me on May 8th ... was it up to me to compose a suitable reply, or would General Dempsey, who probably knew all about it, have sent such a message! A cable to him at GHQ Middle East only produced – late on 10th May – the ugly news that General Dempsey had flown to South Africa.[26]

In fact, a letter to Patrick dated 25 May reveals that he not only knew, but had, as he said, 'my first objective achieved'[27] and he was able to be the first from the Regiment to see His Majesty on one of his immediate duty calls back in the United Kingdom, to thank him for the great honour. On promotion to full General in 1947, he had been appointed ADC General to the King, and regimental lore has it that it was their excellent relationship that finally persuaded His Majesty to accept the post. It made a fine homecoming.

The future was now charted. Civilian life beckoned. The burden of high command could be laid down. New pastures were to be explored. Mountbatten, now Viceroy of India, tried to recruit him, offering a 'vital Governor's appointment' for one year. Dempsey replied cautiously:

> I am intensely interested in the Empire's strategical future in the Middle East – which includes the whole of Africa, the Indian Ocean,

Karachi and the Persian Gulf. I am not interested in those parts of Central, Eastern and Southern India which have no bearing on this. I would therefore be a willing co-operator under you in any matter directly affecting Karachi and that part of N.W. India which might remain in the Empire, and help our strategical interests.[28]

The offer came to nothing, but Mountbatten tried one last shot, telling the Prime Minister and Montgomery that Dempsey's resignation should not be accepted and he should be appointed as CIGS when Montgomery's time was up. It was all to no avail. Dempsey was homeward bound for civilian life. 'He could have run anything,' Pyman had said. Dempsey was now to prove how exactly right he was.

CHAPTER 16

'Sunset'

Dempsey's decision in early 1947 to retire left a gap in the succession plan for CIGS, but he was determined to go. Depressed by the weakness of British policy, and unwilling to involve himself in the in-fighting that he saw as inevitably attendant upon high councils, he declared that he would leave in six months and become Chairman of the Racecourse Betting Control Board. The RBCB, later to become the Tote, was set up in 1928 to handle on-course cash pool bets on approved racecourses. In 1933 it made the first of what were to be many grants to the Hunters' Improvement Society, promoters of point-to-point meetings and pony racing. The Chairman, Sir Reginald Blair, had signalled his intention to retire and Dempsey was delighted to take on a job that combined his love of horses and racing with an agreeable lifestyle. He remarked at the time that, as he would be attending all the race meetings he could anyway for pleasure, it was also nice to feel it was his duty to go.

Writing from London to Pyman in September, three months after retirement, he said;

> I have not really done anything since I came back except put on exactly a stone in weight, and enjoy myself staying with friends in England, Scotland and Ireland. My horse activities take up little of my time, and what there is of it is fun. I am being asked to do a variety of things – write a book (No!), write articles for certain newspapers (No!), help run the Army Cadets (Probably Yes), be chairman of one of the big Hospitals (?) – and so on.
>
> What I really want to do is to find a suitable home in the country; farm a bit, and spend – say – three days a fortnight in London. I hate living in London! I would do that if things in England go right. A very wise man said to me the other day: 'Do not commit yourself to anything just yet. Sit back and watch. Then if things do not go right, you will be free to do whatever is wanted.' Probably very sound advice.[1]

This did not satisfy Pyman, who replied:

> Much as we would all like to see you with a fine country house as
> a firm base, you cannot expect any of your team to agree that you
> should settle down to the life of a country gentleman. However well
> affairs in the Empire go, they cannot go well enough for that.
>
> I can see how wise you were to get away from the circle of the big
> wartime leaders, who have little in front of them but delights from
> self glorification. As you say, the country is tired of all that, so are the
> forces.
>
> The country will need you again soon, and provided that you will
> really listen to the advice of your 'very wise friend', your well wishers
> will meanwhile be satisfied if you concentrate on the second stone.[2]

The reference to the wartime leaders touched on a concern shared by many
that the great Allied achievements were being sullied by the criticisms
expressed in the many memoirs that were now appearing. At first, the
writings of men such as Eisenhower's personal aide, Commander Butcher,
were a matter of mutual regret. Eisenhower even wrote to Montgomery to
apologize for the unfair remarks that were emerging. But as leaders on both
sides of the Atlantic produced their own accounts, and it became apparent
that the façade of unity presented to the outside world in wartime was
just that, each tended to withdraw into his own camp. This exchange of
incivilities was anathema to Dempsey. He expressed his opinion to Brigadier
Molony, a historian of the war: 'Our views are similar. I am one (of very few
I am sorry to say) who believes that what was private once is private still,
and will remain so always. Like you, I deplore many of the books that have
been written, and that is why I have resisted the temptation myself.'[3]

He abhorred the revelation of matters that should have remained
confidential; and he was concerned that the reputation of Montgomery,
whom he revered for his ability as a great wartime commander, was being
tarnished. It was not solely through his memoirs, controversial though
they were, that Montgomery was disappointing Dempsey. The two were in
regular contact, dining together often, and discussing such personal matters
as the desirability of one or the other marrying. But Dempsey was alarmed
at Montgomery's conduct as CIGS.

> I would say that the biggest single stumbling block to progress – as
> regards Men, Money, Planning and everything else – is that Monty
> has (in Boy's words) 'made a complete nonsense of the Chiefs of
> Staff'. In the war, the voice and the judgement of the Chiefs of Staff
> (Brookie and Co) meant something. Today the disjointed voices of

three men pulling in opposite directions mean nothing. And Monty is regarded by the members of the Cabinet as (the word they use) 'irresponsible'.

It is a very great pity that at this time the 'Chiefs of Staff' are not there to help and advise and generally produce a steadying effect on a somewhat rattled government.

Monty. He <u>was</u> happy as CIGS with the thought that one day he would be 'CI Combined Staff'. Now that is not enough, and he is only happy when visualising himself as THE LEADER. It is all highly dangerous, and I don't think he realises that quite a considerable part of the people of England is sick of his publicity, and goes about muttering 'We must not have another Cromwell.'[4]

He was moved to add a later note, to balance his criticism: 'I do not mean it that way. He retains – to a wonderful extent – all his great qualities.'

In 1966, he wrote again to Molony: 'I just felt anxious lest Montgomery's altogether outstanding ability as a commander in the field should be overshadowed by the arrogance which stands out so clearly in your story. It is not easy to convey in print the remarkable hold he had over his troops.'[5]

Years later, as the rows and the controversies continued, Dempsey's patience wore thin. When, in 1967, Montgomery proposed to exclude Freddy de Guingand from his 80th birthday party, Dempsey and Leese threatened to boycott the affair. Montgomery backed down, but Dempsey refused to attend. Nonetheless, he was always careful to distinguish between the Monty of the past from the Monty of the day. Asked to comment on Lewin's forthcoming biography shortly after the birthday incident, Dempsey, who confided that he supposed that he knew Montgomery better than anyone else, from the point of view of an immediate subordinate, wrote:

> My one concern is that you should have the true picture of M as he was during the war. The Americans and other self-seekers have run him down, and belittled his victories in such a way that the younger generations wonder whether he really was much good. And as his military reputation topples, so the achievements of the British soldier topple too. Since the war he has been his own worst advertising agent. I would not attempt to defend that. It is anathema to me. But I will do anything I can to help you establish his genius as a commander in the field.[6]

Dempsey stuck to his resolution not to publish anything and confined himself to commenting briefly to historians such as Liddell Hart and Lewin, whom he judged to be reliable. He declined Liddell Hart's invitation to join the 'Military Commentators' Circle'; he was, as a neighbour put it:

> The General who never wrote a book. He did not disdain the volumes which poured from the pens of his old comrades – indeed he read them appreciatively and enjoyed making guesses, doubtless very shrewd ones, at the identity of the men who reviewed them at length in the weekly paper. But even when the book won his full approval, one felt that he was a little sorry it had been written – or rather sorry that an old friend had written it. He could never avoid the question 'But why, exactly and precisely, did he write this book?' – a question which, in the aftermath of war, is apt to have an uncomfortable answer.[7]

He did take issue privately when Bradley criticized him in *A Soldier's Story*. The issue was the sharing of road space during the breakout from Normandy, following which Dempsey's remarks at a press conference had upset Bradley. Dempsey wrote:

> Dear Brad, no doubt you have very good reasons for the attacks on me which are now being quoted in the English press. They are interesting in that they show what a great difference in outlook there is between American and British generals. We over here place great store on Loyalty, and those of us who had the good fortune to fight alongside such men as Bradley, Hodges, Simpson, Ridgway, Taylor and so on, would hesitate a long time before attacking them in print: they were our friends. I understand there is a lot of money in the sort of stuff you have written, so perhaps that is the reason. But I feel it is letting Ike down very badly for you may remember he was very keen on Anglo-American cooperation and friendship, and I am sure still is.[8]

Offers of high command were made. In 1948, he was proposed as the High Commissioner for Malaya, a vital post in the campaign to counter Chin Peng's communist insurgency. Dempsey considered and, based on his experience as Commander ALFSEA, agreed to take on the post, but with one condition. Singapore would have to be included in his remit. This was not acceptable to the Colonial Office, who had other plans, and the post went to Gerald Templer.

In 1950, Dempsey did agree to take on a 'shadow' post, that of Commander-in-Chief Home Forces. This appointment would only be activated in war, when it was envisaged that a Russian invasion would be countered by a resistance network modelled on parts of the wartime Home Guard. As with everything he did, Dempsey took his duties seriously and set his mind to considering how best such a network could be run. He studied the work of Captain Swire, who had made a reputation as an expert in Home Guard intelligence, and visited Belgium to discuss with Colonel de Greef, the Minister of Defence, his experiences under German occupation.

Not unnaturally for a recently retired senior officer, he was consulted on a variety of subjects, from the future size and strength of the Army to the desirability of officers having university degrees. He was in favour of the latter, but not from an exclusively military university. His view was:

> A great many things go to make up the education of a young man, and it is at the university that many of the desirable influences reach him. You will never get that at an 'Army University'. If we are short of a university in England, we should start another – in fact apart altogether from military interests, I would have thought that this need has already become apparent. When I was commanding a Battalion in 1938-39, I was very keen on the University entry and was always prepared to accept 50% from that source.[9]

In this, Dempsey was ahead of his time. Although a trickle of graduates were commissioned in the 1950s and 1960s, the trickle only became a flood in the 1980s, and today 90 per cent of the Sandhurst intake are graduates. He was often a guest of Normandy Company at Sandhurst and was regularly asked to speak of the campaign at their dinners. He was remembered by the cadets as totally charming and modest, kind and approachable.

Dempsey and Pyman worked together on the Second Army History, not as a way of making money – its distribution was severely restricted and it was graded secret – but as their way of recording the lessons to be learned, and paying tribute to those who had served with them. However, Dempsey not unnaturally had to consider his material future. His letters to his friends betray his longing to settle down after a life of action and, soon after he left the Army, he surprised them and his family by renouncing his bachelor status to marry, in Dublin, Viola O'Reilly, daughter of Captain Percy O'Reilly of Westmeath in the Irish Republic. They had met when Dempsey visited the stables of his old friend and business colleague, Captain Boyd Rochfort, the Queen's trainer, where she was working. Although she was a Catholic ('Were they married in church?' asked an aunt. 'I do hope Viola was given a dispensation to allow this!') Dempsey was happy enough to accompany her to worship in her own church and the marriage, although not blessed with children, was extremely happy. He and 'Tuppeny' as she was always known, shared a love of horses and they agreed to settle down in Berkshire, initially at The Old Vicarage at Greenham, and then for the years until they died, at Coombe House, Yattendon. Berkshire was a natural choice, first for its regimental connection, and second for its proximity to premier racing.

A consideration in the selection of Yattendon was that the entire village is part of the estate of Lord Iliffe. As well as being a pretty village, and preserved against the possibility of unwelcome development, its properties are rented. This was attractive for Dempsey. He had some private means, largely acquired through the buying and selling of horses and the compensation he received when his house at Greenham was requisitioned, and a meagre army pension. He had received only a small gratuity on retirement. In contrast to Earl Haig, to whom a grateful nation had granted £100,000 after the Great War, the senior officers of the Second World War were rather meanly rewarded. Brooke was given £300, of which £200 was needed to pay for his robes as the newly ennobled Lord Alanbrooke. He was so poorly off that he had to sell his beloved bird books to get by. Not unnaturally, some saw publication of their memoirs as a way out of poverty, but for Dempsey this would not do. He was determined that 'what was private would remain private', and took steps to ensure that confidential papers and diaries were destroyed. He had to make a living in other ways.

The RBCB was a natural start point to the world of business, where the 'bottom line' replaced the lives of soldiers as the prime consideration. The Board had two functions: to present an alternative to bookmakers for betting; and to apply a proportion of its income from its betting activities for the good of racing. Although grants were made before the war, racing went into decline during hostilities and revenue suffered. Financially the war was not a disaster for the Board, but grants reduced, and it was not until 1948 that the upturn in racing enabled money to be given for the refurbishment of courses, transporting horses to meetings and the authorities' administrative expenses, such as photo-finish cameras.

Dempsey's term as chairman coincided with the end of the upturn in Tote turnover, partly because of a fall in racecourse attendance. After 1948, turnover hovered around £25 million and grants at around half a million. The press began to ask questions and Dempsey's total integrity was the Board's strongest asset in warding off criticism. It is interesting that the majority of the Board's senior members stepped down as Dempsey took over, and he was able to reassure the public by publishing a breakdown of revenue, expenses and grants. The basic problem was that, while tote payouts were comparatively generous, the majority of the race-going public preferred the fixed odds of the conventional bookmakers.

He was known during his time at the RBCB as tolerant, humorous and kindly, a man who loved racing but could be caustic at times about racing journalists whose writing he thought did damage to the sport. His love of the Turf and its traditions was tempered with a wise radicalism, and his rare causticism was by no means unfair, either to the press, or to its less conformist members.

In 1951, as the system for dividend calculation was amended to give the Tote more generous terms, Dempsey was succeeded by Dingwall Bateson, a lawyer who was said to have quipped, 'A solicitor is a man who calls in a person he doesn't know to sign a contract he hasn't seen to buy property he doesn't want with money he hasn't got.' It would be hard to imagine a greater contrast to Dempsey.

The RBCB, and the County Fire Insurance Company, of which he became a director, had provided the means for a pleasant and moderately rewarding few years in which Dempsey had adjusted to civilian life. It had not been easy. In his first few months of retirement he had expressed his concern at the direction events in Britain were heading:

> Most thinking people believe that there is going to be a row this winter. We must have an end of restrictive practices, 'Coats off, longer hours, pay by results'. That would solve all our troubles … If we really got the coal out of the ground it would go a long way towards adjusting the balance. At present the miners have cornered it, and are sitting on top of the mines saying' "No – you can only have just that much.' If they will not dig it out, we had better get someone who will – ie imported labour. Perhaps we have so raised the standard of living that they do not care about mining any more.
>
> I would say myself that something will happen this winter. Something will touch off a coal strike – then a General Strike: perhaps quite suddenly: and then we shall see. I do not believe we can go on much longer as we are going at present.[10]

These views may seem reactionary to the modern reader, but Dempsey was to show that he understood how to lead successfully in civilian life, just as he had in the Army. He became Chairman of H and G Simonds, then of Greene, King and Sons, and finally Deputy Chairman of the amalgamated Courage, Barclay and Simonds Ltd. For many years he headed these great brewing firms to their benefit and to the benefit of the Regiment. Any soldier of the Berkshires who presented himself at the Reading brewery could be assured of temporary employment and sustenance.

Dempsey's time as Chairman of Greene King, from 1955 to 1969, is remembered for his prolonged and successful maintenance of the firm's independence. In 1980 there were eighty brewery companies in the United Kingdom. Only twenty years previously there had been over ten times that number. To remain independent the firm had to generate sufficient drive to carry through a number of innovations, especially in relation to free trade. A new approach was also needed to extend beer, wine and spirits sales and to introduce new types of beer, so that both financial performance and the range of products offered could stand comparison with its larger rivals. The company, under Dempsey, maintained its traditional ethos of quiet paternalism, never flamboyant, and underwritten by a spirit of service. He was the perfect fit.

Dempsey was now in the ranks of the 'Great and the Good'. He was the head of three military families: The Royal Military Police; The Special Air Service; and The Royal Berkshire Regiment. His interest in, and support for, the Corps of Military Police as it was originally known had been expressed during the war. He is quoted at their museum as saying:

> The Military Policeman became so well known a figure on every road to the battle field that his presence became taken for granted. Few soldiers as they hurried over a bridge, which was a regular target for the enemy, gave much thought to the man whose duty it was to be there for hours on end, directing the traffic and ensuring its rapid passage.

The Royal title was granted, and the name changed to Royal Military Police, in late 1946, and Dempsey became Colonel Commandant in early 1947. One of his early duties, after retirement, was to agree a Corps march. Accompanied by the outgoing and incoming Provost Marshals, Major General Erskine and Brigadier Wheeler, Dempsey visited the Royal School of Military Music at Kneller Hall. There the school band played for them a special arrangement of 'The Watch Tower', based on an old piece of German music by Rudolf Herzer, which they agreed to adopt for the Corps. The march was played on all ceremonial occasions, never with more gusto than at the Centenary parade in 1955. In his address Dempsey said:

> This is a great day for the history of our Corps, and one on which we think back with pride and gratitude on the achievements of our predecessors. We recall their loyalty and steadfastness in the days of peace, and their courage and determination in time of war. As you pass through the Memorial Archway at the close of the parade you will remember these things and resolve that whilst the well-being of the Royal Military Police is in your hands you will not let it own. And in your task you soldiers of today take with you the best wishes of your Old Comrades.[11]

On his retirement as Colonel Commandant in 1957, Dempsey paid generous tribute, as was his wont, to the four Provost Marshals who had commanded the Corps during his tenure. It had been a very happy relationship and Dempsey was remembered by the Corps for 'what he was as a person – a very great gentleman'.

The second military family with which Dempsey was proud to be associated was the Special Air Service. Their own view was that he always had a leaning towards what were called in a derogatory way by some, 'Private Armies'. What was more he was one of the few high commanders who knew how to use them. After the war, the status of the SAS was in doubt and Dempsey's tenure as Colonel Commandant from 1951 to 1960 was a critical period for its survival. In the early 1950s John Woodhouse set up a selection process for potential recruits for the Regiment, then serving in Malaya. Dempsey gave it strong support and, importantly, smoothed out relations with the Airborne Forces Depot, which was to play a part in their training. 'I hope it is clearly understood,' said Dempsey, 'that there is no question of the SAS being taken over, now or in the future, by Airborne Forces.'[12] Of course there had been, but there was no longer. Noting that Dempsey was a professional soldier of the highest order, a quiet man and a splendid leader, the SAS ascribed to his modesty the fact that many of his great achievements went unsung.

The third 'family' was of course Dempsey's beloved Royal Berkshire Regiment. With his Colonelcy came, as an added bonus, the honour of being Colonel of the Lincoln and Welland Regiment, a reserve unit of the Canadian Army, long affiliated to the Berkshires and known as the 'Links and Winks'. For Dempsey, who knew Canadian soldiers so well from working with them and commanding them in battle, this was a special pleasure, and he maintained a warm and close relationship with them right up to his death.

In 1947, as Dempsey assumed the Colonelcy, the announcement was made that, in common with many other regiments, the Berkshires were to lose one of their two regular battalions. The battalion in Germany was to be disbanded. Dempsey wrote to his predecessor:

> It seems to me that we have three great tasks ahead of us: to adjust our outlook and activities to the new Regimental organisation – to see to it that the spirit of comradeship engendered in the war in each of our battalions is carried into the years of peace – and to ensure that the dependants of those Royal Berkshire men who lost their lives in the war are not forgotten.[13]

For the Berkshires, Dempsey felt that special kinship which can only be fully understood by those who have experienced the privilege of serving with a first-class regiment in peace and war. His speech on being admitted as an Honorary Freeman of the Borough of Reading suggests something of the feelings that they invoked. After ascribing his own successes, with typical modesty, to the men he had commanded, he spoke of the Regiment. It was the story of an English county regiment which had been in existence already for more than 200 years. The history of the Royal Berkshire Regiment dated back to 1743 and they had won renown in every corner of the earth, in Russia, China, India, Afghanistan and Persia, from the north to the south of Africa, in America, in the West Indies, and throughout the Continent of Europe. There was scarcely a campaign in which one or other of the battalions had not played its part.

> The county regimental system has truly proved its worth in Britain's wars. It would be a sad and bad day for Britain if ever its infantry regiments ceased to belong to a county, and if the Royal Berkshire Regiment no longer looked to Reading as its home. The Army is passing through difficult days and needs all the support that patriotism, loyalty and tradition can give it.[14]

As his years as Colonel of the Regiment drew to a close, Dempsey reflected:

> I have now gone full circle in my military life. I started as a 2nd Lt in the Royal Berkshire Regiment in 1915. I have been round the circumference since then, and am back where I began with the Berkshire soldiers. I am very fortunate ... and wish to leave it at that.[15]

His status within the Regiment was, and remains, legendary. The few who remember him personally recall his kindness, his charm, his personal interest in everyone and anything connected to the Regiment. Those who did not know him hear of his exploits with wonder.

The last years were quiet and centred on Yattenden. Dempsey became a familiar figure in the village, in his distinctive brown tweed suit. A neighbour described 'a tall, slender man walking so quietly along our lanes; so courteously, as if anxious not to incommode so much as a dandelion; and always with one of those smiles of greeting that belong to the eyes no less than to the lips.'[16]

He and Tuppeny hosted small lunch parties for neighbours and he read the lesson in the lovely village church. He kept in touch with old comrades, particularly Selwyn Lloyd, whom he put up for the Turf Club, and 'Pete' Pyman. When the latter was disabled by the stroke which was to rob him of the chance of becoming CGS, Dempsey was one of the first to visit him in hospital. Pyman's son, then a Sandhurst cadet, was with his father at the time. 'You would have thought he would have no time for me; I was a very junior sprog, but he could not have been nicer. He was utterly charming, and left an impression on me which has never gone away.'[17]

Dempsey continued to enjoy Africa and it was on a visit to his nephew, Michael, in Kenya, that he began to complain of a pain in his back. On his return to England cancer was diagnosed. By an extraordinary coincidence, Miles Dempsey died on 4 June 1969, twenty-five years to the day after the first of the Knight's Vigil services which he had inaugurated at Portsdown on the eve of D-Day. He had attended the commemoration every year, along with many others, such as Maurice Chilton and Selwyn Lloyd, who had been at the original service. Selwyn Lloyd remembered: 'Year by year since then, some of us have returned with him to that parish church to commemorate that occasion and to renew our vows. It could have been an event deserving and receiving public notice, but he forbade any publicity. This was typical.'[18]

Guy Simonds wrote that 'The impact of his loss was all the more poignant to those of us who were revisiting the very places so closely associated with him in the military campaign. The more one got to know Miles, the greater grew one's appreciation of his fine qualities.'[19]

The news of his death created little interest in the press. Obituaries catalogued his career, mentioned his sporting achievements and graded him an outstanding commander. One mentioned that, although he commanded an army in the field with unbroken success for nearly a year in the Second World War, he was comparatively unknown to the general public. Speculating that this was because he never held an independent command, it also pointed out that he was a man who never sought the limelight. Some of the more sensationalist produced stories on the theme that, as one expressed it, 'Lucky Dempsey dies as Monty gardens'. The man to whom Dempsey in large part owed his rise and who, in turn, depended on Dempsey for much of his success, was unaware that his protégé had passed away. Asked about his feelings on the twenty-fifth anniversary of D-Day, Montgomery replied, 'I have nothing to say about it. It is a long time ago. I can only say I am sorry we did not win the peace.'

He was buried in a simple grave in Yattenden churchyard, to be joined some years later by Tuppeny. On every anniversary of his death, a simple cross of remembrance has appeared by his grave, 'From a Normandy Veteran'. His memorial service was held in Farm Street Church, the centre of Jesuit worship in Britain, and was attended by Mountbatten and Montgomery. The Entrance hymn was 'O Son of man, our hero strong and tender, whose servants are the brave in all the earth', Dempsey's favourite. Commenting on the friendship and affection that were so evident at the service, Selwyn

Lloyd remembered that, on his death bed, Dempsey remained in complete command of himself, 'with that last characteristic wave of the hand to the nurse as she went off to see if she could get something to help him'.[20]

So went to his Maker a cheerful Christian who had witnessed stirring times and shaped great events. The long years of apprenticeship, the sharpening of his professional expertise through the dreary years of Britain's military unpreparedness, reached their full flowering in the war. His rise from junior rank to command of half a million men in a few years was unprecedented. His responsibilities were enormous, his achievements remarkable. If Dempsey is not as well known as others of similar, or even junior, rank, it is due, above all, to his modesty. His watchwords were courage, patriotism, integrity, loyalty – old-fashioned virtues out of vogue today. His personality was charming, his manner easy, his relaxations sporting rather than cerebral. He embodied the virtues of the Edwardian gentleman, the product of a close and loving relationship with his mother and brother, his mores moulded by Alington of Shrewsbury, his young manhood tempered in the fires of the Western Front and the close comradeship of his regiment. To those who knew him well, he was the most inspiring of men; to those whose lives he touched he remains someone special. He was a 'very parfait gentle knight'. Tuppenny was especially touched by Boyd Richfort's words: 'He was a wonderful friend ... I never came away from any talk with him without the Certain Conviction that he would do everything he had promised to do, and more – and never to the slightest extent think of his own advantage to the detriment of his colleagues.'[21]

Selwyn Lloyd's tribute catches the man:

I prefer to remember him by his personal qualities. I have never known anyone who got to the point quicker. There was plenty of humour, never any humbug; one felt that here was a first-class intellect dealing with complicated and difficult problems in an exemplary and straightforward manner. I do not think he had any enemies, a remarkable fact in view of the heavy responsibilities he shouldered. He was loved by those who knew him well.

In the later years, after his retirement from the Amy, blessed by a happy marriage, with his business interests and his passion for racing, he continued to command the affection and respect of a very wide circle.

His career and life and philosophy were epitomised by the word integrity, and coupled with it an almost excessive humility.

Of nothing in life am I prouder than that I served under him during great events, and that he was my friend.[22]

Epilogue

On 6 June 1948, many of the 400 men of Dempsey's old headquarters returned to Christ Church. Scouts and guides formed a guard of honour for the General, lining the path to the church. In a service that held poignant reminders of the 'Knights' Vigil' of four years before, the Revd Gilman read the introduction, the Revd J.W.J. Steele, now Assistant Chaplain General, Singapore, read the prayer of Sir Francis Drake and the Bishop of Portsmouth dedicated two stained-glass windows.

The windows are quite unusual for an English church. They depict St Michael and St George, in armour and in an attitude of victory. Beneath the figure of St Michael is a scene of troops wading ashore from an invasion barge, with a destroyer in the background and a bomber overhead. Below St George, tanks are shown going into action. In his dedication, the Bishop said:

> We dedicate these windows to the glory of God, and in memory of Second Army; its task completed; its duty done. To Second Army there was given a glorious part in a great task; to relieve the oppressed; to restore freedom to Europe; and to bring peace to the world. That Army splendidly achieved its purpose and continued steadfastly until victory was won.

A commemorative service has been held at Christ Church on the first Sunday in June ever since. During the service the vicar recalls the service of 1944 and invites the congregation to remember those who took part in its achievements.

> O Lord God, when thou givest to Thy servants to endeavour any great matter, grant us also to know that it is not the beginning, but the continuing of the same, until it be thoroughly finished, which yieldeth the true glory.

The words are a fitting tribute to a fine man. We can but be grateful that, when the hour came, it was given to this courageous, honourable, decent, dedicated soldier to do great deeds on our behalf, and in the cause of free men everywhere.

Notes

Chapter 1
1. Shrewsbury School Magazine, 27 July 1914, by kind permission of the Governors of Shrewsbury School.
2. Nevil Shute, *Slide Rule*, Pan Books, 1968.

Chapter 2
1. J.C. Dunn, *The War The Infantry Knew*, P.S. King Ltd, by kind permission of the Trustees of The Royal Welsh Fusiliers Regimental Association.
2. A.W. Pagan, *Infantry*, Gale and Polden, 1951.
3. Hanbury Sparrow, *The Land Locked Lake*, Craftsman Press, Thailand, 1933.
4. *Ibid.*
5. War Diary of 1st Battalion The Royal Berkshire Regiment, by kind permission of the Trustees of the Rifles Wardrobe and Museum Trust.
6. Dempsey Family Collection, Trench Diary 1918.
7. *Ibid.*

Chapter 3
1. *The China Dragon*, journal of The Royal Berkshire Regiment, by kind permission of the Trustees of the Rifles Wardrobe and Museum Trust.
2. Captains Dempsey and Gueterbock, North-West Persia, notes for a lecture at Staff College, Camberley, 1930, The Wardrobe.
3. *Ibid.*
4. Captain Dempsey, Orders for Outposts, August 1920, The Wardrobe.
5. *Poster of the Indian Revolutionary Organisation*, printed by Turkestan Governmental Publications, Tashkent, 1920, The Wardrobe.
6. Major General Ironside, Order to OC Menjcol, 28 October 1920, The Wardrobe
7. Dempsey Family Collection, Diary for 1921.
8. *Ibid.*
9. *Ibid.*
10. *The China Dragon, op. cit.*
11. *Ibid.*

Chapter 4
1. *The China Dragon, op. cit.*
2. Dempsey Family Collection, letter from Katherine De La Fosse, 1 February 2002.
3. Dempsey Family Collection, letter from Sybil Chilton, 26 June 1925.
4. *The China Dragon, op. cit.*
5. *Owl Pie*, Staff College Journal, 1931, by kind permission of the Joint Services Command and Staff College.

6. Manuscript held by the library, Joint Services Command and Staff College.
7. *Owl Pie, op. cit.*

Chapter 5
1. Letter from Colonel D.F. Salt, *Journal of The Royal Military Police*, by kind permission of the Trustees of the Royal Military Police Regimental Fund.
2. *The China Dragon, op. cit.*
3. *Ibid.*
4. Dempsey Family Collection, Hunting Journal, 1928-39.
5. Salt, *op. cit.*

Chapter 6
1. *Journal of The Royal Military Police, op. cit.*
2. Dempsey Family Collection, letter from PHD, May 1940.
3. Captain P. Birkett Smith, in conversation with author.
4. *Journal of The Royal Military Police, op. cit.*
5. Colonel G. Woolnough MC, in conversation with author.
6. NAO Kew, Citation for DSO, 27 June 1940.

Chapter 7
1. Sir Harold Pyman, *Call to Arms,* Leo Cooper, London, 1971.
2. Interview with Ronald Lewin, Churchill Archive Centre, RLEW 7/7, by kind permission of the Trustees
3. Dempsey Family Collection, letter to PHD, 11 January 1943.
4. RLEW 7/7, *op. cit.*
5. Dempsey Family Collection, letter to PHD, 24 August 1943.

Chapter 8
1. Dempsey Family Collection, letter to PHD, 21 September 1943.
2. John Strawson, *A History of the SAS Regiment,* Secker & Warburg, 1984.
3. Dempsey Family Collection, letter to PHD, 12 October 1943.
4. Dempsey Family Collection, letter to PHD, 29 October 1943.
5. Dempsey Family Collection, letter from Simpson, July 1969.

Chapter 9
1. Notes of conversation Dempsey–Liddell Hart, Liddell Hart Centre for Military Archives, LH 15/15/130/1, by kind permission of the Trustees.
2. Handwritten notes by Dempsey, National Archive Office, Kew, WO 280/5.
3. Bradley, *A Soldier's Story,* Eyre & Spottiswood, 1951.
4. LH 15/15/130/8. The italics are the author's.
5. Notes of conversation Dempsey-Lewin, Churchill Archives Centre, RLEW 7/7.

Chapter 10
1. General Sir Brian Horrocks, *Corps Commander,* Sidgewick & Jackson, 1977.
2. De Guingand, *Operation Victory,* Hodder & Stoughton, 1947.
3. RLEW 7/7.
4. Bradley, *op. cit.*
5. Dempsey Family Collection, letter to PHD, 15 June 1944.
6. LH 15/15/130/1.
7. *Ibid.*
8. Captain Birkett-Smith, letter to author.
9. PJGG 9/8/9.
10. NAO WO 285.

11. Dempsey Press Conference, 1 July 1944.
12. LH 15/15/130/4.
13. Carver, letter to Liddell Hart, 8 May 1952, Liddell Hart Centre for Military Archives. The italics are the author's.

Chapter 11
1. LH 1/230/22.
2. *Ibid.*
3. RLEW 7/7.
4. LH 1/230/22.
5. Selwyn Lloyd, *The Times,* 10 June 1969.
6. LH 15/15/130/5.
7. 'Operations of Second Army in North West Europe', NAO, WO 205/972 B.
8. *The War Diaries of Lord Alanbrooke,* Weidenfeld & Nicolson, 2001.
9. LH 1/230/22.
10. Carlo D'Este, *Eisenhower, Supreme Allied Commander,* Weidenfeld & Nicolson, 2002.
11. NAO WO 285.
12. Whitelaw, *The Whitelaw Memoirs,* Aurum Press, 1989.
13. Imperial War Museum, PP/MCR/C 30 BLM 119.
14. *Ibid.*
15. *Ibid.*
16. Pyman, *op. cit.*
17. LH 9/28/33.
18. Horrocks, *op. cit.*
19. Deedes, W.F.R., *Dear Bill,* Macmillan, 1997.
20. Churchill Archive Centre, SELO 118.
21. Deedes, *op. cit.*

Chapter 12
1. 'Operations of Second Army', *op. cit.*
2. Horrocks, *op. cit.* The italics are the author's.
3. 'Operations of Second Army', *op. cit.*
4. War Diary, *op. cit.*
5. Montgomery, B.L., *The Memoirs of Field Marshal Montgomery of Alamein,* William Collins, Sons and Co Ltd, 1958.
6. Hills, Stuart, *By Tank into Normandy,* Cassell, 2003.
7. *War Diary, op. cit.* The italics are the author's.
8. Horrocks, *op. cit.*
9. LH 15/15/130/7.
10. *Ibid.*
11. War Diary, *op. cit.*
12. Bennett, *Ultra in the West,* Hutchinson, London 1979.
13. Horrocks, *op cit.* The italics are the author's.
14. *RLEW 7/7.*
15. *Ibid.*
16. Horrocks, *op. cit.*
17. *Ibid.*
18. LH 15/15/130/38.
19. Letter Dempsey-Major Ellis, 7 July 1966, NAO Kew.
20. Letter Dempsey-Major Ellis, 19 June 1962, NAO Kew.
21. 'Operations of Second Army', *op. cit.*
22. Letter Dempsey-Major Ellis, *op. cit.*

Chapter 13

1. *The China Dragon, op. cit.*
2. War Diary, *op. cit.*
3. *Ibid.*
4. *Ibid.*
5. IWM BLM 119/32.
6. Hills, *op. cit.*
7. Pyman, *op. cit.*
8. O'Connor, 5/4/86.
9. *Ibid.*
10. *War Diaries of Lord Alanbrooke, op. cit.*
11. Bennett, *op. cit.*
12. Dempsey Family Collection, letter to PHD, 12 April 1944.
13. IWM BLM 97/105.
14. Pyman, *op. cit.*
15. SELO 6/260A.

Chapter 14

1. *Operations of Second Army, op. cit.*
2. *Ibid.*
3. *The War Diaries of Lord Alanbrooke, op. cit.*
4. University of Southampton Library, MB1/C83, by kind permission of the Trustees.
5. Dempsey Family Collection, letter to PHD, undated.
6. O'Connor, S/4/91.
7. *Ibid.*
8. *Ibid.*
9. *Ibid.*
10. *The China Dragon, op. cit.*
11. *Ibid.*
12. Dempsey Family Collection, letter to PHD, 27 January 1946.
13. *The China Dragon, op. cit.*
14. MB1/C83.

Chapter 15

1. Pyman, 7/3/2.
2. *Ibid.*
3. Notes on Talk to GHQ Middle East, NAO Kew, WO 285.
4. *Ibid.*
5. IWM BLM 211/4.
6. IWM BLM 211/9.
7. IWM BLM 211/11.
8. IWM BLM 211/12.
9. IWM BLM 211/17.
10. IWM BLM 211/30.
11. IWM BLM 211/31.
12. Dempsey Family Collection, letter to PHD, 17 November 1946.
13. MB 1/E47.
14. *Ibid.*
15. *Ibid.*
16. Dempsey letter, 23 January 1947, IWM XXO2.
17. Dempsey Family Collection, letter to PHD, 8 December 1946.
18. Pyman 7/2/1.

19. LH 1/270/36.
20. *Ibid.*
21. *Ibid.*
22. Pyman, 7/3/7.
23. Notes for Address, NAO WO 285.
24. Notes for Farewell Dinner, NAO WO 285.
25. *Ibid.*
26. *The China Dragon.*
27. Dempsey Family Collection, letter to PHD, 25 May 1947.
28. MB 1/E47.

Chapter 16
1. Pyman, 7/3/7.
2. Pyman, 7/3/8.
3. Liddell Hart Centre, letter to Brig Maloney, 1 August 1964.
4. Pyman 7/3/7.
5. Liddell Hart Centre, letter to Brig Maloney, 31 August 1966.
6. RLEW 7/7.
7. Dempsey Family Collection, *Yattenden Broadsheet*, July 1969.
8. Eisenhower Library, Dempsey letter to Bradley, 25 May 1951.
9. Pyman 7/7/2.
10. Pyman 7/3/7.
11. *Royal Military Police Journal*, 1955.
12. Strawson, *op. cit.*
13. The Wardrobe, letter to Maj Gen Collins, 5 June 1947.
14. *The China Dragon.*
15. LH 1/230/44.
16. Dempsey Family Collection, *Yattendon Broadsheet, op. cit.*
17. Colonel Pyman, conversation with author.
18. *The Times*, 10 June 1969.
19. Dempsey Family Collection, Simpson letter, *op. cit.*
20. SELO 6/260 A.
21. Dempsey Family Collection, Letter from Boyd Rochfort, June 1969. 22. *The Times*, 10 June 1969.

Select Bibliography

Publications

Alanbrooke, Lord, *War Diaries,* (London 2001)

Barnett, Correlli, *Britain and Her Army,* (London 1970)

Barnett, Correlli, *The Collapse of British Power,* (London 1972)

Baynes, John, *The Forgotten Victor,* (London 1989)

Belchem., David, *Victory in Normandy,* (London 1981)

Bennett, Ralph, *Ultra in the West,* (London 1979)

Boatner, Mark, *The Biographical Dictionary of World War II,* (USA 1996)

Bradley, Omar, *A Soldier's Story,* (USA 1951)

Caddick-Adams, Peter, *General Sir Miles Christopher Dempsey (1896-1969) 'Not a Popular Leader',* (RUSI Journal 2005)

Carver, Michael, *Out of Step,* (Great Britain 1989)

Chandler, David ed, *The Oxford History of the British Army,* (Oxford 1964)

Cloake, John, *Templar, Tiger of Malaya,* (London 1985)

Cohen, Eliot, *Supreme Command,* (USA 2002)

Deedes, W F, *Dear Bill,* (London 1997)

de Guingand, Francis, *Operation Victory,* (London 1947)

D'Este, Carlo, *The Battle for Sicily, 1943,* (London 1988)

D'Este, Carlo, *Eisenhower, Supreme Allied Commander,* (London 2001)

Dunn, Capt J C, *The War The Infantry Knew,* (Great Britain 1958)

Fullick, Roy, *Shan Hackett,* (Great Britain 2003)

Fraser, David, *And We Shall Shock Them,* (Great Britain 1983)

Fraser, David, *Wars and Shadows,* (London 2002)

Hamilton, Nigel, *Monty, Master of the Battlefield,* (Great Britain 1983)

Hamilton, Nigel, *Monty, The Field Marshal,* (Great Britain 1986)

Hart, Stephen, *Collossal Cracks,* (USA 2007)

Hanbury Sparrow, *The Land Locked Lake,* (Thailand 1933)

Hastings, Max, *Armageddon,* (London 2004)

Henderson, Johnny, with Douglas-Home, Jamie, *Watching Monty,* (U K 2005)

Horne, Alistair, *The Lonely Leader,* (London 1994)

Horrocks, Sir Brian, *Corps Commander,* (London 1979)

Horrocks, Sir Brian, *A Full Life,* (London 1960)

Ironside, Edmund, *High Road to Command,* (London 1972)

Irving, David, *The War Between The Generals,* (USA 1981)

Lewin, Ronald, *Montgomery as Military Commander,* (London 1971)

Liddell Hart, B H, *History of the Second World War,* (London 1970)

Mead, Richard, *Churchill's Lions,* (UK 2007)

Montgomery, Field Marshal Viscount, *The Memoirs,* (Great Britain 1958)

North, John, *North West Europe 1944-45,* (London 1953)
Pagan, A W, *Infantry,* (Aldershot 1951)
Pyman, Sir Harold, *Call to Arms,* (London 1971)
Ryan, Cornelius, *A Bridge Too Far,* (UK 1974)
Sebag-Montefiore, *Dunkirk,* (London 2006)
Sheppard, G A, *The Italian Campaign, 1943-45*
Shute, Nevil, *Slide Rule,* (London 1968)
Smart, Nick, *British Generals of the Second World War,* (Great Britain 2005)
Terraine, John, *The Smoke and the Fire,* (Great Britain 1980)
Thompson, Julian, *Dunkirk, Retreat to Victory,* (London 2008)
Thorpe, D R, *Selwyn Lloyd,* (London 1989)
War Diary, *First Battalion The Royal Berkshire Regiment 1914-19*
Whitelaw, William, *The Whitelaw Memoirs,* (London 1989)
Winton, Harold and Mets, David ed *The Challenge of Change,* (USA 2000)

Other Sources
The Dempsey Family Collection. *Private papers of General Sir Miles Dempsey, 1914 -69.*
Liddell Hart Centre for Military Archives. *Dempsey, Pyman and O'Connor papers.*
The Churchill Archives Centre. *The Lewin and Selwyn Lloyd papers.*
Southampton University Library. *The Mountbatten papers.*
National Archives Office. *War Diary, History of Second Army, Dempsey papers.*
Imperial War Museum. *Montgomery papers.*
The Rifles Wardrobe Museum. *Dempsey papers.*

Index

Alington, Cyril, 1–3, 201
American Army: 57
First American Army, 104, 121, 125–6, 133, 135, 146
Third American Army, 125
Fifth American Army, 70, 74
Seventh American Army, 61
Ninth American Army, 149, 153, 155
Divisions:
    7th Armoured, 146–9
    17th Airborne, 153
    82nd Airborne, 134, 139–43
    84th, 149–50
    101st Airborne, 134, 139–40
Antwerp, 131, 133,
Ardennes, 151–2
Arnhem, 101, 131–46, see also
    Browning, Horrocks, XXX
    Corps
Arras, 46
Ayette, 13

Baghdad, 16, 23
Bareilly, 25,
Barber, Colin, General, 129, see also
    15th Division
Barker, Evelyn, General, 149, 155–6, 176–7, see also VIII Corps
Berney-Ficklin, Horatio, General, 61, 66, see also 5th Division
Birkett Smith, Captain, 45, 103
Bolsheviks, 18, 19, 22 Bourlon
    Wood, 11
Bradley, Omar, General, 193
Army Commander, 80–1, 87, 89, 91, 98, 101, 104, 106–107, 109, 113, 119, 124, 126
Army Group Commander, 128, 135, 146, 149
Brereton, Lewis, General, 134–9
British Army:
    Second Army:
        dedication, 202
        D-Day, 80–94
        headquarters, 95–6
        Normandy campaign, 95–127
        planning for D-Day, 80–8
        pre-invasion service, xi
        Seine to the Baltic, 128–161

Eighth Army, 60–1, 84
Fourteenth Army, 164–5, 167–8
I Corps, 83, 100, 104, 108–9, 112, 115
II Corps, 47
VIII Corps, 83, 103–5, 113–7, 120–1, 126, 137, 146, 148–52, 154–7
XII Corps, 84, 112, 115, 120, 124–7, 129–30, 137, 146, 148–9, 152–7
XIII Corps:
    condition 1942, 58
    formations for Sicily, 61
    Italian campaign, 69–79
    Sicily campaign, 61–8
XXX Corps, 83, 96, 99, 100–104, 108, 109, 112, 115, 120–6, 129–31, 146, 148–53, 156
    Arnhem operations, 133–44
Divisions:
    Guards Armoured, 114, 116–7, 120–1, 129, 131, 133, 140–7, 152, 157
    1st Airborne, 61–3, 65, 72, 88, 100–101, 134–45
    2nd, 12
    3rd, 83, 90–1, 99, 104, 108, 117, 140, 148, 157
    4th, 48
    5th, 43–46, 61, 66, 70, 71, 72, 76–7
    6th Airborne, 84, 91, 93, 100, 102, 115, 152–3, 156
    7th Armoured, 100–103–104, 109, 114, 116–8, 121, 140, 147, 152, 155–6
    11th Armoured, 103–105, 114, 116–7, 120–1, 129–31, 140, 156–7
    15th, 103–105, 120, 129, 140, 147–8, 150, 154–6
    42nd, 55
    43rd, 103–104, 121, 123, 126, 129, 140, 142, 147, 149, 152, 157
    46th, 53–4
    49th, 103–105, 112
    50th Northumbrian, 46, 61, 63, 65, 69, 90, 99, 112, 121, 133, 146

51st Highland, 37, 100, 102, 104, 108–9, 112, 115, 117, 147, 154–5
52nd Lowland, 134, 152–7
53rd, 140, 148, 155, 157
59th, 108, 112, 146
78th, 72–6
79th, 108, 149–50, 154
Brigades:
    1 Army Tank, 46
    1st Commando, 154–5
    4th Armoured, 61, 67, 72, 72
    5th, 35, 37
    8th Armoured, 100–101, 105
    10th, 48
    11th, 72
    13th, 42–49, 61, 71, 76
    29th Armoured, 152
    36th, 73
    38th (Irish), 73
    44th Armoured, 61
    99th, 12–13
    143th, 47–8
    227th, 142
Regiments,
    Household Cavalry, 121, 129
    12th Lancers, 45
    13/18th Hussars, 123
    23rd Hussars, 116
    Royal Tank, 45, 61
    County of London Yeomanry, 61
    Sherwood Rangers Yeomanry, 150
    Black Watch, 154,
    Cameronians, 43, 45–8
    Cheshire, 45
    2 Commando, 67
    3 Commando, 65, 73
    Dorset, 142
    Duke of Cornwall's Light Infantry, 5
    Durham Light Infantry, 65, 153
    East Yorkshire, 65
    Gloucestershire, 7
    Inniskilling, 43–7
    King's Royal Rifle Corps, 8
    Manchester, 47
    Parachute, 142

Rifle Brigade, 116, 153
Royal Berkshire, 4, 5, 6, 8, 11, 12, 13, 15, 16, 21, 23, 24, 28, 38, 39, 40, 153, 163
Royal Fusiliers, 8
Royal Irish Fusiliers, 4, 19–20
Royal Welsh Fusiliers, 7
Scots Guards, 121
South Staffords, 62
Special Raiding Squadron, 61, 63, 73–4, 77
Wiltshire, 43, 44–7, 105, 123, 126
York and Lancaster, 1
Royal Field Artillery, 5, 47
Chestnut Troop, 20
Royal Flying Corps, 5
Royal Military Police, 184, 197–8
Broadhurst, Harry, Air Marshal, 78, 81, 87, 95, 104, 112, 140
Brooke, General, 43, 47–8, 52, 54, 76, 80, 118–9, 155, 164, 169
Browning, 'Boy', General, 27, 84, 100, 13–1, 134, 137–44, 164, *see also* Arnhem
Brussels, 131, 152
Bucknall, Gerald, General, 66, 77, 83, 88, 100, 102–105, 109, 121–3, *see also* XXX Corps
Bullen-Smith, Charles, General, 3, 44, 49, 109, 117–8, *see also* 51st Highland Division

Caen, 81, 87–8, 90, 100–8, 112–5, 118–20
Cairo, 173–5
Camberley, 28–34
Cambrai, 11
Canadian Army,
    in UK, 49–53
    First Canadian Army, 117–8, 120, 125, 140, 149
    I Canadian Corps, 50–2
    II Canadian Corps, 110, 112, 115, 117, 120
    VII Canadian Corps, 49
    Divisions:
        1st Canadian, 50, 52, 69–70, 72, 75, 79, 112
        2nd Canadian, 50–2, 108, 112, 117
        3rd Canadian, 83, 90, 99, 100, 104, 110
    Brigades:
        1st Canadian Tank, 72
        2nd Canadian Armoured, 101
        3 Canadian, 71, 76
    Regiments:
        48th Highlanders, 75
        Royal 22e, 75
        West Nova Scotia, 75
Carver, Lord Michael, 109

Champain, General, 18–20
Chilton, Maurice, General, 30–1, 81, 96, 119, 151, 200, *see also* Second Army Christ Church, Portsdown, xi, 200, 202
Churchill, Jack, Lieutenant Colonel, 67
Churchill, Winston, 7, 58, 102, 119–20, 155
Coningham, Air Marshal, 86–7, 102, 104, 113, 119
Cossacks, 18, 19, 21–23
Crerar, Harry, General, 97, 124
Crocker, John, General, 83, 88, 96, 100–101, 108–10, 117, *see also* I Corps
Cunningham, Alan, General, 176–81
Currie, Brigadier, 61, 65, 72

Deedes, 'Bill', 123, 126
de Guingand, Francis, General, 59, 97, 184, 192
Delville Wood, 8–9
Dempsey, Arthur Francis, 1
Dempsey, James, 1, 2, 4, 5, 15, 26–7
Dempsey, Margaret, 1, 5, 12, 26, 45
Dempsey, Miles, General:
    Arnhem, 134–46
    boyhood, 1
    BLUECOAT, 120–1
    breakout from Normandy, 126–9
    Bucknall, General, 121–3
    brigade major, 36–8
    Camberley, 30–4
    Canadians in UK, 49–53
    clearance operations, 146–52
    Cold War strategy, 184–7
    Commander Second Army, 78–9, 80–164
    Commander, 13 Brigade, 43–9
    Commander, XIII Corps, 56–77
    Commanding Officer, 40–2
    D-Day preparation, xi, 80–8
    D-Day, 89–94
    death, 200–201
    Divisional Commander, 54–6
    EPSOM, 103–106
    Falaise, 124–6
    Far East, 164–72
    First World War, 6–14
    German surrender, 157–64
    GOODWOOD, 113–20
    Italian campaign, 69–77
    Keller, General, 110
    marriage, 194
    Middle East, 173–88
    Military Secretary, 34–5
    Normandy campaign, 95–127
    Northern Persia, 17–23
    PERCH, 100–101

Palestine, 174, 176–81
    pursuit from Normandy, 129–33
    Regimental Colonel, 183, 188, 198–9
    retirement, 169, 181–4, 187, 190–200
    Rhine crossing, 153–6
    Sandhurst, 6–8, 24–8
    school, 1–5
    Sicily, 61–8
    South Africa, 40, 184
    See also Montgomery
Dempsey, Patrick:
    early life, 1, 2, 4, 5, 11, 15, 26
    with BEF, 45
    letters from Miles, 45, 59, 67, 71, 74, 76, 99, 157, 169, 181, 183, 188
Dempsey, Viola, Lady, 194, 199, 200–1
Dill, John, General, 30, 42, 51
Dunkirk, 49
Dunn, J.C.Captain, 7
Durnford-Slater, Lieutenant Colonel, 65
Dutch East Indies, 166–69

Eisenhower, Dwight, General, 57, 60, 66, 112, 117, 119, 124, 128, 130–1, 134, 136, 139, 191
Enzeli, 18–9, 22
Erskine, "Bobby", General, 30, 102, 109, 117–8, 123, *see also* 7th Armoured Division
Ervillers, 13
Escarmain, 13
Evelegh, Vyvyan, General, 41, 72, *see also* 78th Division

Falaise, 118, 124–6
Franklyn, Major General, 43, 49, *see also* 5th Division

Gairdner, Charles, General, 58–9
Gale, Richard, General, 89, 93, 152, *see also* 6th Airborne Division
Gavin, James, General, 139, 141, *see also* 82nd Airborne Division
GOLD Beach, 83, 90, 93
German Army:
    in 1917–18, 12
    in 1940, 45–8
    in Sicily, 60
    in Italy, 69, 75
    in Normandy, 81–3, 88, 91–2, 105, 116, 124, 1129, 132–3, 137–8, 161–3
Greene King, 196–7
Gumbinnen, 32

Hanbury-Sparrow, Lieutenant Colonel, 8, 16

Hobart, Percy, General, 85, 108, 150, *see also* 79th Division
Hodges, Bill, General, 126, 146–7
Hopkinson, George, General, 30, 61, 64, *see also* 1st Airborne Division
Horrocks, Brian, General, 31, 35, 38, 56, 79
  XXX Corps Commander, 93, 95–8, 123–4, 130, 132, 137–9, 146, 150, 152–3
  Arnhem operations, 132–46

Indian Army, 17, 20, 168–9
Ironside, Edmund, General, 13, 20–24
Italian campaign, 69–77

JUNO Beach, 83, 90
Jangali, 18

Kazvin 18, 20, 23
Keller, Rod, General, 109–10
Kirkman, Sidney, General, 31, 61, 63–4, *see also* 50th Division

La Vacquerie, 12
Leese, Oliver, General, 79, 89, 164, 181, 183, 192
Leigh-Mallory, Air Marshal, 30, 87, 101, 104, 112
Lloyd, Selwin, Brigadier, 124–5, 151, 157–8, 160–1, 199, 200–201

Malaya, 164–8, 170–1,
Maury, 13
Mayne, Paddy, Lieutenant Colonel, 62, 73
Menjil, 19, 21–23
Mesopotamia, 16–17
Military Secretary, 34
Miraumont, 10
Montgomery, Bernard Law, General:
  Americans, relationship, 67, 87
  Bucknall, General, 122
  Camberley, 34, 37
  CIGS, 173, 176–81
  Commander 3rd Division, 48
  Commander South East Army, 55–6
  D-Day exhortation, xi
  Dempsey, General, relationship, 57–8, 67–8, 78–9, 84, 89, 96–8, 104, 119, 158–9, 176–81, 192, 200
  Italian campaign, 69–77
  Keller, General, 110
  Normandy strategy, 87, 103, 112
  OVERLORD planning, 80–1, 84, 86
  qualities, 56–8
  RAF, relationship, 86–7, 104, 113, 119

Sicily campaign, 58–68
21st Army Group, 112–57
Morgan, Frederick, General, 80, 113, 119
Mountbatten, Louis, Admiral, 164, 166, 168–9, 172, 181–3, 188–9, 200

Nijmegen, 131, 133, 135, 138–43, 146
Norperforce, 18–23

O'Connor, Richard, General, 27, 34, 36, 151, 153, 159, 165–6, 167
  VIII Corps Commander, 79, 83, 98, 103–104, 108, 115–18, 121, 126, 140, 142, 146–9
OMAHA Beach, 91–2
Operations,
  AVALANCHE, 69
  BAYTOWN, 69, 70
  BLUECOAT, 120–4, 128
  CHARNWOOD, 108, 115
  COMET, 135
  EPSOM, 104–106
  GOODWOOD, 111, 113–7, 119–20
  HUSKY, 70
  MARKET GARDEN, 133–46
  MINCEMEAT, 60
  NIPOFF, 171
  NUTCRACKER, 149–50
  OVERLORD:
    preparation 67, 80
    success, 92
    summary, 94
  PERCH, 100–102
  PLUNDER, 153–6
  TUXEDO, 135
  VARSITY, 153–6
  WINDSOR, 107
  ZIPPER, 166
Oppy Wood, 10

Pagan, 'Patsy', Lieutenant Colonel, 7
Palestine, 174, 176–81, 184
Patton, George, General, 61, 87–9, 113
Pelmanism, 24
Persia, 17–23
Ponte Grande Bridge, 62
Primasole Bridge, 64–6
Pyman, 'Pete', General:
  XXX Corps, 96, 122–3
  Second Army, 151, 156, 157–8, 160, 164
  post-war, 172–3, 183–4, 190–1, 194, 199
Pyman, Charles, Colonel, 200

RBCB, 181, 190, 195–6
Reza Khan, 23
Resht, 19, 22

Rhine, 133, 135–6, 144, 146–7, 153–6
Ritchie, Neil, General, 30, 84, 115, 124, 140, 142, 155–6, *see also* XII Corps
Roberts, 'Pip', General. 116–7, 121, 129, *see also* 11th Armoured Division
Royal Marines:
  40 Commando, 73
  47 Commando, 93

Sandhurst, RMC, 2–4, 15, 26–28
Scarpe, 36
Shrewsbury School, xi, 1–3, 15, 183, 201
Serre, 9–10
Shute, Nevil, 3, 5
Sicily, invasion of:
  planning and preparation, 58–62
  assault, 62–5
  advance to Messina, 65–68
Simonds, Guy, General, 69, 75, 79, 110, 115, 150, 200, *see also* Canadian Army
Simpson, William, General, 149
Slim, Bill, General, 164
Somme, 5–12, 129
Special Forces, 77, 157, 198
Staff College, *see* Camberley
Starosselsky, Colonel, 18, 21, *see also* Cossacks
Stokes, V.G. 9, 11, 16
Stopford, 'Monty', General, 43, 169
SWORD Beach, 83, 90
Sylvester, Lindsay, General, 147–9

Tedder, Air Marshal, 86, 102, 112–3, 119
Termoli, 73–4, 76
Thomas, Ivor, General, 126, *see also* 43rd Wessex Division
Troubridge, Admiral, 30, 33, 59, 67, 187

ULTRA, 105, 119, 137–8, 155
Urquhart, Roy, General, 70–1, 101, 142, 145, *see also* 1st Airborne Division

Venlo, 135, 146, 149–51
Vian, Admiral, 81, 99
Villers Bocage, 100–103, 120

Wesel, 135–6, 153–5
Woolnough, George, Captain, 47–8

Yattenden, 195, 199, 200
Ypres-Commine Canal, 47–9